P9-CME-554

More Praise for *Agenda for a New Economy*

"In this new edition of his groundbreaking book, David Korten steps up with a new, practical, and energizing guide we all can use to transform today's economic disaster into a living democracy."
—**Frances Moore Lappé, author of** *Getting a Grip 2* **and** *Diet for a Small Planet*

"What I love about this edition of *Agenda for a New Economy* is that David Korten brings together previously fragmented ideas about how to move forward into a compelling, cohesive framework for personal, community, and government action. This book will get you from 'yes, but how?' to 'yes, and here's how.'"
—**Alisa Gravitz, Executive Director, Green America**

"David Korten has updated and strengthened an already timely and insightful book. No one has done a better job at bringing together the multiple crises—economic, environmental, social, political—in which we find ourselves today. His vision of the path forward is clear and compelling."
—**James Gustave Speth, Dean, Yale School of Forestry and Environmental Studies; former Administrator, United Nations Development Programme; and author of** *The Bridge at the Edge of the World*

"At an urgent moment in human history, David Korten offers a new way to organize our economy that is both inspired and deeply practical. This is a must-read guide to creating a viable future."
—**Stacy Mitchell, Senior Researcher, Institute for Local Self-Reliance; Chair, American Independent Business Alliance; and author of** *Big-Box Swindle*

"Faith communities at their best help us see and believe in what is possible and help us face inconvenient truths and uncomfortable realities. At their worst, faith communities kill dreams and reinforce fantasies. David Korten's new book can help all of us who lead and participate in faith communities to fulfill our best potential and stop playing to our worst. It's urgent, important, clear, and downright inspiring, and it challenges us to pursue what is excellent, mature, and real."
—**Brian McLaren, author of** *A New Kind of Christianity*

"David Korten tells the truth like no one else—a truth our planet needs us to hear."

—Marjorie Kelly, cofounder, Corporation 20/20; founding editor, *Business Ethics* magazine; and author of *The Divine Right of Capital*

"Korten turns conventional economic thinking upside down and inside out. This book reveals what is really going on in the U.S. and global economy—and what can and should be done about it."

—Van Jones, founder, *Green for All* and author of *The Green Collar Economy*

"Just as the global economy crumbles, David Korten's timely plan for a new economy—a locally based living economy—will keep Spaceship Earth on a steady course, while bringing greater equality and strengthening our democratic institutions. And as if that were not enough, it will bring us more joy."

—Judy Wicks, cofounder and Chair, Business Alliance for Local Living Economies

"David Korten shows that patching the tires of a vehicle that's going over a cliff is neither sane nor acceptable. But the financial crisis can be a healing crisis, and Korten gives us prescriptions that could actually give us a thriving and just economy that works for people and the planet.

—Vicki Robin, cofounder, Conversation Cafés and coauthor of *Your Money or Your Life*

"The most important book to emerge thus far on the economic crisis. David Korten provides real solutions."

—Peter Barnes, cofounder, Working Assets, and author of *Capitalism 3.0*

"A great book. Korten provides solutions far beyond economics. If we care about the health, safety, education, and well-being of our society and want to create a world with a semblance of social and economic equity, this book is the next big step in that direction."

—Peter Block, author of *Community* and *Stewardship*

"A stirring defense of life and liberty. Guided by the hand of Adam Smith, David Korten paints a spirited picture of a new economy: in bold strokes, from the Earth up, and for all the people. Obama watchers, take note—page after page, redesign trumps reform and shouts, 'Yes, we can!'"

—Raffi Cavoukian, singer, author, entrepreneur, ecology advocate, and founder of Child Honoring

AGENDA FOR A NEW ECONOMY

OTHER BOOKS BY DAVID C. KORTEN

Community Management

Getting to the 21st Century

The Great Turning

People-Centered Development

The Post-Corporate World

When Corporations Rule the World

AGENDA FOR A **NEW ECONOMY**

From PHANTOM WEALTH to REAL WEALTH

DAVID C. KORTEN

A publication of the New Economy Working Group

Berrett–Koehler Publishers, Inc.
San Francisco
a BK Currents book

Copyright © 2010 by The People-Centered Development Forum

Berrett-Koehler Publishers, Inc., 235 Montgomery Street, Suite 650, San Francisco, CA 94104-2916 • Tel: (415) 288-0260 • Fax: (415) 362-2512 • www.bkconnection.com

ORDERING INFORMATION

QUANTITY SALES. Special discounts are available on quantity purchases by corporations, associations, and others. For details, contact the "Special Sales Department" at the Berrett-Koehler address above.

INDIVIDUAL SALES. Berrett-Koehler publications are available through most bookstores. They can also be ordered directly from Berrett-Koehler: Tel: (800) 929-2929; Fax: (802) 864-7626; www.bkconnection.com

ORDERS FOR COLLEGE TEXTBOOK/COURSE ADOPTION USE. Please contact Berrett-Koehler: Tel: (800) 929-2929; Fax: (802) 864-7626.

ORDERS BY U.S. TRADE BOOKSTORES AND WHOLESALERS. Please contact Ingram Publisher Services, Tel: (800) 509-4887; Fax: (800) 838-1149; E-mail: customer.service@ingrampublisherservices.com; or visit www.ingrampublisherservices.com/Ordering for details about electronic ordering.

LIBRARY OF CONGRESS CATALOGING-IN-PUBLICATION DATA

Korten, David C.
Agenda for a new economy: from phantom wealth to real wealth / David C. Korten. – 2nd ed.
    p. cm.
Includes bibliographical references and index.
ISBN 978-1-60509-375-8 (pbk.: alk. paper)
1. United States – Economic policy – 2001–2009. 2. United States – Economic policy – 2001–2009. 3. Wealth – United States. I. Title.
HC106.83.K67 2010
330.973 – dc22

2010015448

Second Edition

14 13 12 11 10   10 9 8 7 6 5 4 3 2 1

Project management, cover and interior design by Valerie Brewster
Copyediting by Karen Seriguchi, proofreading by Todd Manza, index by George Draffan
Cover image: ChuckStryker/istockphoto

▶•◆•◆•◀

To Steve Piersanti and the incredible staff of Berrett-Koehler, who proposed this book project and supported it above and beyond the call of duty

To the staff and board of *YES! Magazine*, who are communicating a new vision of human possibility to the world

To the staff, board, and local network members of the Business Alliance for Local Living Economies, who are building the New Economy from the bottom up

To the staff of the Institute for Policy Studies, who are helping to frame the New Economy policy agenda and to build a supportive political alliance

To the hundreds of grassroots groups engaged in popular economics education and political mobilization

And to the buccaneers and privateers of Wall Street, whose excesses revealed a financial system so corrupt and detached from reality as to be beyond repair — without them, this call to shut down Wall Street would surely fall on deaf ears

I care not what puppet is placed upon the throne of England to rule this Empire on which the sun never sets. The man who controls Britain's money supply controls the British Empire, and I control the British money supply.

NATHAN MAYER ROTHSCHILD (1777–1836)

All financial innovation involves, in one form or another, the creation of debt secured in greater or lesser adequacy by real assets. . . . All [financial] crises have involved debt that, in one fashion or another, has become dangerously out of scale in relation to the underlying means of payment.

JOHN KENNETH GALBRAITH, *A Short History of Financial Euphoria*

The legal rate [of interest] . . . ought not to be much above the lowest market rate. If . . . fixed so high as eight or ten percent, the greater part of the money which was to be lent, would be lent to prodigals and projectors, who alone would be willing to give this high interest.

ADAM SMITH, *The Wealth of Nations*

I don't think this is just a financial panic; I believe that it represents the failure of a whole model of banking, of an overgrown financial sector that did more harm than good.

PAUL KRUGMAN, "THE MARKET MYSTIQUE," *New York Times*

CONTENTS

ix

ACKNOWLEDGMENTS

Agenda for a New Economy is a book about unrealized possibility. I bear sole responsibility for its contents, but it is the product of many minds and the deeds of many leaders. A few of are mentioned here for their special contributions.

First, I'm indebted to Rabbi Michael Lerner, who shortly before the financial meltdown of September 2008 invited me to write an article for *Tikkun* magazine reviewing books by two influential economists. As the meltdown played out, the article evolved with Michael's guidance to become a call for a basic redesign of our economic institutions and featured a proposed address for delivery by President Obama on a New Economy agenda.

As I was working on that piece with Michael, the Wall Street financial bubble burst and the U.S. Congress rushed through a bill attempting to restore business as usual by bailing out the banks responsible for the crisis. At the same time, *YES! Magazine* editors Sarah van Gelder and Doug Pibel suggested I do a piece for *YES!* on what Congress should be doing to actualize the possibilities of a new economy designed to serve people, community, and nature. The *Tikkun* and *YES!* articles both appeared shortly after the November 2008 presidential election of Barack Obama.

Late in the evening on November 24, Steve Piersanti, the president and publisher of Berrett-Koehler Publishers, with whom I've worked on my most widely read books, sent me an e-mail message saying he had read the *YES!* article and wanted to help get its message out far and wide, perhaps as a short book.

From that moment forward, Steve and the incredible

Berrett-Koehler staff went into overdrive to produce the book in time for a January 23, 2009, launch at the historic Trinity Church in the heart of Wall Street, shortly after Obama's presidential inauguration. I've never in my life worked with such single-minded concentration or experienced such total support from colleagues. I sent Steve chapters on a daily basis, and he invariably responded within a few hours with feedback. Michael Crowley adjusted his holiday vacation to put together the cover text, endorsements, and marketing materials. Karen Seriguchi, who served as copy editor, worked with me literally around the clock for ten days to turn the manuscript into a final edited text. Valerie Brewster of Scribe Typography did the design and composition, and Todd Manza did the proofreading, all in record time. I also owe special thanks to Raffi, who made a special recording of his song "No Wall Too Tall" to celebrate the launch at the Trinity Church

Fran Korten, my life partner and publisher of *YES! Magazine*, advised on the editorial content and protected me from interruptions. Kat Gjovik, director of communications and outreach for the Great Turning Initiative, dealt with all the communications that I put on hold. Susan Gleason, media and outreach manager for *YES! Magazine*, helped organize the launch and related media events. This second edition has been completed on a more conventional publication schedule with the same dedicated support from the same teams at Berrett-Koehler and *YES!*

Others who made important contributions to one or both editions include Gar Alperovitz, Cecile Andrews, Sarah Anderson, Tusi Avegalio, Alissa Barron, Jane Barthelemy, Matthew Bauer, Stephen Bezruchka, Jacob Bomann-Larsen, Ellen Brown, Puanani Burgess, John Cavanagh, Raffi Cavoukian, Barbara Chan, Tiffiniy Cheng, Chuck Collins, Bob Dandrew, Charles Eisenstein, Riane Eisler, Hilary Franz, Alisa Gravitz, Shannon Hayes, Gerri Haynes, Bob Jones, Van Jones, Georgia Kelly, Marjorie Kelly, Dennis Kucinich, Dal LaMagna, Michelle

Long, Derek Long, Jason McLennan, Jerry Mander, Stacy Mitchell, Frances Moore Lappé, Noel Ortega, John Perkins, Barry Peters, Channie Peters, Harry Pickens, Vicki Robin, Bob Scott, Don Shaffer, Vandana Shiva, Michael Shuman, James Gustave Speth, Sarah Stranahan, Lama Tsomo, Roberto Vargas, Meredith Walker, Randall Wallace, Judy Wicks, Sandy Wiggins, Richard Wilkinson, and Stephen Zarlenga.

This second edition of *Agenda for a New Economy* is published as a report of the New Economy Working Group (NEWGroup, neweconomyworkinggroup.org).

I cochair NEWGroup with John Cavanagh, executive director of the Institute for Policy Studies (IPS) in Washington, D.C. Noel Ortega is the NEWGroup coordinator.

NEWGroup is a partnership of IPS (ips-dc.org); *YES! Magazine* (yesmagazine.org); BALLE (livingeconomies.org); the People-Centered Development Forum (pcdf.org); James Gustave Speth, former dean of the Yale School of Forestry and administrator of the United Nations Development Programme; and Gar Alperovitz, professor of political economy, the University of Maryland, and president of the National Center for Economic and Security Alternatives. IPS, which works in partnership with progressive members of Congress and many national groups involved in economic education and policy advocacy, serves as the secretariat. The views expressed are mine and do not necessarily represent positions of NEWGroup or its individual partners.

David Korten
davidkorten.org

PROLOGUE

►•◆•◆•◄

A QUESTION OF VALUES

I wrote the first edition of this book in late 2008, when Wall Street was in the throes of collapse. The phantom wealth machine had been exposed and its devastating effects on the real economy were apparent everywhere.

The book was published just as a new president and a new Congress were taking power. I hoped they might begin to rein in the Wall Street financial institutions that were causing such pain and set us on the path to a much more sensible economy. Flush with the excitement of the moment, I included a chapter with the economic address to the nation that I hoped our youthful, idealistic, articulate new president might give — one that recognized a need to transform the money system, global corporations, and the rules that determine the behavior of both.

I knew the speech was a fantasy but felt it might help readers see more clearly how the New Economy agenda translates into a redirection of public policy.

In the eighteen months since the first edition of this book came out, we have seen with increasing clarity the extent of Wall Street's hold on Washington. Leadership for transformational change must come, as it always has, from outside the institutions of power. It requires building a powerful social movement based on a shared understanding of the roots of the problem and a shared vision of the path to its resolution.

As a society, we cannot create a future that we cannot see in our collective mind. The first edition of *Agenda for a New*

1

Economy presented a framing vision drawn largely from material I had written before the crash. This second edition brings in substantial new material and thinking based on a year and a half of revelations about the Wall Street–Washington political axis, additional reflection, and conversations with knowledgeable and thoughtful colleagues.

A NATIONAL CONVERSATION

Few and fortunate are those whose lives have not been directly touched by the September 2008 Wall Street meltdown and its consequences. The meltdown remains at the center of public awareness and concern. People want to understand what went wrong and how we can set it right. Yet the public commentary centers on finger-pointing. Who knew what, when? Which regulators were asleep at the switch, and why?

A few observers — including Dean Baker (*Plunder and Blunder*), William Black (*The Best Way to Rob a Bank Is to Own One*), Charles Morris (*The Trillion Dollar Meltdown*), Kevin Phillips (*Bad Money*), and Gary Weiss (*Born to Steal*) — provided extensive documentation of the corruption of Wall Street's most powerful institutions even before the September 2008 crash.

There has since been an outpouring of such books and articles, including those by R. P. Bottle (*The Trouble with Markets*), Michael Lewis (*The Big Short*), Martin Lowy (*Debt Spiral*), Simon Johnson and James Kwak (*13 Bankers*), Barry Lynn (*Cornered*), and Janine R. Wedel (*Shadow Elite*). Each pulls back the curtain on Wall Street corruption a bit further and fuels public outrage and disgust with the Wall Street–Washington axis.

Most calls for action, however, seek only to limit the excesses and deceptions of greedy bankers and financiers. We have yet to engage a much-needed national conversation that addresses essential, yet unasked, questions. For example:

1. Do Wall Street institutions do anything so vital for the national interest as to justify opening the national purse strings and showering them with trillions of dollars in order to save them from the consequences of their own excess?

2. Is it possible that the whole Wall Street edifice is built on an illusion that has no substance yet carries deadly economic, social, and environmental consequences for the larger society?

3. Might there be other ways to provide necessary and beneficial financial services with greater effectiveness and at lower cost?

This edition of *Agenda for a New Economy,* as did the first edition, argues that the correct answers are (1) no, (2) yes, (3) yes.

Ultimately, it comes down to a question of the values we believe the economy should serve. Should it give priority to money, or to life? To the fortunes of the few, or the well-being of all?

The Wall Street economy we have is highly effective and efficient at converting real living wealth to phantom financial wealth to make rich people richer. It is a path to collective suicide. Our future and that of our children depend on replacing the values and institutions of the Wall Street economy with the culture and institutions of a New Economy designed to provide an adequate and satisfying livelihood for all people in balanced relationship to Earth's biosphere.

I believe that an honest public examination of these questions will lead to a unifying political consensus that, rather than repair and restrain the Wall Street institutions that brought down the global economy, we can and should replace them with institutions that serve our real values and are appropriate to the needs and realities of the twenty-first century. I have written *Agenda for a New Economy* in the hope that it may help to provoke and frame such a conversation.

Because I am issuing a call to shut down Wall Street, I want to clearly distinguish my position from the declarations of those on the far right who say the "too big to fail" Wall Street banks should been left to collapse as a self-corrective act of market discipline. Although I share the underlying sentiment, I also recognize why those who made the decisions felt compelled to prevent such a collapse. Simply letting the banks fail would almost certainly have brought about a collapse of the global financial system and economy far worse than what we experienced.

Wall Street controls the creation and flow of the money that facilitates the economic transactions on which we depend for meeting most of our material needs. If the institutions of Wall Street suddenly shut down with no alternative in place, we would have only the money in our pockets and would be instantly reduced to bartering for most essentials of daily life, including food and water.

This, of course, is why an otherwise cash-strapped and gridlocked Washington political establishment and a Congress that has difficulty reaching agreement on far smaller issues responded instantly with a massive bailout in the face of public outrage to save Wall Street's largest banks from collapse.

The process of shutting down Wall Street must parallel action to put in place the institutions of a new system for creating and allocating national currencies in ways more responsive to society's needs.

THE STORY OF THE FIRST EDITION

I wrote *Agenda for a New Economy* to open a discussion about why a fundamental redesign of our economic institutions is required and what it might involve. The second edition, as the first, is addressed to people who are acutely aware that things are going badly wrong economically, socially, and environmentally and who are looking for real solutions based on new approaches and institutions.

The first edition of *Agenda for a New Economy* was written and published in immediate response to the meltdown. It was launched at a national theological conference at the historic Trinity Church at the foot of Wall Street in New York City on January 23, 2009, just three days after the inauguration of Barack Obama as president of the United States.

Much of the nation was in a state of euphoria born of hope that our new president would deliver on his promise of change. That hope, combined with outrage at Wall Street excesses, had swept Obama into the White House and should have created fertile ground for serious action on economic reform. Yet the strongest reform proposals on the table as of this writing involve little more than tinkering at the margins to restrain the worst of those excesses.

There are evident political explanations for President Obama's failure in this regard, but they are only part of the story. His options have been severely limited by a very practical reality: neither of the two prevailing schools of economic thought — market fundamentalism or Keynesianism — addresses the underlying institutional, social, and environmental foundations of the problem he faces and therefore provide no framework for the needed system redesign. I take this up in more detail in chapter 17.

In any event, the leadership for institutional transformation rarely comes from those who depend on existing institutions as their base of power. It invariably comes from authentic grassroots movements. Efforts to form a social movement to confront the Wall Street–Washington axis are similarly handicapped, however, by the failure of the prevailing economic models to provide a framework for a comprehensive restructuring.

Most of the elements of the New Economy model are known, but they must be brought together into a coherent guide to action. Fortunately, a number of groups are discussing the problem and organizing to address it. What follows owes much to my participation in these conversations, particularly those of the New Economy Working Group.

WHAT'S NEW?

Much of the second edition is either new or substantially revised to reflect recent events and what I've learned over the past eighteen months.

I've added a new section to chapter 2 on the difference between good debt and bad debt and on Wall Street's language of self-deception. In part II I've also added a new chapter, "Greed Is Not a Virtue; Sharing Is Not a Sin," which provides a brief overview of Wall Street's behavior since the crash and highlights the contrast between the moral values of Wall Street capitalism and those of the New Economy.

The most important new contributions are in the latter part of the book, which has been extensively rewritten and expanded. It is reorganized into three parts. Part III frames the New Economy's "Living-Economy Vision." Part IV translates the vision into an action agenda. Part V outlines a mobilization strategy for implementation.

The agenda, now more coherent and fully developed, builds from a stronger ecological systems perspective and introduces the concept of the living enterprise. I have substantially revised my thinking about the institutional design for a living-wealth money system. The system I'm now proposing is more diverse and decentralized and more supportive of local resilience and self-organization.

There is an assessment in chapter 17 of why President Obama failed to deliver on the hopeful vision of candidate Obama and what we can do about it. I have recast the proposed presidential economic address to the nation (now chapter 15) as the address that we the people must make into a political imperative for either our present or a future president to deliver. If you are looking for an overview of the policy agenda, this is the chapter.

The discussion of story power in chapter 18 goes deeper into the underlying role of culture in shaping collective behavior. A substantially new chapter 19 outlines a threefold social-learning-oriented implementation strategy and includes a new section on institutional change agendas for media, education, religion, and the arts. The scenarios offering fictional accounts of life and money in a New Economy future are pulled together into an epilogue, "The View from 2084." It addresses the question, How will our children live?

I hope these revisions will serve you, the reader, in making your own contributions to changing the economic story and bringing the New Economy into being where you live.

As in the first edition, I have intentionally avoided going into the complex details of the various Wall Street financial schemes and scams. Such inquiry holds its own fascination but distracts from the bottom line message:

> Wall Street operates as a criminal syndicate engaged in financial scams and extortion rackets that impose unbearable costs on society while serving no beneficial function not better served in other ways. The need is not to repair

Wall Street but to replace it with institutions devoted to serving the financial needs of ordinary people in ways that are fair, honest, and consistent with the reality of our human dependence on Earth's biosphere.

For those who want to delve into the arcane details of exactly how the Wall Street scams work, there are other books, such as those mentioned above. *Agenda for a New Economy* is about the bigger picture.

THE PERSONAL STORY THAT FRAMES MY UNDERSTANDING OF HUMAN POSSIBILITY

I grew up in a conservative small town where I learned to value family, community, and nature. I was raised to believe in the special character of America as a middle-class democracy, free from the extremes of wealth and poverty that characterized the world's less advanced nations. In my childhood, my dad, a local retail merchant, taught me that if your primary business purpose is not to serve your customers and community, then you have no business being in business.

My Stanford Business School education taught me to look for the big picture. My doctoral dissertation research in Ethiopia taught me the power of culture in shaping collective behavior.

From my experience as an Air Force captain on the faculty of the Special Air Warfare School and as a military aide in the Office of the Secretary of Defense during the Vietnam War, I learned how the world's most powerful military was thwarted by the self-organizing networks of an ill-equipped peasant army. That experience helps me see the potential of a committed citizenry to likewise thwart the seemingly invincible power of Wall Street.

While serving as a professor on the organization faculty at the Harvard Business School, I learned how the structures of large-scale institutional systems shape behavior and how system structures can be designed to support intended outcomes.

From my fifteen years in Asia with the Ford Foundation and the U.S. Agency for International Development, I experienced the positive power and potential of local community self-organization and the importance of local control of essential economic resources. I learned about strategies for large-scale institutional change from my involvement in both successful and unsuccessful efforts to restructure national resource-management systems in irrigation and forestry to place control in the hands of local communities.

It was during these years in Asia that I became aware of the terrible truth that development models based on economic growth were making a few people fabulously wealthy at an enormous social and environmental cost to the substantial majority. Such things stand out so much more clearly when you are outside your own culture.

In 1992, Fran and I returned to the United States and settled in New York City. There, in our apartment on Union Square between Madison Avenue and Wall Street, I wrote *When Corporations Rule the World.* The research for this book took me into a deep exploration of why the publicly traded limited liability, private-benefit corporation is an inherently destructive anti-market business form. I also came to see how the power of financial markets trumps even the power of global corporations and forces them into the role of economic predator.

In writing *The Post-Corporate World: Life After Capitalism,* I came to see the important distinction between a Wall Street capitalist economy and a Main Street market economy and to appreciate the ways in which properly designed and regulated market systems mimic the organizing dynamics and principles of healthy living systems, which, contrary to the prevailing story, demonstrate life's extraordinary capacity for cooperative self-organization.

I learned from the experience of my daughters, Diana and Alicia, how difficult the Wall Street reengineering of the economy has made it for today's young professionals to establish themselves economically — in contrast to the far easier experience of my generation.

As a founding member of the International Forum on Globalization, I learned about the power of a new story propagated through global citizen networks to thwart the agenda of the world's most powerful corporations and reshape the course of history.

As the cofounder and board chair of *YES! Magazine*, I have come to realize that every act of resistance against what we don't want must be paired with a positive vision of what we do want.

Writing *The Great Turning: From Empire to Earth Community*, I began to place our current human financial, social, and environmental crises in the historical context of five thousand years of organizing human societies as hierarchies of domination governed by institutions that nurture and reward moral, emotional, and behavioral dysfunction.

As a founding board member of the Business Alliance for Local Living Economies, I have been immersed in the experience of communities all across the United States and Canada that are taking control of their economic futures by rebuilding their local economies as they declare their independence from predatory Wall Street corporations.

All these many themes inform and find expression in *Agenda for a New Economy*. Many of them are developed at greater length in my other books mentioned above.

There are many resources for readers interested in the perspective of other writers who are dealing with important aspects of the New Economy. These are some of the many that have contributed to my thinking: Gar Alperovitz, *America Beyond Capitalism*; Riane Eisler, *The Real Wealth of Nations*; Van Jones, *The Green Collar Economy*; Bill McKibben, *Deep Economy*; Stacy Mitchell, *Big Box Swindle*; Michael Shuman, *The Small-Mart Revolution*; and James Gustave Speth, *The Bridge at the Edge of the World*.

Another valuable resource for those who are looking for more information on the people and organizations engaged in creating the New Economy and other initiatives intended to create just, sustainable, and compassionate societies is *YES! Magazine* (yesmagazine.org), which I cofounded and serve as board chair. The quarterly magazine provides in-depth examinations of major issues and new ways to solve them; the Web site provides fresh articles tied to headline news every day.

If you want to get involved in developing your local Main Street economy into a model New Economy, two national organizations can be of help: the Business Alliance for Local Living Economies (livingeconomies.org) and the American Independent Business Alliance (amiba.net). Both are active in the United States and Canada, and both are devoted to strengthening local independent businesses and building "local" as a positive branding identity.

BALLE has a particular focus on developing relationships among local independent businesses to strengthen what it calls the building blocks of healthy local living economies: sustainable agriculture, green building, renewable energy, community capital, zero-waste manufacturing, and independent retail. I am a founding member of the BALLE governing board.

AMIBA has paid particular attention to giving local independent businesses a political voice and eliminating special subsidies and exceptions for box stores to level the playing field for local businesses. I am a member of the AMIBA advisory board.

You also can find a clear articulation of the basic elements of the New Economy on the Web site of the New Economy Working Group, as well as resources and campaigns you can be part of to advance the agenda (neweconomyworkinggroup .org). I blog with modest regularity on yesmagazine.org. You can read about more of my latest activities and thinking on davidkorten.org. You can find group discussion guides for both the first and second editions of *Agenda for a New Economy* and can sign up for our free Great Turning Initiative e-mail newsletter at greatturning.org. I regularly tweet as dkorten and have a Facebook author page.

David Korten
Bainbridge Island, Washington

davidkorten.org
greatturning.org
yesmagazine.org
pcdforum.org

PART I

THE CASE FOR A NEW ECONOMY

If we look upstream for the ultimate cause of the economic crisis that is tearing so many lives apart, we find an illusion: the belief that money — a mere number created with a simple accounting entry that has no reality outside the human mind — is wealth. Because money represents a claim on so many things essential to our survival and well-being, we easily slip into evaluating economic performance in terms of the rate of financial return to money, essentially the rate at which money is growing, rather than by the economy's contribution to the long-term well-being of people and nature.

We can trace each of the major failures of our economic system to the misperception of money as wealth: the boom-and-bust cycles; the decimation of the middle class; families forced to choose between paying the rent, putting food on the table, and caring for their children; the decline of community life; and the wanton destruction of nature.

Once the belief that money is wealth is implanted firmly in the mind, it is easy to accept the idea that money is a storehouse of value rather than simply a storehouse of expectations, and that "making money" is the equivalent of "creating wealth." Because Wall Street makes money in breathtaking quantities, we have allowed it to assume control of the whole economy — and therein lies the source of our problem.

Financial collapse pulled away the curtain on the Wall

13

Street alchemists to reveal an illusion factory that pays its managers outrageous sums for creating phantom wealth unrelated to the production of anything of real value. They merely create claims on the real wealth created by others — otherwise known as counterfeiting, a form of theft.

Spending trillions of dollars trying to fix Wall Street is a fool's errand. Our hope lies not with the Wall Street phantom-wealth machine, but rather with the real-world economy of Main Street, where people engage in the production and exchange of real goods and services to meet the real needs of their children, families, and communities, and where they have a natural interest in maintaining the health and vitality of their natural environment.

Ironically, it turns out that the solution to a failed capitalist economy is a real-market economy much in line with the true vision of Adam Smith. Building a new real-wealth economy on the foundation of the Main Street economy will require far more than adjustments at the margins. It will require a complete bottom-to-top redesign of our economic assumptions, values, and institutions.

Chapter 1, "Looking Upstream," spells out what it means to treat causes rather than symptoms and why restructuring the economy's most powerful institutions is essential.

Chapter 2, "Modern Alchemists and the Sport of Moneymaking," looks at the reality behind Wall Street's illusions and the variety of its methods for making money without the exertion of creating anything of real value in return.

Chapter 3, "A Real-Market Alternative," contrasts the Wall Street and Main Street economies and puts to rest the fallacy that the only alternative to rule by Wall Street capitalists is rule by communist bureaucrats.

Chapter 4, "More Than Tinkering at the Margins," spells out why the "adjustment at the margins" approach favored by establishment interests cannot stabilize the economy, reduce economic inequality, or prevent environmental collapse.

CHAPTER 1

▶•◆•◆•◀

LOOKING UPSTREAM

A man was standing beside a stream when he saw a baby struggling in the water. Without a thought he jumped in and saved it. No sooner had he placed it gently on the shore than he saw another and jumped in to save it, then another and another. Totally focused on saving babies, he never thought to look upstream to answer the obvious question: Where were the babies coming from, and how did they get in the water?

ANONYMOUS

Our economic system has failed in every dimension: financial, environmental, and social. Moreover, the current financial collapse provides an incontestable demonstration that it is unable to self-correct.

Bloomberg News estimated in March 2009 that total federal bank bailout commitments and guarantees topped $12.8 trillion, nearly the equivalent of the total U.S. GDP.[1] Yet private bank credit still wasn't flowing into the real economy more than a year later.

The Bush administration's response to the financial crisis focused on bailing out the Wall Street institutions that bore primary responsibility for creating the crisis; its hope was that if the government picked up enough of those institutions' losses and toxic assets, the banks might decide to open the tap and get credit flowing again. It did not happen, because Wall Street is not in the business of financing the real economy.

The failure of the credit system is only one manifestation of a failed economic system that is wildly out of balance with, and devastatingly harmful to, both humans and the natural environment.

Wages are falling in the face of volatile food and energy prices. Consumer debt, housing foreclosures, and executive pay are setting historic records. The middle class is shrinking. The unconscionable and growing worldwide gap between rich and poor, with its related alienation, is eroding the social fabric to the point of fueling terrorism, genocide, and other violent criminal activity.

At the same time, excessive consumption is pushing Earth's ecosystems into collapse. Climate change and the related increase in droughts, floods, and wildfires are serious threats. Scientists are in almost universal agreement that human activity bears substantial responsibility. We face severe water shortages, the erosion of topsoil, the loss of species, and the end of the fossil fuel subsidy. In each instance, a failed economic system that takes no account of the social and environmental costs of monetary profits bears major responsibility.

Spending trillions of dollars in an effort to restore a failed system to normal function is a reckless waste of time and resources and, in the absence of action to replace the failed system, is the greatest misuse of federal government credit in history. The more intelligent course is to acknowledge the failure and to set about redesigning our economic system from the bottom up to align with the realities and opportunities of the twenty-first century.

We face a monumental economic challenge that goes far beyond anything being discussed by the administration, the U.S. Congress, or the corporate press.

Hope that an Obama administration would take serious action to rein in Wall Street in favor of Main Street began to die even before he took office, when he announced his initial picks for the country's top economic posts. That hope

SYSTEMIC FAILURE

The failure of the phantom-wealth casino economy is evident in:

1. An **economic crisis** created by an unstable global financial system that favors speculation in asset bubbles over investment in the production of beneficial goods and services, drives continuing cycles of boom and bust, mires people and governments in debts they cannot pay, and holds national governments hostage to the interests of global financiers concerned only with maximizing their own profits.

2. A **social crisis** of extreme and growing inequality within and among nations created by a focus on maximizing returns to money—which means to the people who already have the most money. A tiny minority of executives and financiers experience soaring incomes and accumulate grand fortunes at the expense of working people whose wages are largely stagnant or falling relative to the cost of living. The enormous disparities undermine institutional legitimacy, human health, and the social fabric of families and communities and thereby feed violence.

3. An **environmental crisis** of climate chaos, loss of fertile soil, shortages of clean freshwater, disappearing forests, and collapsing fisheries created by an economic system prone to collapse if excessive forms of consumption do not continuously grow. This crisis is reducing Earth's capacity to support life and is creating large-scale human displacement and hardship that further fuel social breakdowns.

continued to fall, along with President Obama's poll numbers, as he backed off from pushing essential Wall Street reforms. Even the Obama administration's $787 billion economic stimulus package did nothing to address the deeper structural causes of our financial, social, and environmental crisis.

On the positive side, however, the financial crisis has put to rest the myths that our economic institutions are sound and that markets work best when deregulated. This opens a window of opportunity to initiate a national conversation about what we can and must do to create an economic system that can work for all people for all time. That window will

REAL WEALTH/LIVING WEALTH

Real wealth has intrinsic value, as contrasted to exchange value. Life, not money, is the measure of real-wealth value. Examples include land, labor, knowledge, and physical infrastructure.

The most important forms of wealth are beyond price and are unavailable for market purchase. These include healthy, happy children, loving families, caring communities, and a beautiful, healthy, natural environment.

Real wealth also includes all the many things of intrinsic artistic, spiritual, or utilitarian value that are essential to maintaining the various forms of living wealth. These may or may not have a market price. They include healthful food, fertile land, pure water, clean air, caring relationships and loving parents, education, health care, fulfilling opportunities for service, and time for meditation and spiritual reflection. For most purposes, real wealth is living wealth, and living wealth is real wealth. Money is neither.

remain open for as long as the nation remains mired in unemployment, housing foreclosures, and unpayable debts — which in the absence of action to implement the New Economy agenda spelled out in part IV, is likely to be a very long time.

TREAT THE SYSTEM, NOT THE SYMPTOM

As a student in business school, I learned a basic rule of effective problem solving that has shaped much of my professional life. Our professors constantly admonished us to "look at

Because of the essential role of caring relationships, the monetization and commodification of real wealth, which generally translates into the monetization and commodification of relationships, tends to diminish their real value. The monetization and commodification of relationships does, however, translate into growth in the gross domestic product and new opportunities for corporate profits. Replacing parental caregivers with paid child care workers is an example.

In contrast to a phantom-wealth economy, money in a real-wealth or living economy is not used as a measure or a storehouse of value but solely as a convenient medium of exchange. A phantom-wealth economy seeks to monetize and commodify relationships to increase dependence on money; a real-wealth economy favors strengthening relationships based on mutual caring to reduce dependence on money.

the big picture." Treat the visible problem — a defective product or an underperforming employee — as the symptom of a deeper system failure. *Look upstream to find the source of the problem and correct the system so the problem will not recur.* It is perhaps the most important lesson I learned in more than twenty-six years of formal education.

Many years after I left academia, an observation by a wise Canadian friend and colleague, Tim Brodhead, reminded me of this lesson when he explained why most efforts fail to end poverty. "They stop at treating the symptoms of poverty, such as hunger and poor health, with food programs and clinics, without ever asking the obvious question: Why do a few people enjoy effortless abundance while billions of others who work far harder experience extreme deprivation?" He summed it up with this simple statement: "If you act to correct a problem without a theory about its cause, you inevitably treat only the symptoms." It is the same lesson my business professors were drumming into my brain many years earlier.

I was trained to apply this lesson within the confines of the business enterprise. Tim's observation made me realize that I had been applying it in my work as a development professional in Africa, Asia, and Latin America. For years, I had been asking the question: What is the underlying cause of persistent poverty? Eventually, I came to realize that poverty is not the only significant unsolved human problem, and I enlarged the question to ask: Why is our economic system consigning billions of people to degrading poverty, destroying Earth's ecosystem, and tearing up the social fabric of civilized community? How must that system and the institutions it comprises change if we are to have a world that works for all people and the whole of life?

Pleading with people to do the right thing is not going to get us where we need to go so long as we have a culture that celebrates, and institutions that reward, the destructive

PHANTOM WEALTH

Also called illusory wealth, this is wealth that appears or disappears as if by magic. The term generally denotes money created by accounting entries or the inflation of asset bubbles unrelated to the creation of anything of real value or utility. The high-tech-stock and housing bubbles are examples.

Phantom wealth also includes financial assets created by debt pyramids in which financial institutions engage in complex trading and lending schemes using fictitious or overvalued assets as collateral for loans in order to feed and inflate asset bubbles to create more phantom collateral to support more borrowing to further feed the bubble to justify outsized management fees.

Those engaged in creating phantom wealth collect handsome "performance" fees for their services at each step and walk away with their gains. When the bubble bursts, borrowers default on debts they cannot pay and the debt pyramid collapses, along with the bubble, in a cascade of bankruptcies.

Those who had no part in creating or profiting from the scam are then left to absorb the losses and to sort out the phantom-wealth claims still held by the perpetrators against the marketable real wealth of the larger society. It is all legal, which makes it a perfect crime.

behaviors we must now put behind us. It is so much more sensible to direct our attention to making the right thing easy and pleasurable by working together to create a culture that celebrates positive values and to foster institutions that reward positive behavior.

WORSE THAN NO THEORY

What my wise colleague did not mention is that placing too much faith in a "bad" theory or story, one that offers incorrect explanations, may be even worse than acting with no theory at all. A bad theory can lead us to false solutions that amplify the actions that caused the problem in the first place. Indeed, a bad theory or story can lead whole societies to persist in self-destructive behavior to the point of self-extinction.

The cultural historian Jared Diamond tells of the Viking colony on the coast of Greenland that perished of hunger next to waters abundant with fish; it had a cultural theory, or story, that eating fish was not "civilized."[2] On a much larger scale, the human future is now in question and the cause can be traced, in part, to economic theories that serve the narrow interests of a few and result in devastating consequences for all.

As we are perplexed by the behavior of the Vikings who perished because of their unwillingness to give up an obviously foolish theory, so future generations may be perplexed by our foolish embrace of some absurd theories of our own, including the theory that financial speculation and the inflation of financial bubbles create real wealth and make us richer. No need to be concerned that we are trashing Earth's life support system and destroying the social bonds of family and community, because eventually, or so the theory goes, we will have enough money to heal the environment and end poverty.

This theory led to economic policies that for decades served to create a mirage of phantom wealth that vanished before our eyes as the subprime mortgage crisis unfolded. It also led us to give control of our political and economic systems to institutions devoted to creating phantom wealth for the exclusive private benefit of their most powerful players.

Even with Wall Street's dramatic demonstration that we

were chasing a phantom, most observers have yet to acknowledge that the financial speculation was not creating wealth at all. Rather it was merely increasing the claims of financial speculators on the shrinking pool of everyone else's real wealth.

A NEW STORY FOR A NEW ECONOMY

A theory, of course, is nothing more than a fancy name for a story that presumes to explain how things work. It is now commonly acknowledged that we humans are on a course of self-destruction. Climate chaos, the end of cheap oil, collapsing fisheries, dead rivers, falling water tables, terrorism, genocidal wars, financial collapse, species extinction, thirty thousand child deaths daily from poverty — and, in the richest country in the world, millions squeezed out of the middle class — are all evidence of the monumental failure of our existing cultural stories and the institutions to which they give rise. We have good reason to fear for our future.

At first, each of the many disasters that confront us appears distinct. In fact, they all have a common origin that our feeble "solutions" fail to address for lack of an adequate theory. *Agenda for a New Economy* is a big-picture story, or theory, of where we went wrong in the design of our economic institutions and what we can do about it. We do, in fact, have the means to create an economic system that takes life as its defining value and fulfills six criteria of true economic health. Such a system would

1. provide every person with the opportunity for a healthy, dignified, and fulfilling life;

2. restore and maintain the vitality of Earth's natural systems;

3. nurture the relationships of strong, caring communities;

4. encourage economic cooperation in service to the public interest and democratically determined priorities;

5. allocate resources equitably to socially and environmentally beneficial uses; and

6. root economic power in people- and place-based communities to support the democratic ideal of one-person, one-vote citizen sovereignty.

A BOOK FOR THOSE LOOKING UPSTREAM

Agenda for a New Economy is a book for people who are looking upstream, not to place blame, but to find real solutions that fulfill a shared human dream of a world that works for all in perpetuity. At its core, it is about the cultural stories that shape our collective values and the institutional systems that shape our relationships with one another and with Earth. The relevance is global, but the primary focus is on the United States because U.S. economic values and institutions are somewhat distinctive and have a powerful global influence.

The justified public outrage against the breathtaking excesses of Wall Street creates an opportunity to mobilize political support for a New Economy that shifts our economic priorities from making money for rich people to creating better lives for all and that reallocates our economic resources from destructive, or merely wasteful, uses to beneficial ones.

To create an economic system that works for all, we need a different design grounded in different values and a different understanding of wealth, our human nature, and the sources of human happiness and well-being. The basic design elements of the New Economy we seek are known, as I will elaborate in subsequent chapters.

We face an urgent need for a national and international discourse on economic policy choices that support a bottom-to-top structural transformation of the economy to strengthen community and reallocate resources to where they best serve. I have written *Agenda for a New Economy* as a contribution to this discourse. I hope you will be encouraged to engage your friends, colleagues, community, and media contacts in discussion about the foundational economic policy choices at hand and will find this book a useful tool.

CHAPTER 2

►•◆•◆•◄

MODERN ALCHEMISTS AND THE SPORT OF MONEYMAKING

Speculators may do no harm as bubbles on a steady stream of enterprise. But the position is serious when enterprise becomes the bubble on a whirlpool of speculation.

JOHN MAYNARD KEYNES

The capitalist ideal is to create money out of nothing, without the need to produce anything of real value in return. Wall Street has turned this ideal into a high-stakes competitive sport. Money is the means of scoring, and *Forbes* magazine is the unofficial scorekeeper issuing periodic reports on the "richest people," ranked in the order of their financial assets. The player with the most assets wins. Because the scoring is competitive, no player has enough money so long as another player in the game has more.

Making money with no effort can be an addictive experience. I recall my excitement back in the mid-'60s, when my wife, Fran, and I first made a modest investment in a mutual fund and watched our savings grow magically by hundreds and then thousands of dollars with no effort whatever on our part. We felt as if we had discovered the philosopher's stone that turned cheap metals into gold. We got a case of Wall Street fever on what by current standards was a tiny scale.

Of course, most of what we call magic is illusion. When the credit collapse pulled back the curtain to expose Wall Street's inner workings, all the world was able to see the extent to which Wall Street is a world of deception, misrepresentation, and insider dealing in the business of creating phantom wealth without a corresponding contribution to the creation of anything of real value. It was such an ugly picture that Wall Street's seriously corrupted institutions stopped lending even to each other for the very good reason that they didn't trust anyone's financial statements.

PHANTOM WEALTH

In business school, I learned the art of assessing investment options to maximize financial return. My teachers never mentioned that what we were really learning was to maximize returns to people who had money, that is, to make rich people richer. Nor did they mention that if pursued mechanically, the methods we were learning might result in the creation of phantom wealth. That concept didn't exist.

Buried in the details of our calculations, no one asked, What is money? Why should we assume that maximizing

---

PHANTOM-WEALTH EXUBERANCE

The illusions of Wall Street are captured in the titles and publication dates of popular books such as:

Dow 36,000: The New Strategy for Profiting from the Coming Rise in the Stock Market (2000)

Dow 30,000 by 2008: Why It's Different This Time (2004)

Why the Real Estate Boom Will Not Bust (2006)

financial return maximizes the creation of real value? I don't recall whether such questions ever occurred to me. If they did, I would have kept them to myself for fear of being dismissed as hopelessly stupid.

Nor did our teachers ever point out, perhaps because they didn't recognize it themselves, that money is only an accounting chit with no existence or intrinsic value outside the human mind. Certainly, they never told us that money is a system of power and that the more dependent we are on money as the mediator of human relationships, the more readily those who have the power to create money and to decide who gets it can abuse that power.

If we had been paying close attention, we might have noticed that many fortunes were the result of financial speculation, fraud, government subsidies, the sale of harmful products, and the abuse of monopoly power. But this was rarely mentioned.

It is easy to confuse money with the real wealth for which it can be exchanged — our labor, ideas, land, gold, health care, food, and many other things of value in their own right. The illusions of phantom wealth are so convincing that most Wall Street players believe the wealth they are creating is real. They are standing so far upstream, they may never see the babies floating downstream that the system they serve is throwing into the water.

The market, of course, makes no distinction between the dollars acquired through means that enrich society, those created by means that impoverish society, and those simply created out of thin air. Money is money, and the more you have, the more the market eagerly responds to your every whim. To believe that paper or electronic money is real wealth, rather than simply a coupon that may be redeemed for goods and services of real intrinsic value, is to accept illusion as reality.

Those who create and benefit from phantom wealth's financial returns may never realize that their gain is unfairly diluting everyone else's claim to the available stock of real wealth. They also may fail to realize that Wall Street and its international counterparts have generated total phantom-wealth claims far in excess of the value of all the world's real wealth, thus creating expectations of future security and comforts that can never be fulfilled.

The Edmunds Fallacy

While doing the research in 1997 for *The Post-Corporate World: Life after Capitalism,* I came across an article in *Foreign Policy* by John Edmunds, then a finance professor at Babson College and the Arthur D. Little School of Management, titled "Securities: The New World Wealth Machine." I was stunned. *Foreign Policy* is a highly respected professional journal with a strict review process. Yet here in its pages was an article recommending that the production of real goods and services should be regarded as passé because national economies can and should be organized around the inflation of financial-asset bubbles. The following is an excerpt:

> Securitization — the issuance of high-quality bonds and stocks — has become the most powerful engine of wealth creation in today's world economy. Financial securities have grown to the point that they are now worth more than a year's worldwide output of goods and services, and soon they will be worth more than two years' output. While politicians concentrate on trade balances and intellectual property rights, these financial instruments are the leading component of wealth today as well as its fastest-growing generator.
>
> Historically, manufacturing, exporting, and direct investment produced prosperity through income creation. Wealth was created when a portion of income was diverted from consumption into investment in

buildings, machinery, and technological change. Societies accumulated wealth slowly over generations.

Now many societies, and indeed the entire world, have learned how to create wealth directly. The new approach requires that a state find ways to increase the *market value* of its stock of productive assets. [Emphasis in the original.] ... Wealth is also created when money, foreign or domestic, flows into the capital market of a country and raises the value of its quoted securities....

Nowadays, wealth is created when the managers of a business enterprise give high priority to rewarding the shareholders and bondholders. The greater the rewards, the more the shares and bonds are likely to be worth in the financial markets.... An economic policy that aims to achieve growth by wealth creation therefore does not attempt to increase the production of goods and services, except as a secondary objective.[1]

Professor Edmunds is telling government policymakers that they should no longer concern themselves with producing real wealth by increasing the national output of goods and services that have real utility. They should put all that aside. They can grow their national economies faster with less exertion by securitizing real assets so that investors can put them into play in financial markets and pump up their value to create gigantic asset bubbles.

At first I thought perhaps this was a parody intended to expose the irrationality of the exuberance surrounding the inflation of financial bubbles. Or might an editor with a droll sense of humor have let it through to see whether anyone was paying attention? But the next issue of *Foreign Policy* featured sober commentaries on the article by two other scholars, neither of whom took exception to the obviously flawed logic.

Rarely have I come across such a clear example of the

THE POLICY PREFERENCE FOR PHANTOM WEALTH

In recent decades, the Federal Reserve has allied with the U.S. Treasury Department and Wall Street banks to give the creation of phantom wealth priority over the production of real wealth. Rather than attempt to dampen asset bubbles like the tech-stock bubble of the 1990s and the housing bubble of 2000s, the Fed pursued cheap money policies to encourage borrowing by speculators to support continuing inflation. The growing power and profits of Wall Street signaled the success of these policies.

Meanwhile, the U.S. industrial sector was decimated as production was outsourced to low-wage economies to increase share prices. In many cases, Wall Street inflated the stock prices of its favored companies, which then gave them the power to buy up other companies. WorldCom's highly valued stock, for example, allowed it to purchase MCI and a dozen other companies. Later, the market turned down and WorldCom was forced into bankruptcy. Stock bubbles create major market disruptions.

The subprime mortgage boom was built on creating overvalued assets that served as collateral for more borrowing to create more overvalued assets. Federal bailouts to save overleveraged financial institutions when the bubble bursts represent another resource-allocation distortion.

widespread belief, seemingly pervasive on Wall Street, that inflating asset bubbles creates real wealth. Apparently, even the editors of *Foreign Policy* and their editorial reviewers failed to recognize what I'll call the "Edmunds fallacy" for the sake of giving it a shorthand name. Asset bubbles create only phantom wealth that increases the claims of the holder to a society's real wealth and thereby dilutes the claims of everyone else. Edmunds did not invent this fallacy, but its publication in *Foreign Policy* lent it new intellectual respectability and apparently stirred the imagination of Wall Street insiders.

In his 2008 book *Bad Money,* the journalist and former Republican Party political strategist Kevin Phillips notes that the Edmunds article was widely discussed on Wall Street and implies that it may have inspired the securitization of housing mortgages.[2] If it did, then measured by the costs to society of the fraud it helped to inspire, it might be judged the most costly academic thesis of all time.

The Edmunds article reminded me of a conversation I'd had some years earlier with Malaysia's then minister of forestry. He told me in all seriousness that Malaysia would be better off once all its trees were cut down and the proceeds were deposited in interest-bearing accounts, because interest grows faster than trees. An image flashed into my mind of a barren Malaysian landscape populated only by banks, their computers happily whirring away calculating the interest on those deposits. This is exactly the kind of disaster to which the Edmunds fallacy leads.

No matter who or what inspired the securitization of housing mortgages, Edmunds's logic is the underlying logic of Wall Street. Forget production and the interests of working people, communities, and nature. Focus on driving up the market price of financial securities by whatever means. The subprime mortgage debacle was a hugely costly test of a badly flawed theory.

Securitizing Subprime Mortgages

After the terrorist attacks of September 11, 2001, the U.S. Federal Reserve sought to counteract the resulting economic disruption by lowering interest rates. By July 2003, they were down to 1 percent, which was below the rate of inflation. The negative cost of borrowing set off a housing bubble and an orgy of leveraged buyouts. Wall Street investment banks invented creative instruments that justified the collection of fees for themselves, allowed them to pass the risks to others, and kept off their own books their position in what came to be called toxic assets.

The availability of cheap mortgages stimulated the housing market, which in turn inflated housing prices. The faster the bubble of easy profits grew, the faster new money flowed in to inflate it even more. Pundits and politicians, embracing the Edmunds fallacy, celebrated as wealth creation the growth in housing prices and sales financed by debt that borrowers had no means to repay.

Banks enlisted independent brokers to sign up borrowers, on commission. The banks bundled the mortgages into securities they sold to investment banks that sliced and diced them, packaged them into complex securities, and then sold them to hedge funds whose math wizards packaged them into even more complex securities that no one really understood.

These securities were "insured" against loss by other highly leveraged Wall Street institutions, such as AIG, which pocketed the premiums but kept only minimal reserves to cover potential losses, on the theory that housing prices could only go up. The investment banks and hedge funds that created the securities claimed that insurance eliminated the risk of holding such securities and hired ratings agencies to certify their claims. The securities were then sold to pension funds, endowment funds, mutual funds, and others as high-yield, risk-free investments. The players at each step along the way made a fortune from the collection of fees and commissions while passing the risks on to the next guy.[3]

In the home mortgage industry of an earlier time, local banks made loans to local borrowers and carried the risk on their books. If a homeowner could not meet the mortgage payments, the bank that made the loan bore the loss. This encouraged a careful review of mortgage applications to assure the financial solvency of the borrower.

In the "modernized" financial system, the bank captures a fee for signing up the borrower. Because the risk associated with a potential default is passed to others, the bank has no incentive to exercise due diligence, an obvious system design flaw. According to the famed international financier George Soros, "Credit standards collapsed, and mortgages were made widely available to people with low credit ratings. [Thus the term *subprime mortgage*.] . . . 'Alt-A' (or liar loans), with low or no documentation, were common, including, at the extreme, 'ninja' loans (no job, no income, no assets), frequently with the active connivance of the mortgage brokers and mortgage lenders."[4] The norm was clear. Just get a signature on a mortgage document and collect the fee. The bigger the loan, the bigger the fee. No worry if the borrower can't pay. That will be the next guy's problem.

Of course, if worst came to worst, the government could likely be pressured into a bailout by the threat that if the government didn't pick up the losses, retirees would lose their pensions, banks would stop making loans, and the economy would collapse.

The details are far more complex than what I've outlined here, but that is the essence of what happened. When obviously unqualified borrowers defaulted, the whole house of cards came tumbling down and the phantom wealth that Wall Street had created through mortgage securitization disappeared even more rapidly than it had magically appeared — as did the trillions of dollars of government bailout money that followed. The only winners were the bankers and financiers responsible for creating the crisis, who walked way with vast fortunes skimmed off as fees and bonuses, even after the bubble burst.

A Bubble Is Just a Bubble

Contrary to Edmunds's "logic," an asset bubble, real estate or otherwise, does not create wealth. A rise in the market price of a house from $200,000 to $400,000 does not make it more functional or comfortable. The real consequence of a real estate bubble is to increase the financial power of those who own property relative to those who do not. Wall Street encouraged homeowners to monetize their market gains with mortgages they lacked the means to repay except by further borrowing, which it then converted into worthless toxic securities and sold to the unwary, including the pension funds that many of those who borrowed against their inflated home values counted on for their retirement.

When the housing bubble inevitably burst, dazed homeowners walked away, many in financial ruin, from properties on which they owed more than the market value. Securities based on those mortgages lost value, and the overleveraged Wall Street players could not meet their financial commitments to each other. In the face of escalating defaults, the whole system of interlocking credit obligations collapsed and Wall Street institutions turned to taxpayers for a bailout.

The government responded with trillions of dollars in public bailout money. The recipient institutions held extravagant parties, increased executive bonuses and dividends, and financed acquisitions. The bailout money seemed to vanish as quickly as the phantom wealth of the housing bubble. Credit, however, remained frozen.

Debt Slaves to Wall Street

Why do we tolerate Wall Street's reckless excess and abuse of power? In part, it is because so many people of influence have bought into the Edmunds fallacy. Many actively celebrate the Wall Street production of phantom wealth and our growing reliance on other countries to produce the goods and services we consume. By the prevailing story, we, the United States, serve the global economy by specializing in making money and consuming the goods that others produce. In the fantasy world of Wall Street, this all makes perfect sense.

If you have difficulty understanding the Wall Street logic, which is taught in many economics and finance courses, it may be because you are in touch with reality. No matter what Wall Street says, a bad loan is still a bad loan no matter how many times it has been sliced, diced, and repackaged into ever more complex derivatives certified by Standard & Poor's as AAA.

Even more, however, we tolerate Wall Street and rush to bail it out because it controls the issuance of credit and thereby our access to money in a world that has made us dependent on money for almost every aspect of our lives. Furthermore, many of us depend on private retirement accounts that in turn depend on the success of Wall Street's money games.

Here is a simple description of how the money-creation process works.

ALCHEMISTS IN EYESHADES

Most people think of accounting as a rather boring subject, but pay attention here, because nearly every dollar in circulation has been created by a private bank with a deceptively simple accounting sleight of hand. Understand how it works and you understand why our current system of debt money created by private banks for private gain makes it possible for a few people to acquire obscene amounts of unearned money while sticking the rest of us with the bill.

My college economics professors taught us that banks are financial intermediaries between savers and borrowers: A saver makes a deposit and the bank lends that money to a borrower to finance a business or home. But that isn't the way it really works.

Unless you are holding a long-term certificate of deposit, you have immediate access to the money you deposit in your bank. If you borrow money from the bank, you also have immediate access to the funds in the account that the bank created in your name when it made the loan. When a loan is issued, the bank's accountant enters two numbers in the bank's accounting records: She records the borrower's promise to repay the loan as an asset, and the money the bank puts into the borrower's account as a liability.

At first glance, it looks like these entries cancel each other out, which in a sense is true. The key is that neither entry existed previously. With the accountant's entries, the bank created new money from nothing in the amount of the loan principal and caused the amount of money in the economy as a whole to increase. At the same time, the borrower acquired a legal obligation to repay the principal with interest.

This, in fact, is how all money (except for coins and some special notes) is created. It should be noted that the bank-created money is purely electronic. There isn't even a paper record.

Needless to say, granting banks the right to create money with a computer keystroke and then lend it out at interest makes banking very profitable, and Wall Street, which owns the banks, enormously powerful. Unless this power is limited and used with great care, it leads to financial instability and inequality, creates an economic growth imperative, and distorts economic priorities, all costs to society I explain in chapter 7, "The High Cost of Phantom Wealth." The consequences can become truly devastating when banks discover the profit potential in putting this money-creation power at the service of financial speculators and predators engaged in the creation of phantom wealth and ignore the underlying assumptions of the debt/credit money system we have left it to them to manage.

FROM GOOD DEBT TO BAD DEBT

The debt-based money system that is the foundation of Wall Street's control of the economy and society is based on an underlying logic. So long as its practice is true to that logic, the debt model of money creation can be a driving engine of real-wealth production — up to the point at which the economy encounters the limits of the planet.

Driven by greed and blinded by hubris, Wall Street forgot the logic and created a debt bomb that guaranteed economic and financial collapse.

The Logic of Productive Saving and Investment

The logic of the debt-based money system assumes that the financial system receives the savings of working people and in turn lends those savings to entrepreneurs and enterprises to finance capital investment projects that expand society's pool of real wealth.

This logic assumes that savers are deferring immediate consumption so that the economic resources that otherwise would be directed to their consumption are instead devoted to creating new capital assets that support greater future production. It further assumes that the benefits of this new real wealth are shared equitably among those who contributed to its creation: The savers who defer their consumption receive a fair share as interest. The entrepreneurs who convert the savings into productive capacity receive a fair share as profit. The workers who provide the labor receive a fair share as wages, and the governments that provide the supporting infrastructure receive a fair share as taxes.

The operation of the financial system was more or less consistent with this logic from the 1940s through much of the 1970s. Then the orgy of deregulation described in chapter 5 allowed it to morph from a servant system into a predator system devoted to making money without the bother of financing productive enterprise.

The Illogic of Negative Saving and Consumer Debt

In October 2008, *BusinessWeek* called attention to what it called a gigantic credit bubble, "consumption that was not justified by income growth," and estimated that for U.S. consumers the total gap between income and consumption over the previous ten years totaled some $3 trillion dollars.[5] That gap was one of the many conditions for financial disaster resulting from the creation of phantom-wealth illusions but, of course, it was and continues to be highly profitable for Wall Street.

Anytime debt exceeds the capacity to repay it, there is a problem for someone. When the total debt of a society is greater than the total market value of all its real resources, it means that the expectations of the holders of the debt — for example people whose retirement savings are invested in supposedly safe derivatives based on toxic assets — cannot be fulfilled. The society faces the difficult task of determining whose claims and expectations will be fulfilled and whose will not.

In the current instance, there is a deeper issue. *Business-Week* was talking about *consumer* debt. The logic of the money system assumes that debt is a means by which savings are translated into investment in expanding productive output.

In our current case, the money lent comes from an accounting entry, not from savings, and it is used to fund consumption, not production. The debt and the expectations of those who hold it grow exponentially, but actual production does not. This creates an ever-greater disconnect between expectations and the real wealth available to satisfy them.

It is the same situation when the government spends beyond its income to finance nonproductive consumption items such as an outsized military establishment and Wall Street bailouts. Deficit spending by government may be justified for investments in various forms of real productive capital, such as infrastructure, education, health, research, and environmental rejuvenation. These build the society's productive capacity and thereby contribute to the creation of corresponding real wealth. By contrast, wars deplete real wealth, and Wall Street bailouts, in the absence of corrective structural reforms, simply revive the predatory phantom-wealth machine.

Although this may sound a bit complicated, the basics are simple. Borrowing for investment in productive capacity is a generally beneficial path. Borrowing for current consumption is bad because it creates no new value and creates debts that can only be rolled over into ever-greater debt that the borrower has no way to repay.

We are in trouble as a nation not because our expenditures exceed our income but because the excess expenditure is for consumption rather than for investments that support increased future output. Furthermore, we make up the difference between our consumption and our production with imported goods purchased on credit extended by the producing countries. The more we allow cheap products from abroad to crowd out domestic jobs and businesses, the more dependent we become on imports, the faster our foreign debt grows, and the faster our capacity to repay the debt declines.

These systemic imbalances create ever-growing instability

on a path to ultimate collapse. It is also a path to a condition of permanent servitude called debt slavery, which I put in historical context in chapter 14.

The Language of Self-Deception

One of the main reasons we tend not to see such irrational and destructive dynamics is that the deceptions are built right into our language. We refer to speculation as "investment" and to phantom wealth as "capital." The practice of equating money with financial capital comes from a time when savings, representing deferred consumption, were used to invest in new productive capacity. In the global casino economy, that idea of savings seems a bit quaint, yet we continue to use the old linguistic conventions.

This obfuscation of the language is an important contributor to the mistaken perception that as a global society we are getting richer, when in fact we are getting poorer in ways that put the future of our species at risk.

▸•◆•◆•◂

Wall Street, as economic system or syndicate, is extremely good at what it is designed and managed to do: make a few people fabulously wealthy without the exertion and distraction of producing anything of real value. From the perspective of the beneficiaries, money is money, and those who have lots of it can indulge themselves in luxuries beyond the imagination of the kings and emperors of previous times.

The major failing of the existing financial system from the perspective of its Wall Street beneficiaries is the tendency for asset bubbles to collapse and wipe out large portions of their asset statements, even forcing them to sell off estates, yachts, and private jets at fire-sale prices.

In the bigger picture, even when the bubbles are expanding, Wall Street's gain is a net loss for the rest of the society because Wall Street's growing claims on the real wealth of society dilute the claims of others. The social costs of growing inequality and the environmental costs of the related profligate consumption fall on those who don't have the money to live in splendid isolation from the resulting social and environmental breakdown.

The idea that economic growth will bring up the bottom and finance environmental restoration has no substance. The so-called rising tide lifts only the yachts and swamps the desperate, naked swimmers struggling for survival, and no amount of money can heal the environment in the face of unrestrained growth in material consumption.

For the winners, it works out fine in the short term that growth in Wall Street financial assets plays out for the rest of society as growing inequality. A wealthy class needs a servant class, and what remains of the world's real wealth need only be shared among the very rich.

Fortunately for the rest of us, there is an alternative to Wall Street phantom-wealth capitalism: a real-market economy.

CHAPTER 3

►·◆·◆·◄

A REAL-MARKET ALTERNATIVE

Communism forgets that life is individual. Capitalism forgets
that life is social, and the kingdom of brotherhood is found neither in the thesis of communism nor the antithesis of capitalism
but in a higher synthesis . . . that combines the truths of both.

MARTIN LUTHER KING JR.

Americans have long been told that the only alternative
to the rapacious excess of capitalism is the debilitating repression of communism. This sets up a false and dangerously self-limiting choice between two extremes, both of
which failed because they created a concentration of unaccountable power that stifled liberty and creativity for all but
the few at the top.

The alternative to both of these discredited experiments
in centralized power is an economic system that roots power
in people and communities of place and unleashes our innate
human capacity for cooperation and creativity. We have a historic opportunity to bring such an economy into being. The
key is the often-mentioned distinction between our existing
Wall Street and Main Street economies.

WALL STREET VERSUS MAIN STREET

Wall Street and *Main Street* are names given to two economies
with strikingly different priorities, values, and institutions.

They are distinct but interconnected, and they are often in competition.

Wall Street

Wall Street refers to the institutions of big finance and the captive corporations that serve them. They may be located anywhere, not just on the famous street in New York City that has become a global symbol of capitalist excess.

Wall Street is a world of pure finance in the business of using money to make money by whatever means for people who have money. Any involvement in the production of real goods and services is purely an incidental byproduct. Maximizing financial return is the game. To that end, Wall Street institutions have perfected the arts of financial speculation, corporate-asset stripping, predatory lending, risk shifting, leveraging, and debt-pyramid creation. Successful players are rewarded with celebrity, extravagant perks, and vast financial fortunes.

Wall Street players justify their actions with the claim that they are creating wealth for the benefit of society, a convenient bit of self-delusion. We noted in the previous chapter, however, that money isn't wealth. It is only an accounting chit, a number of value only because by social convention we are willing to accept it in return for things of real value.

Main Street

Main Street is the world of local businesses and working people engaged in producing real goods and services to provide a livelihood for themselves, their families, and their communities. Main Street is more varied in its priorities, values, and institutions. Like the diverse species of a healthy ecosystem, its enterprises take many forms, from sole proprietorships and family businesses to cooperatives and locally owned and locally rooted privately held corporations. Achieving a positive financial return is an essential condition of staying in business, but most Main Street businesses function within a framework of community values and interests that moderate the drive for profit.

I grew up in a small town in which my family had a successful retail music and appliance business. My dad took great pride in standing behind and servicing everything he sold. I recall the not infrequent experience of his answering the phone during dinner and asking Mother to keep his dinner warm as he got up to open the store for a customer with an urgent need. One, I remember, was from a local musician who had broken his guitar pick and needed a replacement for a job he was playing that night. At that time, a pick was probably no more than a 10-cent item.

I understood that business was a service to the community and that that was what businesspeople provided. Many Main Street business owners continue to this day to embrace a similar commitment to community service, including the twenty-one thousand members of the Business Alliance for Local Living Economies already engaged in building the New Economy. This commitment is an essential part of what distinguishes Main Street from Wall Street.

CORPORATIONS

So, what of corporations? Many of them produce beneficial goods and services that we need in our daily lives. Where do they fit between Wall Street and Main Street? The answer is, "It depends."

The legal form of the modern publicly traded limited liability corporation was invented a bit more than four hundred years ago when the king of England issued a charter to the East India Company. He thereby granted a group of investors, including himself, an exclusive Crown-protected license to colonize the lands of Asia and expropriate their resources through trade and military force.

The corporate charter suits this purpose well: It creates the legal capacity to amass under unified management the power of virtually unlimited financial capital; moreover, the shareholders who benefit are exempted from liability for the consequences of management's actions beyond the amount of their investment. It is an open invitation to abuse to which even saints are prone to succumb.

That said, there are incorporated businesses with identifiable responsible owners who live in the communities in which their businesses are located and who operate their corporations as responsible members of their community. These corporations are properly considered part of the Main Street economy.

Once a corporation sells its shares publicly through Wall Street exchanges or to Wall Street private equity investors, however, it becomes an agent of Wall Street. Whatever values it may have had before are, in all probability, subordinated to Wall Street interests and values. The production of goods and services becomes incidental to the primary business purpose of making money. As a onetime executive of the Odwalla corporation told me, "So long as we were privately owned by the founders, we were in the business of producing and marketing healthful fruit juice products. Once we went public, everything changed. From that event forward, we were in the business of making money."

Notwithstanding the title of my first book on the global economy, *When Corporations Rule the World,* the real economic power in this country resides with Wall Street institutions that buy and sell major corporations as if they were mere commodities. Any chief executive officer of a Wall Street–traded corporation that puts social or environmental considerations ahead of financial return will soon find

FREEDOM TO COMMIT FRAUD

The term *free market* is a code word for an unregulated market that allows the rich to consume and monopolize resources for personal gain free from accountability for the broader social and environmental consequences. A free market rewards financial rogues and speculators who profit from governmental, social, and environmental subsidies, speculation, the abuse of monopoly power, and financial fraud, creating an open and often irresistible invitation to externalize costs and increase inequality.

Markets work best within the framework of a caring community. The stronger the relations of mutual trust and caring, the more the market becomes self-policing. The need for formal governmental oversight and intervention is minimal. An economy of powerful corporations governed by a culture of greed and a belief that it is their legal duty to maximize returns to shareholders is a quite different matter, and it is difficult for even the strongest of governments to control.

himself cast out through a revolt of institutional shareholders or a hostile takeover.

Visit a contemporary corporate headquarters and you see people, buildings, furnishings, and office equipment. By all appearances, the people are running things. An organizational chart will show clear lines of authority leading to a CEO who in turn reports to a board of directors. It is easy to think of a corporation as a community of people. That is, however, a misleading characterization, because the people are all employees of the corporation and paid to serve its financial interests. If the corporation is Wall Street owned, they are bound to serve Wall Street interests, and their employment is solely at Wall Street's pleasure.

The publicly traded limited liability corporation is most accurately described as a pool of money with special legal rights and protections. Even the CEO and directors can be dismissed without notice or recourse. In theory, it is the shareholders whom management serves; however, because most shares are held in trust by various institutional investors, the real shareholders are generally invisible even to the corporate officers.

In effect, management is hired by money to nurture money's growth and reproduction in disregard of all other considerations. The result is a global capitalist economy destructive of both life and the human soul.

THE MARKET ALTERNATIVE

Defenders of capitalist excess insist that capitalism is synonymous with markets and private ownership. If not entirely false, this claim is at best seriously misleading, and it obscures our ability to see an obvious nonrepressive alternative.

The theory of the market economy traces back to the eighteenth-century Scottish economist Adam Smith and the publication in 1776 of his *Inquiry into the Nature and Causes of the Wealth of Nations*. Considered by many to be the most influential economics book ever written, Smith's seminal text articulates the powerful and wonderfully democratic ideal of a self-organizing economy that creates an equitable and socially optimal allocation of society's productive resources through the interaction of small buyers and sellers making decisions based on their individual needs, interests, and abilities.

Market theory, as articulated by Smith and those who subsequently elaborated on his ideas, developed into an elegant

ADAM SMITH'S VISION

Adam Smith envisioned a world of local-market economies populated by small entrepreneurs, artisans, and family farmers with strong community roots, engaged in producing and exchanging goods and services to meet the needs of themselves and their neighbors. This was a vision of the Main Street economy of Smith's time.

Contrary to popular misconception, Adam Smith was not the father of capitalism. He would have taken offense at the title, because the values of capitalism as we know it were not his values. He had a substantial antipathy toward corporate monopolies and those who use their wealth and power in ways that harm others. He believed that people have a natural and appropriate concern for the well-being of others and a duty not to do others harm. He also believed that government has a responsibility to restrain those who fail in that duty.

and coherent intellectual construction grounded in carefully articulated assumptions regarding the conditions under which such self-organizing processes would indeed lead to socially optimal outcomes. Market fundamentalists, whose views are shaped more by ideology than by fact-based science, generally ignore the essential conditions of efficient market allocation. For example:

- Buyers and sellers must be too small to influence the market price.
- Income and ownership must be distributed equitably with no extremes of wealth or poverty.
- Complete information must be available to all participants, and there can be no trade secrets.

- Sellers must bear the full cost of the products they sell and incorporate it into the sale price.

- Investment capital must remain within national borders, and trade between countries must be balanced.

- Savings must be invested in the creation of productive capital rather than in speculative trading.

Although not a perfect match, a vital community-centered Main Street aligns with these principles surprisingly well. Wall Street does not. Wall Street abhors real markets and builds its business model around the systematic violation of these market principles.

Wall Street does, however, conform to the original definition of *capitalism*, which historians have traced to the mid-1800s, long after Adam Smith's death. In its early use it referred to an economic and political regime in which the ownership and benefits of capital are appropriated by the few to the exclusion of the many who through their labor make capital productive.[1] This is a near-perfect characterization of Wall Street.

CAPITALISM CLOAKED IN MARKET RHETORIC

Capitalism's claim to the mantle of the market has no more substance than the claim of the rogue in the tale of "The Emperor's New Clothes," who declared that he had cloaked the ruler in a fine gown. In selectively culling bits and pieces of market theory to argue that the public interest is best served by giving globe-spanning megacorporations a license to maximize their profits without public restraint, capitalism has distorted market theory beyond recognition to legitimize an ideology without logical or empirical foundation in the service of a narrow class interest.

Table 3.1 provides an overview of some of the major differences between the Wall Street capitalist economy we

Table 3.1 Wall Street Capitalism versus Main Street Markets

	Wall Street capitalism	Main Street markets
Dominant driver	Making money	Creating livelihoods
Defining activity	Using money to make money for those who have money	Employing available resources to meet the needs of the community
Firm size	Very large	Small and medium
Costs	Externalized to the public	Internalized by the user
Ownership	Impersonal and absentee	Personal and rooted
Financial capital	Global with no borders	Local/national with clear borders
Purpose of investment	Maximize private profit	Increase beneficial output
The role of profit	An end to be maximized	A means to sustain viability
Efficiency measure	Returns to financial capital	Returns to living capital
Coordinating mechanisms	Central planning by mega-corporations	Self-organizing markets and networks
Cooperation	Can occur among competitors to escape the discipline of competition	Occurs among people and communities to advance the common good
Purpose of competition	Eliminates the unfit	Stimulates efficiency and innovation
Government role	Protect the interests of property	Protect the common interest
Trade	Free and unregulated	Fair and balanced
Political orientation	A democracy of dollars	A democracy of persons

have and the kind of Main Street market economy we need to encourage.

Like cancer cells that attempt to hide from the body's immune system by masking themselves as healthy cells, capitalism's agents attempt to conceal themselves from society's immune system by masquerading as agents of a healthy market economy. Capitalism has become so skilled in this deception that we now find our economic and political leaders committed to policies that serve the pathology at the expense of the healthy body. To restore health we must recognize the diseased cells for what they are and either surgically remove them or deprive them of access to the body's nutrients.

Under a socialist system, government consolidates power unto itself. Under a capitalist model, government falls captive to corporate interests and facilitates the consolidation of corporate power. In a true market system, democratically accountable governments provide an appropriate framework of rules within which people, communities, entrepreneurs, and responsible investors self-organize in predominantly local markets to meet their economic needs in socially and environmentally responsible ways.

RULES MAKE THE DIFFERENCE

Capitalism — rule by big money — is what happens to a market economy that lacks appropriate rules. Economic power becomes increasingly concentrated and delinked from public accountability. The power holders rewrite the rules to secure for themselves the financial gains of their decisions while passing the costs to others. Focused on generating financial gains for the rich and powerful in disregard of real-world consequences, the economic system neglects the production of real wealth in favor of producing phantom wealth. A lack of market rules is the cause. The implementation of market rules is the antidote.

Free market ideologues will shout that government is restricting individual liberty. But liberty can be abused, particularly when combined with a massive concentration of unaccountable financial power. As Adam Smith himself acknowledged in *The Theory of Moral Sentiments,* an essential responsibility of government is to step in when required to constrain those who abuse their liberty in ways that harm others.

Proper market rules preclude speculation, the acquisition of monopoly power, and the destruction of real wealth to create phantom wealth. They support an economy that functions more like a healthy ecosystem than a cancer. They create a powerful bias in favor of Main Street and real wealth.

A true market economy absolutely needs government, not to direct every aspect of the economy but to set the framework of rules that provide a context within which the daily decision making of people and businesses balances individual and community interests. If market fundamentalists complain that such interference inhibits financial "innovation," so be it. That is the intention. Most Wall Street financial innovations are nothing more than complex variations on the basic Ponzi scheme and should be illegal.

▶•◆•◆•◀

In the Wall Street economy, money is both means and end, and the primary product is phantom wealth — money disconnected from the production or possession of anything of real value. The Main Street economy is largely engaged in creating real wealth from real resources to meet real needs. Wall Street is very good at making rich people richer, but it has no concern for the health of people, community, or nature except as sources of short-term profit.

The difference between the Wall Street and Main Street economies is the difference between a capitalist economy and a true market economy. The former monopolizes resources under the central control of global corporations to maximize the profits of the already rich. The latter facilitates radically decentralized economic self-organization to optimize the use of local resources to meet local needs.

Capitalism is what happens to a market economy in the absence of clear market rules fairly and uniformly enforced by democratically accountable governments. If government doesn't make and enforce the rules necessary to maintain fair and efficient market allocation, the market's most powerful corporate players make their own rules to suit their financial advantage, and society pays the price.

Draw back the curtain, as the credit collapse has done, to reveal the inner workings of Wall Street capitalism, and it begins to look less like a legitimate business enterprise and more like a criminal syndicate engaged in counterfeiting, predatory lending, usury, tax evasion, fraud, and extortion. It may be legal, because Wall Street writes its own rules, but it should be illegal and treated accordingly. The nearest equivalent in nature is a cancer that drains the body's energy but produces nothing useful in return.

You "fix" a criminal syndicate by shutting it down through the enforcement of laws that protect the public interest. You "fix" a cancer by removing it and rebuilding the healthy tissue. Main Street is the healthy tissue on which to rebuild the tissues of a healthy economy, but supporting its full development will require more than tinkering at the margins.

CHAPTER 4

▶•◆•◆•◀

MORE THAN TINKERING AT THE MARGINS

We are told routinely that the first priority must be a strong economy. Yet, we know now that we should seek first a strong society, strong nature, and a strong democracy. Today's economy offers little help in these regards. We must move beyond it. We need to reinvent the economy, not merely restore it.

JAMES GUSTAVE SPETH, FORMER ADMINISTRATOR,
UNITED NATIONS DEVELOPMENT PROGRAMME

When economic failure is systemic, temporary fixes, even very expensive ones like the Wall Street bailout, are like putting a bandage on a cancer. They may create a temporary sense of confidence, but the effect is solely cosmetic.

Unfortunately, even influential pundits who recognize the seriousness of the environmental and social dimensions of the current economic crisis generally limit their recommendations to a tune-up of the existing system. It is rare indeed to hear establishment voices call for a redesign of our economic institutions.

Jeffrey Sachs and James Gustave Speth are both influential establishment authors who in recent books present nearly identical statements of the need for action to reverse environmental damage and eliminate poverty. Their recommendations, however, are worlds apart. Sachs focuses on the symptoms and prescribes a bandage. Speth takes a holistic approach, looks upstream for the cause, and prescribes a cultural and institutional transformation.[1]

I contrast the perspectives of Sachs and Speth on three defining economic issues in Table 4.1. The differences are instructive, because we must learn to distinguish those who would lull us into believing we can get by with adjustments at the margins, à la Sachs, the neoclassical economist, from those who offer serious solutions based on a deep system redesign, à la Speth, the systems ecologist.

SACHS: PAINLESS FINE-TUNING

Jeffrey Sachs, an economist by training and perspective, is known for his work as an economic adviser to national governments and an array of public institutions. The *New York Times* once described him as "probably the most important economist in the world."[2]

Sachs opens *Common Wealth: Economics for a Crowded Planet* (2008) with a powerful and unequivocal statement that raises expectations of a bold break from those he refers to as "free-market ideologues":

> The challenges of sustainable development — protecting the environment, stabilizing the world's population, narrowing the gaps between rich and poor, and ending extreme poverty — will take center stage. Global cooperation will have to come to the fore. The very idea of competing nation-states that scramble for markets, power, and resources will become passé.... The pressures of scarce energy resources, growing environmental stresses, a rising global population, legal and illegal mass migration, shifting economic power, and vast

Table 4.1 Tinkering versus Transforming

	Marginal adjustment (Sachs)	System redesign (Speth)
Economic growth	Growth in GDP is a valid measure of human progress, prosperity, and increased well-being. More is generally better. Given a combination of market forces, the provision of public incentives, and a proper mix of technology, there is no inherent environmental limit to economic growth.	Economic growth is disrupting the values and living systems essential to human well-being. Beyond a minimal threshold of consumption, distributing wealth equitably and building community, rather than increasing the consumption of stuff, is the key to increasing human health and happiness.
Equity	Poverty, not equity, is the issue, and the proper response is to kick-start the growth process within the world's remaining pockets of absolute poverty by introducing technologies and social services funded by foreign aid.	Extreme poverty is the inevitable other side of the coin of extreme wealth and can be resolved only through redistribution from those who have more than they need to those who have less.
Governing system	The institutions of capitalism as currently constituted can resolve environmental and social problems through a combination of voluntary action, modest public expenditure, and fine-tuning at the margins.	The operating systems of capitalism must be fundamentally redesigned to internalize costs, distribute ownership, and establish accountability for the human and natural consequences of economic decisions.

inequalities of income are too great to be left to naked market forces and untrammeled geopolitical competition among nations.[3]

That declaration would have served equally well as an opening statement for Speth, who agrees that government must play an essential role, and that nations must cooperate, in any effort to effect meaningful solutions. From there, however, we might wonder whether they live in different worlds.

The Tech Fix

Sachs assures us that we can end environmental stress and poverty with modest investments in existing technologies to sequester carbon, develop new energy sources, end population growth, make more efficient use of water and other natural resources, and jump-start economic growth in the world's remaining pockets of persistent poverty. In a 2007 lecture to the Royal Society in London, Sachs made clear his belief that there is no need to redistribute wealth, cut back material consumption, or otherwise reorganize the economy:

I do not believe that the solution to this problem is a massive cutback of our consumption levels or our living standards. I think the solution is smarter living. I do believe that technology is absolutely critical, and I do not believe . . . that the essence of the problem is that we face a zero sum that must be redistributed. I'm going to argue that there's a way for us to use the knowledge that we have, the technology that we have, to make broad progress in material conditions, to not require or ask the rich to take sharp cuts of living standards, but rather to live with smarter technologies that are sustainable, and thereby to find a way for the rest of the world, which yearns for it, and deserves it as far as I'm concerned, to raise their own material conditions as well. The costs are much less than people think.[4]

Far from calling for a restraint on consumption, Sachs projects global economic expansion from $60 trillion in 2005 to $420 trillion in 2050. Relying on what he calls a "back-of-the-envelope calculation," he estimates that the world's wealthy nations can eliminate extreme poverty and develop and apply the necessary technologies to address environmental needs with an expenditure of a mere 2.4 percent of the projected midcentury economic output. Problem painlessly solved, at least in Sachs's mind.

Growth as Usual

Sachs gives no indication of why, if we can stabilize population and meet the needs of the poor with a modest expenditure, we should need or even want a global economy seven times as large as its present size. Like most other economists, and indeed the general public, Sachs simply assumes that economic growth is both good and necessary. It apparently never occurs to him to question this assumption, which Speth demonstrates to be false.

Furthermore, because Sachs maintains that the poorest of the poor can be put on the path to economic growth with no more than a very modest redistribution, he seems to assume that consumption will continue to increase across the board. He says nothing about what forms of consumption can continue to multiply without placing yet more pressure on already overstressed natural systems. Unless the already affluent are driving even bigger cars, living in bigger houses, eating higher on the food chain, traveling farther with more frequency, and buying more electronic gear, what exactly will they be consuming more of? From what materials will it be fabricated? What energy sources will be used? In what way will this increased consumption improve their quality of life? Sachs fails to consider such questions.

Nor does Sachs mention the realities of political power and resource control — for example, the reality that in most instances, poor countries are poor not because they receive too little foreign aid but because we of the rich nations have used our military and economic power to expropriate their resources to consume beyond our own means. It is troubling, although not surprising, that Sachs's reassuring words get an attentive hearing among establishment power holders.

SPETH: REDIRECTION AND REDESIGN

James Gustave Speth, who has degrees in law and economics, has had a distinguished career as the founder and former head of the World Resources Institute, the administrator of the United Nations Development Programme, and dean of the Yale University School of Forestry. Speth writes from the perspective of a systems ecologist.

The End of Growth and Capitalism

In stark contrast to Sachs, Speth concludes in *The Bridge at the Edge of the World: Capitalism, the Environment, and Crossing from Crisis to Sustainability* (2008) that "the planet cannot sustain capitalism as we know it." He recommends that "the operating system of capitalism" be redesigned to support the development of local economies populated with firms that feature worker and community ownership and that corporations be chartered only to serve the public interest.

Rather than settle for a simplistic back-of-the-envelope projection, Speth takes a hard look at the research on GDP growth and environmental damage. He notes that despite a slight decline in the amount of environmental damage per increment of growth, growth in GDP always increases environmental damage. The relationship is inherent in the simple fact that GDP is mostly a measure of growth in consumption, which is the driving cause of environmental decline. Speth is clear that even though choosing "green" products may be a positive step, not buying at all beats buying green almost every time:

> To sum up, we live in a world where economic growth is generally seen as both beneficent and necessary — the more, the better; where past growth has brought us to a perilous state environmentally; where we are poised for unprecedented increments in growth; where this growth is proceeding with wildly wrong market signals, including prices that do not incorporate environmental costs or reflect the needs of future generations; where a failed politics has not meaningfully corrected the market's obliviousness to environmental needs; where economies are routinely deploying technology that was created in an environmentally unaware era; where there is no hidden hand or inherent mechanism adequate to correct the destructive tendencies. So, right now, one can only conclude that growth is the enemy of environment. Economy and environment remain in collision.[5]

After examining the abuses of corporate power, Speth endorses the call to revoke the charters of corporations that grossly violate the public interest, and to exclude or expel unwanted corporations, roll back limited liability, eliminate corporate personhood, bar corporations from making political contributions, and limit corporate lobbying.

Health and Happiness

Speth is clear that we are unlikely as a species to implement the measures required to bring ourselves into balance with the environment so long as economic growth remains an overriding policy priority, consumerism defines our cultural values, and the excesses of corporate behavior are unconstrained by fairly enforced rules. To correct our misplaced priorities, he recommends replacing financial indicators of economic performance, such as GDP, with wholly new measures based on nonfinancial indicators of social and environmental health — the things we should be optimizing. Speth quotes psychologist David Myers, whose essay "What Is the Good Life?" claims that Americans have

> big houses and broken homes, high incomes and low morale, secured rights and diminished civility. We were excelling at making a living but too often failing at making a life. We celebrated our prosperity but yearned for purpose. We cherished our freedoms but longed for connection. In an age of plenty, we were feeling spiritual hunger. These facts of life lead us to a startling conclusion: Our becoming better off materially has not made us better off psychologically.[6]

This is consistent with studies finding that beyond a basic threshold, equity and community are far more important determinants of health and happiness than income or possessions. Indeed, as Speth documents, economic growth tends to be associated with increases in individualism, social fragmentation, inequality, depression, and even impaired physical health.

Social Movements

Speth gives significant attention to social movements grounded in an awakening spiritual consciousness, which are creating communities of the future from the bottom up, practicing participatory democracy, and demanding changes in the rules of the game.

Many of our deepest thinkers and many of those most familiar with the scale of the challenges we face have concluded that the transitions required can be achieved only in the context of what I will call the rise of a new consciousness. For some, it is a spiritual awakening — a transformation of the human heart. For others it is a more intellectual process of coming to see the world anew and deeply embracing the emerging ethic of the environment and the old ethic of what it means to love thy neighbor as thyself.[7]

▶•◆•◆•◀

By this time, given the strength of the evidence to the contrary, it is difficult to take seriously anyone who assumes, without question, that the global economy can expand to seven times its current size between now and 2050 without collapsing Earth's life support system. Unfortunately, Jeffrey Sachs demonstrates the intellectual myopia common to many professional economists whose ideological assumptions trump reality.

When we seek guidance on dealing with the complex issues relating to interactions between human economies and the planetary ecosystems in which they are embedded, we are best advised to turn to those like James Gustave Speth, who view the world through a larger and less ideologically clouded lens — and who, not incidentally, recognize the distinction between real wealth and phantom wealth.

It is instructive, however, that not even Speth addressed what has become the elephant in the middle of the room — one that had not yet moved to the forefront of the public consciousness at the time he and Sachs were writing their respective books. The elephant — an out-of-control and out-of-touch financial system devoted to speculation, inflating financial bubbles, stripping corporate assets, and predatory lending — was dramatically exposed by the credit collapse. Though costly, the collapse thus has been something of a blessing. It has brought into sharp relief previously obscure but crucial system design choices relating to our financial institutions that we otherwise might not have recognized until they had done so much damage to the economy, our communities, and the environment that recovery would not be possible.

PART II

THE CASE FOR REPLACING WALL STREET

▸•◆•◆•◂

Efforts to fix Wall Street miss an important point. It can't be fixed. It is corrupt beyond repair, and we cannot afford it. Moreover, because the essential functions it does perform are served better in less costly ways, we do not need it.

Wall Street's only business purpose is to enrich its own major players, a bunch of buccaneers and privateers who find it more profitable to expropriate the wealth of others than to find honest jobs producing goods and services beneficial to their communities. They walk away with their fees, commissions, and bonus packages and leave it to others to pick up the costs of federal bailouts, gyrating economic cycles, collapsing environmental systems, broken families, shattered communities, and the export of jobs along with the manufacturing, technology, and research capacities that go with them.

Even more damaging in some ways than the economic costs are the spiritual and psychological costs of a Wall Street culture that celebrates greed, favors the emotionally and morally challenged with outsized compensation packages, and denies the human capacity for cooperation and sharing. Running out of control and delinked from reality, Wall Street has created an *Alice in Wonderland* phantom-wealth world in which prospective financial claims and the expectations that go with them exceed the value of all the world's real wealth by orders of magnitude.

We can no longer afford to acquiesce to a system of rule by those engaged in the pursuit of phantom wealth far beyond any conceivable need — and to no evident end other than to accumulate points in a contest for the top spots on the Forbes list of richest people.

Chapter 5, "What Wall Street Really Wants," explains why there is no limit to Wall Street greed and how its institutions use the economic and political muscle of their monopoly control of the creation and allocation of money to get what they want: Everything!

Chapter 6, "Buccaneers and Privateers," provides an evocative history of the role that licensed pirates and chartered corporations played in the transition from rule by kings — who found them a cheap substitute for official navies and a useful means of circumventing parliamentary oversight — to rule by global financiers.

Chapter 7, "The High Cost of Phantom Wealth," describes how Wall Street players reap enormous financial rewards for creating phantom expectations through their use of complex financial instruments that defy understanding.

Chapter 8, "The End of Empire," describes Wall Street's rule by the power of money as an extension of five thousand years of imperial rule by kings and emperors who wielded the power of the sword.

Chapter 9, "Greed Is Not a Virtue; Sharing Is Not a Sin," looks at what events since the September 2008 crash reveal about the profound ethical issues before us and the inability of Wall Street to face up to its culpability and play a constructive role in a search for real solutions.

CHAPTER 5

►•◄•◄•◄

WHAT WALL STREET REALLY WANTS

The Bankers own the earth. Take it away from them, but leave them the power to create money, and with the flick of the pen they will create enough money to buy it back again.

ATTRIBUTED TO SIR JOSIAH STAMP, DIRECTOR, BANK OF ENGLAND 1928–1941

The Wall Street money game is a power game as old as empire. And like Monopoly, the popular board game, the game isn't over until the winner has it all. So what does Wall Street want? Everything. And the crash of 2008 did nothing to diminish that drive.

The basic question is whether our institutions should be designed to meet the needs of all or to facilitate the Wall Street drive to get it all. Wall Street's answer is clear.

TWO GREAT ARCS

The Nobel Prize–winning economist Paul Krugman opens *The Conscience of a Liberal* with a personal reflection on growing up during the post–World War II years believing that a bipartisan political consensus framed by the New Deal of the Roosevelt administration was what America is about. Only when the New Deal consensus fell apart did he begin to see the deeper truth.

There have been two great arcs in modern American history — an economic arc from high inequality to relative equality and a political arc from extreme polarization to bipartisanship and back again. These two arcs move in parallel: The golden age of economic equality roughly corresponded to the golden age of political bipartisanship.[1]

These arcs, by Krugman's reckoning, are creations of intentional political action. The middle class was created in the space of a very few years through New Deal legislation that established Social Security and other safety-net programs, implemented a highly progressive taxation of income and estates, supported unions, and raised the floor on wages

HOW WALL STREET SEES ITSELF

We, the Wall Street money managers, are society's most valuable citizens. We provide capital, manage risk, maintain liquidity in capital markets, and assure the efficient allocation of investment resources needed to create jobs, support innovation, and grow the economy. We are entitled to the fruits of the wealth we create, for as we make our deals, the wealth pie expands, the benefits trickle down, and the lives of all improve.

We fulfill our moral duty to God and country by maximizing individual financial gain, thereby maximizing the pool of wealth available to all. Those who sacrifice a margin of financial gain for a supposed higher good deprive society of the growth in wealth it might otherwise enjoy, and they thereby engage in an immoral act.

Individualism is the foundation of prosperity and liberty. Government is the enemy of both.

to narrow the wealth and income gap between the upper and lower economic classes.

Once in place, this legislative framework was maintained for a time by a new social consensus. Eventually, however, the legislative framework of the midcentury was reversed by the intentional actions of an alliance of corporate CEOs, religious fundamentalists, antitax libertarians, and neocon militarists. Krugman concludes that market forces did not create the middle class and will not restore it.

"MODERNIZING" THE ECONOMY

They began mobilizing in the 1970s and launched a political takeover during the 1980s under the banner of the Reagan revolution.

Wall Street corporate interests provided the money and largely controlled the real agenda. The religious fundamentalists provided the votes in return for lip service to a conservative social agenda on abortion, family planning, and gay marriage. The libertarians provided the ideological framework. The neocons provided justification for outsized military expenditures that swelled the profits of the defense industry and secured corporate access to resources and markets. The alliance played up cultural and racial divisions to fragment opposition and divert attention from the real agenda of the moneyed interests, which was to roll back the New Deal restraints on the concentration of economic power and reclaim the power and privilege they had enjoyed during the earlier Gilded Age.

Once in power, the Reagan administration ended robust antitrust enforcement in the United States. This unleashed a flood of corporate mergers and acquisitions in a consolidation of Wall Street power. Between 1980 and 2005, there were some 11,500 bank mergers in the United States, an average of 442 per year. To give the remaining banks greater power, capital ratios were reduced to give them greater lending capacity.[2] As the banking system consolidated, its focus shifted from providing financial services for productive activity on Main Street to funding speculation on Wall Street. Banks called it "financial innovation."

Rolling Back New Deal Reforms

Basic derivative securities are not new and can provide a useful service. For example, commodity futures are a form of derivative that, when properly regulated, can help both farmers and food processors reduce risk by locking in prices before a harvest. In the 1990s, ever more complex and exotic derivatives of ever less utility to the real-wealth economy began to proliferate.

During the Clinton administration, the Commodity Futures Trading Commission initiated modest regulatory measures. It was blocked, however, by Treasury Secretary Robert Rubin, Deputy Treasury Secretary Larry Summers, and Federal Reserve chair Alan Greenspan on the ground that the market can regulate itself and any such action would stifle financial innovation. In 2000, Senator Phil Gramm pushed through legislation that prohibited the regulation of derivatives.

An explosive growth of derivatives followed, resulting in the complex entanglement of Wall Street institutions that created the systemic risk that ultimately threatened the entire global economy and forced massive public bailouts. Most derivatives trades served no purpose other than generating commissions and speculative profits.

As the attention of the larger banks turned to the easy and profitable business of financing the derivatives markets, their interest in Main Street was reduced to extracting as much money as possible to put into play in the global casino. Because the derivatives shifted the risk to others, and the primary interest of the bankers was to maximize their bonuses, the ability of those to whom they were peddling mortgages and consumer debt to repay them was immaterial.

In 2004, at the urging of Goldman Sachs and other big investment banks, the established requirement that investment banks maintain a 12-to-1 leverage ratio of debt to equity was repealed, leaving them free to make much greater use of borrowed money. At the time, Goldman Sachs was headed by Hank Paulson, who went on to become secretary of the treasury under George W. Bush.

In 1995, soon after he was appointed treasury secretary by President Clinton, Robert Rubin recommended to Congress that it "modernize" the country's financial system by repealing the Glass-Steagall Act, a Depression-era law that mandated the separation of commercial banking and investment banking.[3] Before he joined the Clinton administration as assistant to the president for economic policy and director of the National Economic Council, Rubin was cochair of Goldman Sachs. Rubin's recommendation received strong support from Allan Greenspan and from Larry Summers, who was then Rubin's deputy and eventual successor at Treasury.

On April 6, 1998, Citicorp (the parent of Citibank) announced a merger with Travelers, the world's largest financial services company. It was the largest corporate merger in history and exactly the kind of merger that Glass-Steagall was intended to prevent. Indeed, the merger was arguably illegal. Citicorp and Travelers launched an intensive campaign to repeal Glass-Steagall with the support of Treasury Secretary Rubin. The Fed, chaired by free market fundamentalist Alan Greenspan, had been systematically eroding Glass-Steagall compliance and on September 23, 1998, approved the merger to form Citigroup.[4]

Rubin resigned from his Treasury post on July 2, 1999, and soon thereafter joined Citigroup as a board member and high-level adviser. The repeal of Glass-Steagall was signed into law by President Clinton on November 12, 1999. Rubin reportedly received more than $126 million in cash and stock during his eight-year tenure at Citigroup.[5] This is an iconic example of the revolving door that links the interests and players in a Wall Street–Washington axis of corruption.

The election of 2008 brought to power a young, brilliant, and dynamic new president who embodies the diversity and global perspective that must define the twenty-first century and made the Democratic Party the majority in the Congress. Yet the Wall Street agenda continues to prevail for an all too evident reason.

According to the Center for Responsive Politics, Goldman Sachs staff donated nearly $4.5 million dollars to the Democratic Party in the run-up to the 2008 election. As a group, they contributed nearly $1 million of that to Barack Obama. That made them Obama's largest private contributor and the biggest business donor to the Democrats in 2008. The sums involved are a pittance in the world of Wall Street, but politicians do pay attention to their largest donors, and Goldman Sachs is only one of many Wall Street players who recognize that giving a few million dollars to Washington politicians can be a highly profitable investment.

It is common for Wall Street players to defend their outrageous actions with a claim that everything they do is legal. That doesn't mean much when you have such power to change the rules. The crucial difference between ordinary street crime and Wall Street crime is that those who commit street crimes rarely have the means to change the laws they find inconvenient.

Making Finance the Dominant Sector

Certainly, rolling back the policies and gains of the Roosevelt New Deal was a central agenda item for the right-wing coalition. At least equally important was the effort of its Wall Street wing and captive regulators — the Federal Reserve and the U.S. Treasury Department — to restructure the U.S. economy in the name of modernization. Their goal was to make finance the economy's dominant and most profitable sector — and they were stunningly successful.

In 1950, arguably the peak of U.S. global power, manufacturing accounted for 29 percent of the U.S. gross domestic product and financial services for 11 percent. By 2005, manufacturing accounted for only 12 percent of the GDP and financial services for 20 percent — more than manufacturing, health, and wholesale/retail.[6] Even more than making our living selling ourselves goods made in China, we have made our living trading pieces of paper — correction: trading numbers encoded in computer files.

Actions to achieve this shift included the removal of restrictions on debt-equity ratios, consumer interest rates, and lending practices, and the formation of huge financial conglomerates that merge banking, insurance, securities, and real estate interests in a densely interconnected web of insider deals. Financial reporting requirements were simultaneously relaxed. These actions cleared the way for the subprime mortgage feeding frenzy that gave us the credit meltdown described in chapter 2.

Hedge funds, the high rollers at the leading edge of the speculative frenzy, proliferated from a couple hundred in the early 1990s to some ten thousand in mid-2007, by which time they had more than $1.8 trillion in financial assets under management. "Like digital buccaneers, and hardly more restrained than their seventeenth-century predecessors," wrote political commentator Kevin Phillips, "they arbitraged the nooks and crannies of global finance, capturing even more return on capital than casino operators made from one-armed bandits and favorable gaming-table odds."[7]

BANKING ON SPECULATION

Leveraging — also known as borrowing — became the name of the Wall Street game. Banks, backed by the Federal Reserve, used their power to create money to feed the speculative frenzy by creating a complex pyramid of loans to each other. In 2006, by Phillips's calculations, the U.S. financial sector debt, which consists largely of financial institutions lending money to other financial institutions to leverage financial speculation, totaled $14 trillion, which was 32 percent of all U.S. debt and 107 percent of the U.S. GDP.[8] According to the Virginia-based Financial Markets Center, in the late 1960s,

> U.S. banks began borrowing Eurodollars in huge volumes from their offshore branches.... In each decade since 1969, the ratio of financial sector debt to GDP has nearly doubled.... With financial institutions channeling half of new lending to other financial firms, credit markets increasingly are being used less to facilitate economic activity and more to leverage bets on changes in asset prices.[9]

The Wall Street alchemists used a combination of complex derivative instruments, creative accounting tricks, and their capacity to create money from nothing by issuing loans to create phantom financial assets that served as collateral to support additional borrowing to create more phantom assets to serve as collateral to support additional borrowing to.... Apparently, some major portion of this trading of loans between financial institutions even involved institutions borrowing from their own branches, essentially using creative accounting to create their own money to support their gambling habit. Talk about insider trading!

Gambling with borrowed money is highly risky for both lender and borrower. But the Wall Street players convinced themselves they had eliminated the risk. In their hubris, they seem to have truly believed that they had mastered the art of creating wealth from nothing.

At the time of its collapse, Lehman Brothers was leveraged 35 to 1, which means it financed its gambling in the global financial casino with thirty-five dollars in borrowed money for every dollar of equity. This can be highly profitable in a rising market. It is disastrous when the market is falling and the highly leveraged bets start going bad. Just as gains are leveraged during the rise, so too are the losses leveraged during the decline. When others start demanding payment, liabilities can quickly exceed a firm's net equity, which throws the firm into insolvency, as Lehman Brothers and much of the rest of Wall Street learned.

They justified their innovations in part with the argument that such innovations reduced risk. In fact, they were simply passing the risk to the credulous. In the end, the managers who made the losing bets walked away with impressive fees collected during the good times and left to others the messy work of sorting things out when Wall Street's sophisticated version of a Ponzi scheme collapsed. In 2007 alone, the fifty highest-paid private investment fund managers walked away with an average of $588 million each in annual compensation — 19,000 times as much as an average worker earns. The top five each took home more than $1.5 billion.[10]

In effect, the outsized Wall Street compensation packages represented a looting of the equity that should have been serving as reserves to cover potential losses from the risks inherent in their high-stakes bets. When the bets started going bad, the firms whose equity reserves had been looted went into default. With their bailouts, the Federal Reserve and the Treasury Department — essentially trying to make up for the looted funds — stepped in to cover the losses that should have been covered by the equity that the managers expropriated.

The year 2008 was a bad one for the hedge fund set, with

compensation for the top players down some 50 percent from 2007. Thanks to the public bailout, however, fund managers set new compensation records in 2009. The average compensation for the top twenty-five fund managers was $1 billion each. The biggest winner, David Tepper, walked away with $4 billion for winning his bet that the government would step in and buy up distressed assets — in effect, he got a direct transfer from the taxpayers.[11]

Wall Street has a simple rule: Capture the gains, pass the risk to others. It appears to be perfectly legal; it should be cause for hard time — and at the least for an effort by government to recover the looted funds on the basis of a dereliction of fiduciary responsibility.

WINNING THE CLASS WAR

Wall Street has been engaged in class warfare pure and simple. It uses its control of the money supply and its political influence to ensure that Wall Street players capture virtually all the benefits of productivity gains in the Main Street economy as interest, dividends, and financial service fees. The creation of phantom wealth further dilutes Main Street claims on real wealth relative to the claims of Wall Street.

This effort to achieve an upward redistribution of wealth was so successful that, from 1980 to 2005, the highest-earning 1 percent of the U.S. population increased its share of taxable income from 9 percent to 19 percent. Most of that gain went to the top tenth of 1 percent and came from the bottom 90 percent.[12] In 2007, the top 400 U.S. tax returns reported an average annual income of $345 million; $12.7 million was the average for the top 427 returns in 1955, adjusted to 2007 dollars.[13]

The measures used to achieve this remarkable outcome included managing monetary policy to maintain a target level of unemployment, managing trade and tax policies to facilitate the corporate outsourcing of jobs to low-wage economies, suppressing labor unions, limiting the enforcement of laws against hiring undocumented immigrant workers, and using accounting tricks that understate inflation to suppress inflation-indexed wage and Social Security increases.

As wages fell relative to inflation, and as public services were rolled back, the household savings rate fell apace. From the beginning of 1959 to the end of 1993, the U.S. household savings rate never fell below 5 percent of disposable household income and often exceeded 10 percent. Since 1999 it has never exceeded 3.5 percent.[14]

Desperate to find ways to make ends meet, households that experienced shrinking real incomes turned from saving to borrowing. Eager to capitalize on the opportunity thus created, Wall Street used aggressive marketing and deceptive lending practices to encourage people to run up credit card and mortgage debts far beyond their means to repay. As the borrowers inevitably fell behind in their payments, Wall Street hit the victims with special fees and usurious interest rates, creating a modern version of debt bondage. Far from trickling down, wealth rushed upward in a gusher.

As Wall Street exported its modernization plan to the world, the wealth gap widened almost everywhere. The export process began with the World Bank and International Monetary Fund encouraging poor countries to fund their development with foreign borrowing. Local elites loved the access to cheap credit and the opportunity to skim off fees and bribes. Foreign contractors got lucrative contracts for large loan-funded projects. And big banks had new customers for loans. It was a win-win all around — except for the poor, who got only the bill.[15]

After the borrowing countries were loaded up with loans far beyond their ability to repay, the World Bank and IMF stepped in as debt collectors and told them:

> Sorry, but since you can't repay, we are here to restructure your economies so we can get back the money you owe us. Eliminate social spending. Cut taxes on the rich to attract foreign investment. Sell your natural resources to foreign corporations. Privatize your public assets and services. Gear your agriculture and manufacturing to production for export to subsidize consumption in rich countries. [Of course they didn't use the term *subsidize*. They probably talked about comparative advantage.] And open your borders to foreign imports. [In theory, this was to help domestic manufacturers be more competitive in foreign markets by facilitating duty-free import of inputs.]

Almost every element of the "structural adjustment" worked to the favor of global corporations.

Eventually the Wall Street players realized they could use multilateral trade agreements to circumvent democracy and restructure everyone's economy at the same time. It worked brilliantly.

In 2005, *Forbes* magazine counted 691 billionaires in the world. In 2008, only three years later, it counted 1,250 and estimated their combined wealth at $4.4 trillion. According to a United Nations University study, the richest 2 percent of world's people now own 51 percent of all the world's assets. The poorest 50 percent own only 1 percent.[16] A 2008 International Labour Organization study reported that in approximately two-thirds of the countries studied, income inequality increased between 1990 and 2005. This was in part the result of an overall fall in labor's share of total income relative to that of managers and investors.[17]

An extreme and growing concentration of privatized wealth and power divides the world between the profligate and the desperate, intensifies competition for Earth's resources, undermines the legitimacy of our institutions, drives an unraveling of the social fabric of mutual trust and caring, and fuels the forces of terrorism, crime, and environmental destruction.

Did the institutions of global finance intend these social and environmental outcomes? Presumably not. They were simply rewriting the rules of commerce to increase their own gains. The titans of Wall Street are much too focused on competing to be the top billionaire to notice the devastated environment or the penniless people at the bottom who have nothing left to be expropriated.

The business press has reported that some hedge fund managers are taking up philanthropy to aid the poor. If any of them have noticed a connection between the power games they play on Wall Street and the condition of the desperately poor they presume to help, I've not seen any mention of it.

▶•◆•◆•◀

The driving dynamic of unregulated markets is to destroy the market discipline that makes the market an innovative and efficient instrument of resource allocation and to take control of government to implement an agenda of elite privilege. Environmental balance, a just distribution of wealth, and achievement of the democratic ideal of one-person, one-voice will come only through political action by a strong political movement.

Wall Street presents itself to the public as a financial services sector concerned with and committed to the well-being of people, family, and community. The public-relations image has little foundation in reality. Its real intentions are revealed in what it does, not what it says. Its actions reveal a cultural-institutional complex devoid of morality, which cares for nothing but acquiring money and power by any means.

CHAPTER 6

▶•◆•◆•◀

BUCCANEERS AND PRIVATEERS

Advocates of capitalism are very apt to appeal to the sacred
principles of liberty, which are embodied in one maxim:
The fortunate must not be restrained in the exercise of
tyranny over the unfortunate.

BERTRAND RUSSELL

The presidency of Ronald Reagan is commonly referred to as the Reagan "revolution," which sought a restoration of traditional conservative values and free markets. The aggressive deregulation efforts begun under Reagan and carried forward by the Bush and Clinton administrations did indeed restore some traditional conservative values, but perhaps not the ones most U.S. conservatives intended.

Note that the term *conservative* originally referred to the monarchists who fought efforts to establish the democratic accountability of kings. As Wall Street was deregulated, the economy regressed to a state reminiscent of an earlier day when the seas were ruled by buccaneers and privateers.

Buccaneer is a colorful name for the pirates of old. The ultimate libertarians, they pursued personal fortune with rules of their own making. They were in their time an iconic expression of "free market" capitalism in its purest form.

Privateers, the forerunners of publicly traded corporations, were pirates to whom a king granted legal immunity in return for a share of the booty.

Wall Street hedge fund managers, day traders, currency traders, and other unlicensed phantom-wealth speculators are the independent, unlicensed buccaneers of our day. Wall Street banks are the commissioned privateers who ply a similar trade with state backing. The economy is their ocean. Publicly traded corporations serve as their favored vessels of plunder, leverage is their favored weapon, and the state is their servant-guardian.

Here in brief is the fascinating story of the adventurous forebears of today's Wall Street swashbucklers.[1]

LAUNCHING THE COLONIAL ERA

From the decline of the Roman Empire until 1500, Europe was burdened by the turmoil of endless and pointless wars in which rival noble factions fought one another to exhaustion in a competition to expand their personal power. Imperial rulers enlarged their domains primarily by pushing their borders outward through the military conquest of contiguous territories. The vanquished people and their lands were brought under the central military and administrative control of the city in which the ruling king or emperor resided.

Continuing violence and chaos led to a yearning for monarchs with the power to restore order within stable borders, giving rise to what historians call the modern era. Once the continent was divided into relatively stable domains, Europe's kings satisfied their ambitions for imperial expansion by projecting their power over long sea routes to establish dominion over distant lands, peoples, and resources.

National military forces and colonial administrations remained important to this new model of empire, but for the most part the European kings of the modern era projected their power and augmented their treasuries by granting commissions to favored adventurers, brigands, and corporations who worked for their own account.

Thus began the historic transition from rule by imperial monarchs to rule by imperial corporations, and from the rule of the sword to the rule of money.

ADVENTURERS ON THE HIGH SEAS

Most of us know the period of Europe's drive for colonial expansion primarily by the names of the great adventurers commissioned and financed by their sovereigns to carry out expeditions of discovery, plunder, and slaughter.

In search of a westward sea route to the riches of Asia, Christopher Columbus landed on the island of Hispaniola (present-day Haiti and the Dominican Republic) in the West Indies in 1492 and claimed it for Spain. Hernando de Soto made his initial mark trading slaves in Central America and later allied with Francisco Pizarro to take control of the Inca empire based in Peru in 1532, the same year the Portuguese established their first settlement in Brazil. Soto returned to Spain one of the wealthiest men of his time, although his share in the plunder was only half that of Pizarro.[2] By 1521, Hernán Cortés had claimed the Mexican empire of Montezuma for Spain.

The vast amounts of gold that Spain ultimately extracted from South and Central America ruined the Spanish economy and fueled inflation throughout Europe. With so much gold available to purchase goods produced by others, Spain became dependent on imports and its productive capacity atrophied. The result was an economic decline from which Spain never recovered.

The pattern is disturbingly similar to that of the current

import-dependent U.S. economy—the primary difference being that U.S. imports are financed not by stolen gold but by foreign debt.

Although licensed by the Crown, the celebrated adventurers of old operated with the independence and lack of scruples of crime lords, competing or cooperating with one another for personal gain and glory as circumstances dictated. Their mission was to extract the physical wealth of foreign lands and peoples by whatever means — including the execution of rulers and the slaughter and enslavement of Native inhabitants — and to share a portion of the spoils with their sovereigns.

The profits from Spain's conquests in the Americas inspired the imperial exertions of the English, Dutch, and French, who soon divided Africa, Asia, and North America into colonies from which to extract plunder and profits from the monopoly control of trade for the benefit of the mother state.

PRIVATEERS

The competition for foreign spoils among the European powers led to the embrace of the ancient practice of privateering — essentially, legalized piracy — as a major instrument of state policy and a favored investment of both sovereigns and wealthy merchants. Why endure the arduous exertions of expropriating the wealth of foreign lands through conquest and trade when it was much easier to attack and plunder the ships carrying the spoils expropriated by others on their way back to European ports?

Monarchs often found it advantageous to grant a license to privately owned, financed, and captained armed vessels to engage in this profitable enterprise. These privateers offered important advantages to cash-strapped rulers. They provided revenue with no cash outlay, and official responsibility could be disavowed more easily than if the warships of the Crown had pillaged the victim vessels.

Crew, captain, private investors, and the commissioning king divided the revenues from the booty while the king's license lent a patina of legality to the acts of plunder and granted the ships safe harbor in their home ports. A new era was in gestation, from which Wall Street eventually emerged.

Some privateers operated powerful naval forces. In 1671, Sir Henry Morgan (yes, appreciative kings did grant favored privateers titles of nobility in recognition of their service) launched an assault on Panama City with thirty-six ships and nearly two thousand brigands, defeating a large Spanish force and looting the city as it burned to the ground.[3]

Tax records for 1790 indicate that four of Boston's top five taxpayers that year obtained their income in part from investments in privateering—they included John Hancock, famed for his outsized signature on the Declaration of Independence.[4]

In 1856, the major European powers, with the exception of Spain, signed the Declaration of Paris, declaring privateering illegal. The United States, which relied heavily on privateers as its primary source of naval power and as a major source of commercial profits in its early years, did not stop commissioning privateers until the end of the nineteenth century.[5]

CHARTERED CORPORATIONS

Eventually, the ruling monarchs turned from swashbuckling adventurers and chartered pirates to chartered corporations as their favored instruments of colonial expansion, administration, and pillage. It is instructive to note that in England this transition was motivated in part by the country's incipient step toward democracy.

By the beginning of the seventeenth century, the English parliament, whose establishment was one of the first modern efforts to limit the arbitrary power of the king, had gained the authority to supervise the Crown's collection and expenditure of domestic tax revenues. Chafing under this restriction, sovereigns such as Elizabeth I, James I, and Charles I found that by issuing corporate charters that bestowed monopoly rights and other privileges on favored investors, they could establish an orderly and permanent source of income through fees and taxes that circumvented parliamentary oversight. They also commonly owned personal shares in the companies to which they granted such privileges.[6]

In addition, chartered corporations sometimes assumed direct responsibility for expenses that otherwise would have fallen on the state, including the costs of maintaining embassies, forts, and other naval, military, and trade facilities. English corporations were at times even given legal jurisdiction over Englishmen residing in a given territory.

Corporations chartered by the British Crown established several of the earliest colonial settlements in what later became the United States and populated them with bonded laborers — many involuntarily transported from England — to work their properties. The importation of slaves from Africa followed.

The East India Company (chartered in 1600) was the primary instrument of Britain's colonization of India, a country the company ruled until 1784 much as if it were a private estate.[7]

In the early 1800s, the East India Company established a thriving business exporting tea from China, paying for its purchases with illegal opium. China responded to the resulting social and economic disruption by confiscating the opium warehoused in Canton by the British merchants. This precipitated the Opium War of 1839–42, which Britain won.

The Dutch East India Company (chartered in 1602)

established its sovereignty over what is now Indonesia and reduced the local people to poverty by displacing them from their lands to grow spices for sale in Europe. The French East India Company (1664) controlled commerce with French territories in India, East Africa, the East Indies, and other islands and territories of the Indian Ocean.

The new corporate form was a joint stock company, which combined two ideas from the Middle Ages: the sale of shares in public markets and the protection of owners from personal liability for the corporation's obligations. These two features enabled a single firm to amass virtually unlimited financial capital, assured the continuity of the firm beyond the death of its founders, and absolved the owners of personal liability for the firm's losses or misdeeds beyond the amount of their holdings in the company.

Furthermore, separating owners from day-to-day management allowed for a unified central direction that was difficult when management control was divided among a number of owner-partners.

It is no exaggeration to characterize these forebears of contemporary publicly traded limited liability corporations as, in effect, legally sanctioned and protected crime syndicates with private armies and navies backed by a mandate from their home governments to extort tribute, expropriate land and other wealth, monopolize markets, trade slaves, deal drugs, and profit from financial scams.

▶•◆•◆•◀

Publicly traded limited liability corporations of gigantic scale now operate with substantial immunity from legal liability and accountability even in the countries that issue their charters. They have become the defining institutions of our day. Wall Street is their symbolic seat of power, and they have reversed their relationship to the state.

Wall Street now commissions the state to finance and field the armies that protect its interests and to staff the diplomatic establishment that negotiates treaties in its favor. From time to time, using its ability to crash the economy at will, it extorts protection money in the form of bailouts and Federal Reserve cash infusions. To maintain the state's loyalty, it begrudgingly shares a fraction of its booty in the form of taxes and offers tribute to its politicians as travel perks and campaign contributions.

As did their swashbuckling forebears, Wall Street's buccaneers and privateers seek self-enrichment by plundering wealth they had no part in creating, enjoy substantial legal immunity, and acknowledge no duty or accountability other than to themselves. Their success carries a heavy price tag for the rest of us.

CHAPTER 7

▶•◆•◆•◀

THE HIGH COST
OF PHANTOM WEALTH

Financial capitalism is a system of irresponsibility and . . .
is amoral. It is a system where the logic of the market
excuses everything. . . . Either we re-found capitalism or
we destroy it.

PRESIDENT NICOLAS SARKOZY OF FRANCE

"We have always known that heedless self-interest was bad
morals," said Franklin Delano Roosevelt in 1937. We know
now that it is bad economics.

PAUL KRUGMAN

Wall Street's relentless drive to have it all not only has had devastating economic, social, and environmental consequences but also has destroyed the integrity of money, created expectations that society has no means to fulfill, and sacrificed the health and happiness of nearly everyone. The full costs are beyond comprehension.

PHANTOM EXPECTATIONS

It is a curious thing that, unless we stuff it in a mattress, we expect whatever money we don't immediately spend to grow in perpetuity without effort on our part. We do not expect the same of real wealth. Buildings must be maintained.

Machinery must be replaced. Knowledge must be updated. The trust and caring of a community must be continuously renewed. Skills must practiced. Even wild spaces must be protected from predators, particularly human. All of these require a real investment of time and life energy. Effortless perpetual growth defies the physical law of conservation of energy. Only phantom wealth can grow effortlessly and perpetually.

As our phantom wealth grows, so too do our expectations regarding what constitutes our rightful claim to society's real wealth. Unless we are voluntary simplicity initiates, we are inclined to increase our consumption in tandem with growth in our income, placing an ever-greater burden on the planet. So often, we say with pride, "I can afford it," without asking whether Earth can afford it.

Because our economic system gives priority to creating phantom wealth, presumed entitlements now far exceed the real wealth available to satisfy them. This can create quite a shock when those of us with financial assets decide to convert our share of the phantom-wealth pool into payments for rent, food, health care, and other needs, if a lot of others make the same decision at the same time.

The financial planner Thornton Parker has pointed out that this is likely to be an issue for baby boomers who built up financial assets during the stock market boom in anticipation of a comfortable retirement. Just as their collective decision to put money into the stock market during their working years helped inflate share prices, so their collective decision to take it out during their retirement will deflate those prices, leaving these retirees in potentially desperate straits.[1]

Wall Street's phantom-wealth machine has created prospective claims and related expectations far out of proportion to the real wealth available to satisfy them.

The problem is not confined to prospective retirees and

retirement accounts. It applies as well to the endowments of foundations, universities, and other nonprofits. It applies to the public trust funds of libraries and municipalities, college savings funds, the reserve accounts of insurance companies, personal trust funds, and much else.

Perhaps the major challenge to the call to shut down the Wall Street phantom-wealth machine is the understandable and serious cry, "But what about our 401(k)s and our university and foundation endowments?" The answer is that so long as these funds are invested with Wall Street institutions engaged in phantom-wealth creation, they rest on nothing more than financial bubbles and creative accounting, and their value can evaporate overnight.

We must build our old-age security and our crucial nonprofit organizations on more solid foundations. In chapter 14, I'll say more about better options for dealing as a society with such things as retirement, home purchases, and insurance than those offered by Wall Street. As for the American dream of living off financial returns in work-free luxury, it is a fantasy that can be achieved by the very few at the expense of the many.

There is no way to tell by how much the claims of financial-asset holders exceed the real wealth available to fulfill them, but the evidence suggests the difference is considerable. No one is even asking how the inevitable loss of unfulfillable expectations might be fairly distributed. A given dollar doesn't come with a marker that identifies it as a phantom dollar or a real one.

DELINKED FROM REALITY AND OUT OF CONTROL

The financial figures that get thrown around in relation to the credit crash and financial bailout of 2008 defy both reality and imagination. The financial assets of the richest 1 percent of Americans before the crash totaled $16.8 trillion.[2] This represents what they understood to be their rightful claim against the world's real wealth. To put that in perspective, the estimated 2007 U.S. gross domestic product was $13.8 trillion, and the total federal government expenditures that fiscal year were $2.7 trillion.[3]

These sums all seem trifling, however, compared with the $55 trillion in credit default swaps outstanding at the time of the subprime mortgage meltdown, to which they made a major contribution.[4] These are essentially insurance contracts that presumably eliminate the risk from the toxic mortgage derivatives. They involve bets and counterbets that may partially cancel each other out if anyone can untangle them — but many of the parties to them have gone bankrupt. Because the transactions were never reported to any central clearinghouse and many of them are carried off the books of the institutions that hold them, no one really knows how much is actually at risk or who owes what to whom.

All we know for sure is that $55 trillion is a great deal of money. It pales into insignificance, however, when compared with the $648 trillion that the Bank for International Settlements reports as the total notional value of all outstanding over-the-counter derivatives as of June 2008.[5] That renders insignificant even the $16 trillion that evaporated between mid-September and the end of November 2008 as the market value of the world's publicly traded corporations' share prices fell by 37 percent.[6]

Is your head spinning? Is your brain shouting, "This doesn't make any sense"? Trust your brain. It is working. Welcome to the *Alice in Wonderland* world of phantom wealth.

A quick note is in order here on the Wall Street bailout figure of $12.8 trillion noted at the beginning of chapter 1. Perhaps you recall the public outrage in October 2008 when the U.S. Congress passed a bill authorizing the Treasury Department to spend $350 billion to bail out Wall Street financial institutions, with another $350 billion in the pipeline subject to congressional approval. So what is this $12.8 trillion?

Some of it is in established government guarantee and insurance programs, including other Treasury Department programs. The FDIC was on the hook for $2.0 trillion, and the Federal Housing Administration for $0.3 trillion. The bulk of it, $7.8 trillion, was from the Federal Reserve,[7] which acts independently and which routinely makes massive financial commitments to the banking system without any congressional approval or oversight process.

Mostly, the Fed creates its own money as it sees fit, with a few simple accounting entries. In most instances, no one seems to know where any particular funding comes from, where it is going, or how it is being used. Indeed, the Fed has stood firm against bipartisan calls from Congress for a federal audit and Freedom of Information lawsuits by Bloomberg News and other news agencies seeking a release of records on who has received what commitments and on what terms. The Fed argues that making such information public would endanger public faith in the banking system. Given how low public faith in the banking system is now, that is an alarming admission.

If you don't understand how Wall Street really works, don't feel bad. I've come to doubt that anyone really understands it. The accounting involves so much smoke and mirrors it may be beyond understanding.

It isn't necessary to know the details to recognize that we are dealing with a system that is delinked from reality and is operating with no one at the helm. Nor does it take special genius to recognize that when folks are moving around trillions of dollars in secret transactions and cannot explain in a credible way where the money is coming from or where it's going, and cannot make a credible case that it is serving a beneficial purpose, they are probably up to no good.

Now I want to turn to what I believe to be the most important of all the many design flaws of Wall Street's phantom-money machine.

PERPETUAL GROWTH ON A FINITE PLANET

The unrealistic expectation that money should grow perpetually and effortlessly is more than a cultural issue. It is built into the design of the Wall Street money machine. Do you recall the description in chapter 2 of how banks create money with a few computer strokes when they issue a loan? Recall that 32 percent of all outstanding U.S. debt is money that financial institutions owe to each other. By making such loans, banks bulked up their financial statements, expanded the total amount of money in play in the Wall Street casino economy, and increased the number and size of the transactions that generated the management fees that paid the bonuses. Recall also that when banks issue loans, they are

GROWTH AND JOBS

There is a connection between growth and jobs, but only because Wall Street has the system gamed to assure that all the gains from increased productivity go to managers and shareholders rather than to labor.

Thus, the total number of jobs will decline and unemployment will increase over time if the economy is not growing at a rate at least equal to the increase in productivity. This problem is easily avoided if productivity gains instead translate into greater time for working people to devote to family, community, and other quality-of-life pursuits.

creating money with simple accounting entries. Yes, much of the phantom-wealth thing is mainly fancy accounting.

Banks were in fact creating money so fast that the Federal Reserve stopped reporting the most meaningful index of the amount of money in circulation, what economists call M3, on March 23, 2006. Some observers believe the Fed stopped reporting it because the amount of money had begun to grow so fast as to cause public alarm and undermine confidence in the dollar.

Phantom Money and Unreported Inflation

John Williams, a consulting economist who has spent years studying the history and nature of economic reporting, tracks economic statistics that the government has either stopped issuing or has seriously distorted. Using the same methodology the Fed once used to compile its M3 index, Williams reports that the rate of growth was running from 5 to 7 percent in 2005. It then began a steady acceleration to a peak annual rate of over 17 percent at the beginning of 2008, just before the credit collapse kicked in.[8]

When the money supply expands faster than productive output, price inflation usually results. According to the official Consumer Price Index, inflation was running at a rate of 2 to 4 percent at the beginning of 2008. Williams compiles his own consumer price index using the same methodology that the government used up until the 1980s, when it decided to start cooking the books to hide evidence of economic mismanagement and hold down automatic wage and Social Security indexing. According to Williams the actual rate of inflation at the beginning of 2008 was in the range of 12 to 13 percent. What you experience every time you go shopping is true.

Surprised? Yes, successive Wall Street–dominated presidential administrations, both Republican and Democratic, have been cooking the books on inflation, money, unemployment, and the GDP for decades. Our economy is in far worse shape than the official statistics reveal. But I stray from our topic.

Inflation of the money supply far in excess of real economic expansion — and the resulting real rate of inflation in consumer prices — is yet another cost of Wall Street's phantom-money orgy. The inflationary phantom money that banks have been creating to fund Wall Street gamblers is one of the several vehicles by which Wall Street takes money out of Main Street pockets and puts it in Wall Street pockets.

Credit Crunch in a World Awash in Money

It is odd that we experienced an economic collapse in 2008 because of a credit crunch, an inability to borrow, at a time when the world has been awash not only in debt but also in money. *BusinessWeek's* July 11, 2005, cover story shouted "Too Much Money" and spoke of a savings glut. Its June 11, 2008, European issue reiterated the theme, "Too Much Money, Inflation Goes Global."

Most discussion of the financial crisis focuses on the details and misses the big picture. The problem is twofold. The economic system is awash in money, but this money is in the wrong places. Second, virtually every dollar in the system is borrowed, because we rely on banks to create our money by lending it into existence. No debt, no money.

As wages fall relative to inflation, the bottom 90 percent of the population is increasingly dependent on borrowing from the top 10 percent to cover daily consumption. But when the less fortunate can't repay their loans, the rich people stop lending. Most loans continue to be repaid, but because the default rate is rising and the crazy system of derivatives trading makes it impossible to separate good debts and responsible borrowers from bad debts and deadbeats, banks are afraid to lend to anyone. As the good loans are repaid, the supply of money shrinks because new loans are not being issued.

In turn, the demand for real goods and services begins to fall because people don't have the money to pay for them. Businesses lay off workers, who consequently cannot repay their debts or even put food on the table. The problem appears to be a lack of money, even though the total money in the financial system is far more than enough to cover real-wealth exchanges in a rational real-wealth economy. The money, however, is locked up in the Wall Street casino economy rather than circulating in the real Main Street economy. Pouring bailout money into Wall Street does zilch for Main Street.

It all traces back to a system that issues money as debt to the casino economy rather than to the productive economy.

Why Debt and the Economy Have to Grow

Because of how our financial system is designed, the economy has to grow or collapse. The growth may or may not provide employment, meet real needs, or reduce poverty — it must only meet the demand of the banking system for its pound of flesh.

Because the bookkeeping entry a bank makes when it issues a loan creates only the principal, the economy must grow fast enough to generate sufficient demand for loans in order to create the money required to make the interest payments in an ever-escalating spiral. Otherwise, debts go into default and the financial system and the economy collapse. The demand for the eventual repayment with interest of nearly every dollar in circulation virtually assures that the economy will fail unless the GDP and income inequality are constantly growing. If you are a Wall Street banker competing for points in the power game, it does not get sweeter than this.

Unfortunately for the rest of us, this demand for perpetual growth simply to keep the bankers happy results in a serious distortion of priorities. To avoid an economic collapse, policy-makers base their choices not on what will maximize the well-being of all but on what will create sufficient demand for additional borrowing to put enough money in circulation to pay the interest due to bankers on the loans already out-standing. The result is ever-increasing debt *and* the acceler-ating destruction of the natural environment and the human social fabric.

It gets even worse. Given Earth's material limits and the amount of debt already in play, there is no way that the pro-ductive economy can expand at sufficient rate to keep the game going. The necessary growth in debt must therefore come from the casino economy and its seemingly limitless ability to create phantom wealth by pumping up finan-cial asset bubbles and loan pyramids — the ultimate Ponzi scheme.

It is illogical and deeply destructive to design an economic system in a way that creates an artificial demand for perpetu-al growth on a finite planet. It is even more pernicious when the defining purpose is to make the already rich even richer relative to everyone else.

By contrast, nothing in the design of the formal economic system allows those with little or no access to money even to give voice to their needs, much less fulfill them. They survive only by scratching out their living at the extreme margins of society in informal or "underground" economies of their own creation. These are design failures of the first order. To heal our sick society, we must redesign our economic system to remove these and other glaring defects, not only to secure our collective survival but also to achieve health and happiness.

HEALTH, HAPPINESS, AND KEEPING UP
WITH THE JONESES

In a society defined by extreme inequality, our perception of our worth and our relationships with others are almost inevitably shaped by our position in the prevailing hierarchy of power and privilege. In this situation, we easily fall into the trap of valuing ourselves by our net worth and material possessions rather than by our intrinsic self-worth.

Once in the trap, we will likely seek to endear ourselves to those above us even as we scheme to displace them and occupy their more elevated chair. Likewise, we may display contempt, whether overtly or subtly, for those below as a way of affirming and justifying our own status. Because financial fortunes are fluid and great phantom-wealth fortunes can evaporate overnight for reasons wholly beyond our control, even those in a position of financial advantage experience continuous, sometimes extreme, anxiety, with serious consequences for physical and emotional health.

In an equitable society in which all people are valued for who they are rather than what they own, our natural concern is for the well-being of the group rather than for our particular position within it, because we truly rise or fall together. Seeking our place of service to the well-being of the whole thus becomes more important than defending and improving our position in a power hierarchy. Rather than anxiety, we feel calm exhilaration. Our blood pressure falls and our health and happiness improve. This is all confirmed by a wealth of scientific studies that document the benefits of equality for individual well-being.[9]

When Ed Diener and his colleagues at the University of Illinois compared the life-satisfaction scores of groups of people of radically different financial means, they found four groups clustered at the top, with almost identical scores on a 7-point scale. One cluster of respondents, which comprised people on *Forbes* magazine's list of the richest Americans, had an average score of 5.8. Ah, so money does bring happiness — *at least when you are at the very tip-top of the hierarchy.*

The other three top-scoring clusters, by contrast, were groups known for their modest, egalitarian lifestyles and strength of community. These were the Pennsylvania Amish (5.8), who favor horses over cars and tractors; the Inuit of northern Greenland (5.9), an indigenous hunting and fishing people; and the Masai (5.7), a traditional herding people in East Africa who traditionally live without electricity or running water in huts fashioned from dried cow dung. These are all communities in which people care for one another and share their resources, and in which economic distinctions are minimal.[10]

By definition, the Forbes 400 list is limited to four hundred people. We cannot all be on it. We could all, however, be living in equitable, caring, sharing communities and enjoying the associated health and happiness benefits. We need only to create societies that put less emphasis on making money and more on cultivating caring place-based communities that distribute wealth equitably.

Wall Street is bad for our health and happiness, not only because it has given us a health care system that places greater priority on Wall Street profits than on our well-being, but even more because it destroys a sense of community, creates a narcissistic culture, and rewards predatory competition.

REAL WEALTH WITH NO LIMITS

It is time to stop managing the economy for the benefit of Wall Street bankers and speculators, to ask what we really want from life, and to redesign our economic institutions accordingly. In so doing, we should look very closely at evidence demonstrating that once a basic level of material well-being is achieved, the major improvements in our health and happiness come not from more money and consumption but rather from relationships, cultural expression, and spiritual growth.

These forms of real wealth are most valuable and fulfilling when they are dissociated from money and financial transactions — and they make little or no demand on environmental resources. The title of the classic ballad comes to mind: "The Best Things in Life Are Free." Those words carry a lot of truth. What are the things that give you enduring pleasure? The material needs of people who are secure in their identity and sense of self-worth can be met in quite modest ways, freeing our energy for the things that bring us real joy.

The cover story of the winter 2009 issue of *YES! Magazine* is about Dee Williams, a young woman who loves her life in an 84-square-foot house on wheels. It cost her $10,000 to build, including the photovoltaic panels that generate her electricity.[11]

I'd give you odds that she is happier than most of the billionaires that Robert Frank writes about in *Richistan*, who spend their lives rushing between gigantic homes and estates in their private jets and yachts, occupied all the while with making deals by phone and computer to pay the bills.[12]

▶•◆•◆•◀

Our economy needs a serious makeover. It is a design issue. We have for too long put up with an economic system designed to make money for rich people and maintain them in a condition of obscene excess by confining billions to lives of desperation and reducing Earth to a toxic waste dump. We can do better. And it's about time we do so. We've put up with such nonsense for five thousand years. Finally, we have the means to choose a different way.

CHAPTER 8

>•◆•◆•◄

THE END OF EMPIRE

I think a pivotal point in our [human] story is the period of
European expansion and colonization, which touched every
single person on the planet and brought about the changes
that we're struggling with today. All our social movements
since that time have been a response — the anti-colonialism
movement, the struggle against slavery, the labor movement, women's movement, the ecological movement.

CARL ANTHONY, *Yes! Magazine*

Look still further upstream beyond Wall Street — even beyond
the money-is-wealth illusion — and we find the yet bigger
picture — a five-thousand-year history of rule and expropriation by rulers intent on securing their privilege and pamper-
ing their egos by any means. Call it the era of Empire.[1]

In an earlier time, rulers were kings and emperors. Now
they are corporate CEOs and hedge fund managers. Wall
Street is Empire's most recent stage, and hopefully the last,
in this tragic drama.

Five thousand years is enough. This is an epic moment.
We now have the imperative and the means as a nation and a
species to end the era of Empire and liberate ourselves from
a needless tragedy. Here is the larger story of what is at stake.

THE TURN TO EMPIRE

By the accounts of imperial historians, civilization, history,
and human progress began with the consolidation of dominator
power in the first great empires. Much is made of their

101

glorious accomplishments and heroic battles as imperial civilizations rose and fell.

Rather less is said about the brutalization of the slaves who built the great monuments, the racism, the suppression of women, the conversion of free farmers into serfs or landless laborers, the carnage of the battles, the hopes and lives destroyed by wave after wave of invasion, the pillage and gratuitous devastation of the vanquished, and the lost creative potential.

In the Beginning

According to the cultural historian Riane Eisler, "One of the best-kept historical secrets is that practically all the material and social technologies fundamental to civilization were developed before the imposition of a dominator society."[2] By her account, early humans evolved within a cultural and institutional frame that nurtured a deep sense of connection to one another and to Earth. They chose to cooperate with life rather than to dominate it.

The domestication of plants and animals, food production and storage, building construction, and clothing production were all discoveries and inventions of what Eisler characterizes as the great partnership societies. These societies also developed the institutions of law, government, and religion that were the foundations of complex social organizations. They cultivated the arts of dance, pottery, basket making, textile weaving, leather crafting, metallurgy, ritual drama, architecture, town planning, boat building, highway construction, and oral literature.[3] Indeed, without these accomplishments, the projection and consolidation of imperial power would not have been possible.

The Dynamics of Power

Then, some five thousand years ago, our ancestors in Mesopotamia, the land we now call Iraq, made a tragic turn from partnership to the dominator relationships of Empire. They turned away from a reverence for the generative power of life, represented by female gods or nature spirits, to a reverence for hierarchy and the power of the sword, represented by distant, usually male, gods. The wisdom of the elder and the priestess gave way to the arbitrary rule of powerful, often ruthless, kings. Societies became divided between rulers and ruled, exploiters and exploited.

Mesopotamia, Egypt, and Rome were three of history's most celebrated empires. Each had its moments of greatness, but at an enormous cost in lives, natural wealth, and human possibility, as vain and violent rulers played out the drama of Empire's inexorable play-or-die, rule-or-be-ruled, kill-or-be-killed competition for power. The underlying dynamic favored the ascendance to power of the most ruthless, brutal, and mentally deranged.

Rule by Psychopaths

Social pathology became the norm as the god of death displaced the goddess of life and as the power of the sword triumphed over the power of the chalice. The creative energy of the species was redirected from building the generative power of the whole to advancing the technological instruments of war and the social instruments of domination. Resources were expropriated on a vast scale to maintain the military forces, prisons, palaces, temples, and patronage for retainers and propagandists on which imperial rule depends.

Great civilizations were built and then swept away in successive waves of violence and destruction. Once-great powers, weakened by corruption and an excess of hubris, fell to rival rulers, and the jealous winners sought to erase even the memory of those they vanquished. The sacred became the servant of the profane. Fertile lands were converted into desert by intention or rapacious neglect. Rule by terror fueled resentments that assured repeating cycles of violent retribution. War, trade, and debt served as weapons of the few to expropriate the means of livelihood of the many and reduce them to slavery or serfdom.

The resulting power imbalances fueled the delusional hubris and debaucheries of psychopathic rulers who fancied themselves possessed of divine privilege and otherworldly power. Attention turned from realizing the possibilities of life in this world to securing a privileged place in the afterlife.

Ruling elites maintained cultural control through the institutions of religion, economic control through the institutions of trade and credit, and political control through the institutions of rule making and organized military force. Although elite factions might engage in ruthless competition with one another, they generally aligned in common cause to secure the continuity of the institutions of their collective privilege, often using intermarriage as a mechanism of alliance building.

If many of the patterns associated with ancient kings, pharaohs, and emperors seem strangely familiar to our own time of the democratic ideal, it is because — as elaborated in chapter 6 — the dominator cultures and institutions of Empire simply morphed into new forms in the face of the democratic challenge.

A NEW NATION IS BORN

More than two millennia passed between the end of the early democratic experiment of ancient Athens in 338 BCE and the beginning of the West's next democratic experiment, marked by the signing of the Declaration of Independence of the United States of America in 1776.

Resistance from Below

It is axiomatic that democracy cannot be imposed from above or abroad. True democracy is born only through its practice.

It is a remarkable fact that the American Revolution did not start as an armed rebellion. It originated in a process that looked rather more like a raucous social movement. For all their diversity and lack of experience with organized self-rule, the grassroots rebels who initiated and led the revolution in its earliest manifestations demonstrated a capacity to express the popular will through self-organizing groups and networks — long one of democracy's most meaningful and effective forms of expression.

When the British changed the rules of engagement from nonviolence to violence, the rebels felt compelled to respond in kind.

As the violence escalated, it created a situation that both allowed and compelled the elites of the Continental Congress to assert their authority by raising an army that assumed control of the rebellion and restored imperial order under a new command.

Democracy Betrayed

After independence was won, the colonial elites who had inserted themselves to take control of what was a self-organized rebellion turned their attention to securing their hold on the institutions of government. The human rights that had been carefully delineated in an earlier Declaration of Colonial Rights, and the principle so elegantly articulated in the Declaration of Independence that all men are created equal and enjoy a natural right to life, liberty, and the pursuit of happiness, fell by the wayside.

The focus shifted to securing the interests of industrialists, bankers, and slave-owning plantation owners and to assuring that the powers of government would remain in the hands of white men of means. Empire morphed once again into a new form, but it remained true to the essential organizing principle of domination. Genocide against Native Americans continued, as did the enslavement of blacks, the denial of the basic rights and humanity of women, and the denial of a just share of profits to those who toil to make capital productive.

Imperial Plutocracy

What the founders brought forth is best described as a constitutional plutocracy with an agenda of imperial expansion. The British lost to the rebels in the American Revolution, but Empire remained robust in a new nation that ultimately became the greatest imperial power the world had ever known.

The new nation joined together the peoples of thirteen colonies settled on a narrow bit of land along the east coast of North America. This land had been taken by force and deceit from its indigenous inhabitants, and much of it continued to be worked by slaves.

When its leaders decided the lands they occupied were insufficient to their needs, they supported an imperial westward expansion, using military force to expropriate all of the Native and Mexican lands between themselves and the far distant Pacific Ocean.

Global expansion beyond territorial borders followed. The United States converted cooperative dictatorships into client states by giving their ruling classes a choice of aligning themselves with U.S. economic and political interests and sharing in the booty or being eliminated by assassination, foreign-financed internal rebellion, or military invasion. Following World War II, when the classic forms of colonial rule became unacceptable, international debt became a favored instrument for gaining leverage over local economies. Subsequently, economies were forced open to foreign corporate ownership and control through debt restructuring and trade agreements.

THE LONG STRUGGLE

The stirring rhetoric of the Declaration of Independence, a revolution, and the U.S. Constitution all failed to bring democracy to North America. They did, however, inspire and lend legitimacy to a long popular struggle of more than two centuries, a global movement that gradually narrowed the yawning gap between political reality and the democratic ideal in the face of determined and often bloody elite opposition. Within the larger historical context, the accomplishments of the American Revolution, though incomplete, were monumental.

Power of the People

Two centuries of struggle reduced monarchy to little more than a historical curiosity. In the United States, a clear separation of church and state secures freedom of religious conscience and worship. Since the founding, a system of checks and balances has successfully barred one elite faction from establishing permanent control of the institutions of government. Active genocide against Native Americans ended, and genocide against any group is now universally and globally condemned. Slavery is no longer a legally protected institution and is culturally unacceptable.

Native Americans, people of color, people without property, and women have the legal right to vote and to participate fully in the political process. Pervasive though it remains in practice, open discrimination to deny the political rights of any group is culturally unacceptable.

That we now take these accomplishments for granted underscores how far we have come.

A Taste of the Possible

Many of us who grew up in the United States in the post–World War II years came to accept democracy and economic justice as something of a birthright secured by the acts of the founding fathers. We were raised to believe that we were blessed to live in a classless society of opportunity for all who were willing to apply themselves and play by the rules.

The experience of the middle class in those years seemed to confirm this story. Those of us who were a part of it, and I include myself here, were inclined to dismiss people who spoke of issues of class as malcontents who would rather promote class warfare than accept responsibility for putting in an honest day's work.

Sure, there had been problems in the past, but thanks to America's intellectual genius and high ideals, we had resolved them and rendered them irrelevant to our present. In our arrogance, we even believed it our responsibility to make the rest of the world more like us. During my years of work in Africa, Asia, and Latin America in service to this agenda, I came to realize how wrong we were.

The middle-class ascendance in post–World War II America was an extraordinary demonstration of the possibilities of democracy and the idea that everyone should share in the benefits of a well-functioning society. Unfortunately, it turned out to be only a temporary victory in the war of the owning class against the rest.

All the disparate historic struggles to achieve justice for workers, women, and people of color, as well as the struggles for peace and the environment, are subtexts of a larger meta-struggle against the cultural mindset and institutions of Empire.

Divided We Fall, United We Stand

The owning classes have long recognized that any political unification of the oppressed places their imperial class privilege at risk. The separate claims of identity politics based on race, gender, and occupational specialization are tolerable to Empire, because they emphasize and perpetuate division. Discussion of class, however, is forbidden, because it exposes common interests and unifying structural issues around which a powerful resistance movement might be built.

Beneath the political stresses that at times threaten to tear our nation apart, we can see the emergent outlines of a largely unrecognized consensus that the world most of us want to bequeath to our children is very different from the world in which we live. Conservatives and liberals share a sense that the dominant culture and institutions of the contemporary world are morally and spiritually bankrupt, unresponsive to human needs and values, and destructive of the strong families and communities we crave and our children desperately need. Deceived by the divide-and-conquer tactics of imperial politics, each places the blame on the other rather than forming a united front to reject Empire's lies and uniting to achieve our common dream.

To raise healthy children we must have healthy, family-supportive economies. This can be achieved only by stripping imperial institutions of their unaccountable power and bringing about an equitable redistribution of real wealth. The struggle for the health and well-being of our children is potentially the unifying political issue of our time and an obvious rallying point for mobilizing a political majority behind a New Economy agenda.

EPIC OPPORTUNITY

It is fortunate that at the precise moment we humans face the imperative to make a collective choice to free ourselves from Empire's seemingly inexorable compete-or-die logic, we have achieved the means to do so. Three events have created possibilities wholly new to the human experience and have forever changed our perception of ourselves and our possibilities.

1. The United Nations was established in 1945. This made it possible for the first time in human history for representatives of the world's nations and people to meet in a neutral space to resolve differences through dialogue rather than force of arms.

2. The first human ventured into space in 1961, allowing us to look back and see ourselves as one people sharing a common destiny on a living spaceship.

3. In the early 1990s, our communications technologies gave us for the first time the capacity to link every human on the planet into a seamless web of nearly costless communication and cooperation.

Geographical isolation once served well Empire's need to keep us divided. That barrier is no more.

The world's estimated 1.7 billion Internet users, a quarter of all the people in the world, are learning to function as a dynamic, self-directing social organism that transcends boundaries of race, class, religion, and nationality to serve as a collective political conscience of the species.[4] On February 15, 2003, more than 10 million people demonstrated the power and potential of this technology when they took to the streets of the world's cities, towns, and villages in a unified call for peace in the face of the buildup to the U.S. invasion of Iraq.

A unified demonstration of political sentiment on this scale and geographic scope would have been inconceivable prior to the Internet. This monumental collective action was accomplished without a central organization, budget, or charismatic leader, through social processes never before possible. It was not only a demonstration of the transformative power of our newly acquired technologies but also an expression of the awakening of a new human consciousness to our shared interests and common destiny — and a foretaste of the possibilities for new and radically more democratic ways of organizing human affairs.

▶•◆•◆•◀

Most of the economic, social, and environmental pathologies of our time — including sexism, racism, economic injustice, violence, and environmental destruction — originates upstream in institutions that grant unaccountable power and privilege to the few and assign the majority to lives of hardship and desperation. The history of the United States demonstrates a simple but profound truth: economic democracy — the equitable distribution of economic power — is an essential foundation of political democracy.

Among the founding fathers of the United States, Thomas Jefferson sought to close the divide between owners and workers by making every worker an owner. Alexander Hamilton sought to secure the position of an elite ruling class by assuring that ownership was firmly concentrated in its hands. Hamilton served as the first secretary of the treasury and laid the foundation of the financial system we now know as Wall Street.

Jefferson had it right, but the Hamiltonians have been winning. Fortunately, the struggle is not over, and the financial crash and its aftermath — particularly the continued obscenity of billion-dollar Wall Street bonuses juxtaposed with deep unemployment, foreclosures, and bankruptcies — creates a rare opportunity to rally political support for measures to actualize the Jeffersonian ideal of a middle-class economic democracy.

A façade of political democracy has cloaked the extent to which Wall Street financial interests control our lives and run Washington, D.C., as a wholly owned subsidiary. That cloak has now been pulled away to reveal how far we remain from the democracy we thought we had. Wall Street has so eroded the economic, social, and environmental foundations of its own existence that its fate is sealed. The unanswered question is only whether it will maintain its grip until it brings down the whole of human civilization in an irrevocable social and environmental collapse or will be swept away by the already emergent values and institutions of a New Economy. Wall Street's days are numbered. Ours need not be.

CHAPTER 9

▶•◆•◆•◀

GREED IS NOT A VIRTUE; SHARING IS NOT A SIN

The 2008–2009 economic crisis presents us with an enormous opportunity: to rediscover our values — as people, as families, as communities of faith, and as a nation. It is a moment of decision we dare not pass by.

JIM WALLIS

No man can serve two masters: for either he will hate the one, and love the other; or else he will hold to the one, and despise the other. Ye cannot serve God and mammon.

JESUS TO HIS DISCIPLES, MATTHEW 6:24

It is really quite simple: Society works better and life is more pleasant for everyone when people share and cooperate. Far from a new discovery, this has been a defining message of religious leaders down through the ages.

Humanity's most celebrated teachers are those who spoke what others knew in their hearts to be true but were afraid to express because that truth contradicted the practice and often the words of those in positions of power. That is our situation today.

Speaking truth requires more courage than special talent. I find that my message resonates with many people, but not because I am revealing something astonishing or new. To the contrary, it is because I'm speaking what they already know to be true but have dared not express in public because it seems so at odds with conventional wisdom. As we each find the courage to give public voice to our inner truth, we empower others to do the same, and together we can change the world.

We humans are living out an epic morality play of five thousand years' duration that pits good, that which serves life, against evil, that which destroys life. Good is represented by the forces of mutual caring, cooperation, and responsibility in the service of life. Evil is represented by the forces of domination, unbridled competition, and individual greed in the service of money.

Individual greed will surely be with us so long as there are humans, but if we are to survive and prosper, we must recognize that greed is a sin, not a virtue — a form of addiction and a sign of psychological dysfunction. Any public subsidy for persons so encumbered should be limited to payment for rehabilitation services as part of a national health care program.

Here is a brief review of what events since the crash reveal about the profound moral issues at stake in the work at hand.

WALL STREET WELFARE QUEENS

As of spring 2010, the Wall Street economy was in apparent recovery. The Dow Jones Industrial Average had gained 62 percent from its ten-year low on March 9, 2009, to mid-March 2010. Wall Street bonuses for 2009 were up 17 percent over 2008. Banks too big to be allowed to fail at the time of the September 2008 crash were even bigger and more confident that government would bail them out when their gambling habit got them in trouble.

Bank of America, Wells Fargo, and JPMorgan Chase accounted for 26 percent of U.S. mortgages and 21 percent of U.S. deposits in 2007. Considered too big to fail following the market crash, each received federal bailout funds, which they used in part to fund major acquisitions with government blessing. Bank of American acquired Merrill Lynch, Wells Fargo took over Wachovia, and JPMorgan Chase took over Bear Stearns. In 2009, with their new acquisitions, these three banks accounted for 42 percent of mortgages and 34 percent of deposits.[1]

As of March 2009, Bloomberg.com estimated that the federal government bailout commitments and guarantees totaled $12.8 trillion; the 2008 U.S. GDP was $14.2 trillion.[2] (See chapter 7 for more details.) This, in essence, amounts to committing the nation's entire economic output to backing Wall Street's questionable bets. Quite a sum, given that Wall Street arguably serves no useful purpose not better served in other ways — the subject of chapter 14.

The "genius" for financial innovation and risk management that Wall Street regularly touts as its gift to the world consists mainly of finding new ways for an unethical trader to capture the profits from questionable financial transactions and shift the risk to others. The consequences for society are a revealing lesson in the importance of positive moral practice.

Thanks to these generous public subsidies, the Wall Street welfare queens are back to their usual business of speculating on asset bubbles, churning out phantom wealth unrelated to the production of anything of value while driving working people further into debt and rewarding themselves with billion-dollar compensation packages.

In the words of economics Nobel laureate Joseph Stiglitz:

> Under the threat of a collapse of the entire system, the safety net — intended to help unfortunate individuals meet the exigencies of life — was generously extended to commercial banks, then to investment banks, insurance

THE UNSPOKEN STORY OF PUBLIC DEBT

It is public knowledge that the Federal Reserve has been extending credit—money it creates with an accounting stroke—to member banks, which now include the infamous Goldman Sachs, at nearly zero percent interest. The reason, we are told, is to help them rebuild their capital and get credit flowing into the real economy.

There is rarely public mention of how the banks use this credit to rebuild their capital and the fact that it represents a direct but off-the-books taxpayer subsidy—off the books because it is not identified as a subsidy in public reports. Here is how it works.

The banks use some substantial portion of this money to buy securities issued by the Treasury Department. These securities cover the deficits created by the costs of the Wall Street bailouts and the economic stimulus package made necessary by the failure of Wall Street banks to keep credit flowing in the economy. Because these securities pay a substantially higher interest rate than the rate that the Fed charges the banks, holding Treasury bonds purchased with the Fed's virtually free money yields the banks a tidy, effortless, and risk-free profit.

As Allan H. Melzer, a Fed historian and professor at Carnegie Mellon University in Pittsburgh, told *Business-Week*, "You can make three percentage points, which is a lot for a bank, for doing nothing. Why should the banks take risks?"[3]

What makes this outrageous is that, instead of giving money to the banks, the Fed could just as easily have given it directly to the Treasury Department. The government—and therefore the taxpayers—rather than the banks would have received the free money and saved a bundle.

firms, auto companies, even car-loan companies. Never has so much money been transferred from so many to so few.

We are accustomed to thinking of government transferring money from the well off to the poor. Here it was the poor and average transferring money to the rich. Already heavily burdened taxpayers saw their money — intended to help banks lend so that the economy could be revived — go to pay outsized bonuses and dividends. Dividends are supposed to be a share of profits; here it was simply a share of government largesse.[4]

Yet there has been no expression of thanks, humility, remorse, or apology from Wall Street power brokers even as the rest of the country bears the burden of continued record job losses, unemployment, foreclosures, and bankruptcies.

To the contrary, they remain self-righteously defiant even as it becomes ever more evident to the public that their primary occupation is creating pyramids of phantom wealth, shifting the risk to the public, and sucking excessive interest and fees from Main Street.

There is a widespread sense that with Wall Street's apparent recovery, the window of opportunity for serious structural change has passed. Such a judgment, however, is premature.

THE WINDOW OF OPPORTUNITY

Wall Street's apparent recovery is largely an illusion created by a combination of public bailouts and deceptive bookkeeping. Even after massive bailout subsidies, Wall Street asset statements include huge sums in overvalued toxic securities and uncollectable receivables.

According to a December 2009 *BusinessWeek* report, Citibank was holding $182 billion in risky assets. The Fed's financial stress test of the nineteen biggest banks in May 2009 estimated that their total losses through 2010 might reach $600 billion. Barclays Bank in the U.K. estimated that these banks have so far recognized only 20 percent of these risky assets in their financial statements.[5]

According to the Bank for International Settlements, the total notional amount of over-the-counter derivatives still outstanding totaled an eye-popping $604.6 trillion in June 2009,[6] compared with an estimated 2009 gross world product of $58 trillion.

These schemes connect the world's largest financial institutions in a seamless web of systemic risk that continues to present a global security threat that dwarfs that posed by a few hundred terrorists living in remote areas of Pakistan and Afghanistan. The faster the government puts money in to keep their giant Ponzi scheme afloat, the faster the insatiable Wall Street welfare queens transfer it to their private accounts. Eventually, if left unchecked, this process has to reach a point at which all the financial resources of all the world's governments cannot prevent a collapse.

Meanwhile, people continue to struggle with the realities of their own unemployment, foreclosures, and bankruptcies or those of their relatives, friends, and neighbors; hear daily revelations of scandalous Wall Street bonuses; and get hit with predatory credit card fees.

Until the big banks are broken up and replaced with financial institutions rooted in and accountable to the communities they serve, we can expect Wall Street's unrepentant misappropriation to repeat endlessly, at enormous cost to society.

Far from closing, the window of opportunity for serious change continues to widen as public awareness of Wall Street corruption grows and outrage builds. The far right has been effective in focusing the outrage on government for funding bailouts with taxpayer money. The counterstrategy is not to defend the indefensible actions of government but rather to focus attention on the life-destroying Wall Street–Washington axis that serves the greed of the few at the expense of the well-being of all.

GLOBALIZING THE SEVEN DEADLY SINS

Capitalism is the institutional embodiment of greed, and Wall Street is its contemporary institutional manifestation. It operates by the moral code of an organized crime syndicate and subverts the values and institutions of both markets and democracy. Far from being ashamed of its ways, it champions them as virtues. What Wall Street considers virtues are actually the seven deadly sins identified by Christian tradition.

Table 9.1 lists the seven deadly sins, along with a note on how each is manifested by capitalism, contrasted with the corresponding seven life-serving virtues of New Economy institutions and practice.

By capitalism's perverse moral logic, if you buy toxic assets from me based on my assurance that they are sound, even if I know they are not, the fault resides not in my lie but rather in your trust in my word. When the assets prove worthless and threaten both your solvency and mine, it leaves no mark on my conscience to warn government in effect, *If you don't buy up my toxic assets and make me whole so that I can return to my trade in toxic assets, I will stop lending and crash the economy.*

In recent years, capitalism has acted through its Wall Street institutional missionaries to take its campaign of moral perversion global. For example, in the international forums in which trade agreements are negotiated, its representatives have succeeded in winning provisions that say in effect, *If a country introduces regulations to prevent a foreign corporation from harming or killing people with its toxic products*

Table 9.1 From Sins to Virtues

Seven Deadly Sins Promoted by Capitalism as Virtues	Seven Life-Serving Virtues Affirmed by the New Economy
PRIDE: Uncommon wealth is a mark of superior intelligence, contribution, and merit and is the proper due of those who have it.	HUMILITY: Every person has a gift. The joy of meaningful service that comes from sharing our personal gift is its own reward.
GREED: If any legal activity makes a profit, you have a moral duty to society to engage in it. In a winner-take-all world, if you don't get the prize, someone else will.	SHARING: Earth's wealth is our common heritage. Preserving and sharing it is our moral duty, a source of true joy, and the foundation of a secure and healthy world.
ENVY: If another has more than you, then you are his inferior until you match or exceed what he has.	LOVE: Those who recognize that all beings are connected know that what we do to and for others we do to and for ourselves.
ANGER: If you do not destroy those who attack you or compete for your wealth or reputation, they will destroy you.	COMPASSION: Life is better for everyone when we treat one another with understanding, respect, and caring.
LUST: Self-indulgence is our nature and the path to fulfillment. Cultivate and fulfill your natural desires for sexual and material gratification.	SELF-CONTROL: Obsessive behavior limits the development of our capacity for the responsible self-mastery of a fully developed human consciousness.
GLUTTONY: If a little is good, then more is better.	MODERATION: Keep your needs modest and take only what you need.
SLOTH: A life of idle luxury is the ultimate personal achievement and a sign of superior worth and status.	PASSION: Life is joyful and exuberant. Engage it fully and with passion in service to yourself and others.

Source: This table is inspired by and draws on "The Seven Deadly Sins," *White Stone Journal*, http://whitestonejournal.com/index.php/seven-deadly-sins (accessed March 2, 2010).

or discharges, the country's government must compensate the corporation for the profits it estimates it will lose.

The following are other examples of Wall Street's global campaign of moral perversion.

- It uses its control of media outlets, advertising, and politicians to shape and spread a global culture of greed, materialism, ruthless competition, individualism, and moral irresponsibility.

- Through the pursuit and celebration of financial gain at any cost, it provides role models for immoral behavior.

- It undermines democracy and the legitimacy of government by buying politicians to do its bidding.

- It uses student loan programs to get the best and brightest youth mired in debt that can be repaid only by selling themselves to jobs that serve Wall Street interests.

- It buys up and monopolizes control of the world's land and water resources in anticipation of extracting monopoly profits by charging what the market will bear as scarcity increases.

- It uses its financial power and creative accounting skills[7] to manipulate markets and obscure market signals, as when helping the Greek government hide its debt[8] or helping corporate CEOs hide their insider bets against the future of their own companies.[9]

- It buys the deeply discounted debt obligations of hapless underwater homeowners and countries on the open market and then demands full-value payment from governments or philanthropists who step in to lend a helping hand to the afflicted.

When governments seek real solutions to high-priority problems, Wall Street uses its lobbying power to block action on all solutions except those that contribute to its own bottom line. We see that in the United States in President Obama's initiatives on:

- Health insurance reform, where Wall Street forced off the table the public nonprofit single-payer health insurance option that is the only way to truly assure everyone access to adequate health care at a bearable cost. It allowed consideration only of a limited, expensive, government-subsidized private insurance program.

- Climate change, where Wall Street forced off the table the option of taxing carbon energy at the source and distributing the proceeds equally on a per person basis, which would have been simple, effective, and equitable. It allowed consideration only of an ineffective cap-and-trade system that offers countless opportunities for profitable fraud and speculation.

- The financial crisis, where Wall Street demanded and received expensive public bailouts for failed banks but recoiled in horror at "socialist" plots to regulate Wall Street or spend public money on direct economic stimulus programs that fund real-wealth local economies to create jobs and rebuild the nation's physical, social, and natural capital.

These and other capitalist attacks on human interests and the natural world are playing out around the world. We look to government to defend the public interest, but we allow government to be taken over by institutions of greed for whom the only interest worthy of government action is their own private financial interest.

It need be so no longer. Change is possible, and it is our right and responsibility as citizens to make it happen.

▸•◆•◆•◂

The apparent Wall Street recovery is solely the product of a combination of public guarantees, public bailout money, and deceptive accounting entries that place much of the nation's economic output for years to come in hock to predatory Wall Street welfare queens and missionaries of greed. Such actions have continued to raise public awareness that the Wall Street–Washington axis is the institutional embodiment of evil in our time and a mortal threat to human security and viability.

The actions of Wall Street's most powerful players and their Washington accomplices have been so extreme, so shameless, and so contrary to public well-being that it is almost as if they wanted to keep the window of opportunity for transformative change open by making sure that no one could fail to recognize the depths of the system's moral corruption.

Let us rise to the occasion. We must now move forward with a New Economy agenda to dismantle and replace Wall Street institutions that champion the seven deadly sins of pride, greed, envy, anger, lust, gluttony, and sloth with New Economy institutions that champion the life-affirming virtues of humility, sharing, love, compassion, self-control, moderation, and passion.

PART III

A LIVING-ECONOMY VISION

▸•◆•◆•◂

We humans are awakening to the reality that we are living beings and that healthy living systems self-organize to function as sharing, cooperative, dynamically balanced communities. Nature's closest equivalent to the corporate-driven global economy is the suicidal, malignant cancer that seeks its own unlimited growth without regard for the harm this does to the body that provides its nourishment. Our future depends on getting with nature's program and organizing ourselves to live in a dynamic, balanced partnership with Earth's biosphere.

This New Economy will look a great deal more like Adam Smith's version of a market economy in which local artisans, merchants, and farmers self-organize to meet the needs of their community than the Wall Street version in which global corporations compete to be the most efficient at converting real-wealth living capital into phantom-wealth money. In our time, Smith's vision translates into a planetary system of bioregional economies that mimic the fractal structure and dynamics of Earth's biosphere, with recurring patterns of self-organizing, ecologically balanced self-reliance on a progressive scale from the global to the local.

The full-scale, modern version of Smith's vision lies beyond the horizon of our experience. To navigate our way to its realization, we must form in our collective mind an image of its institutions and priorities, much as the ancient indigenous navigators of the South Pacific trained themselves to see in their mind unknown islands far beyond the horizon of their experience or normal vision.

Chapter 10, "What People Really Want," cites evidence that the human brain is wired to support caring and sharing and that we humans have long dreamed of a world of vital, healthy children, families, communities, and natural environments: the world we must now create to secure our future.

Chapter 11, "At Home on a Living Earth," makes the case that our future depends on a conscious collective choice to transform the culture that frames our understanding of our individual and shared priorities.

Chapter 12, "New Vision, New Priorities," summarizes the foundational design principles that the culture and institutions of a planetary system of living, real-wealth economies must honor and outlines opportunities to reallocate real resources on the path to a New Economy.

CHAPTER 10

▶•◆•◆•◀

WHAT PEOPLE REALLY WANT

> At this stage of history, one of two things is possible: Either the general population will take control of its own destiny and will concern itself with community interests guided by values of solidarity and sympathy and concern for others, or alternatively there will be no destiny to control.
>
> NOAM CHOMSKY

Empire's greatest tragedy is the denial and suppression of the higher-order possibilities of our human nature. The culture and institutions of the Wall Street economy cultivate and reward our capacity for individualistic greed, hubris, deceit, ruthless competition, and material excess.

They communicate the message in both subtle and unsubtle ways that this is our human nature and that it is all for the good because individualism, competition, and greed drive economic innovation and growth. Our capacities for sharing, honesty, service, compassion, cooperation, and material sufficiency are denied and discouraged, even punished.

The touts of Wall Street would have us believe "there is no alternative." Former British prime minister Margaret Thatcher gave it a name: TINA. To accept TINA is to give up all hope of a future for our children.

Like most imperial propaganda, TINA is a lie. We have the means to build a New Economy that cultivates the best rather than the worst of our nature and thus to realize a long-cherished human dream.

127

Wall Street propagandists have so successfully conditioned our minds that as a society we celebrate the "success" of an economy that is literally killing us. Here is the real story of our human nature.

OUR HUMAN NATURE

We humans are complex beings of many possibilities. Empire has demonstrated our capacity for psychopathology. By way of contrast, most people daily demonstrate, to one extent or another, our capacity for caring, sharing, peacemaking, and service. The former are the possibilities of our lower nature; the latter, the possibilities of our higher nature. Both possibilities are within our means.

Cultivating Our Possibilities Rather Than Our Pathologies

The human capacity to choose is perhaps the most distinctive characteristic of our nature. What we are depends in substantial measure on what we choose to be — not only by our individual choices but also by how we shape the collective cultures and institutions that in turn shape our individual behavior.

In previous chapters, we have seen the devastating consequences of a collective choice for cultures and institutions that for five thousand years have suppressed the full realization of our higher nature.

Given that this pattern has survived for so long even in the face of determined popular struggle, we might be forgiven for assuming that it is immutable and that we are incapable of living any other way. Such assumptions are in error. Cultures and institutions are collective human creations. We can change them through intentional collective action.

We have been trapped in Empire's pernicious rule-or-be-ruled, kill-or-be-killed, play-or-die dynamic by geographic and cultural barriers that have kept us divided and unable to embrace our true nature and common interest. On those historic occasions when we succeeded in breaching these barriers to organize in rebellion, we too often saw the goal as being to gain control of the institutions of Empire's power. Those who successfully claimed that power with the intention of transforming it all too often became its captives and, wearing a cloak of a different color, assumed the throne previously occupied by another.

The communication technologies of the Internet now in place create a potential for collective dialogue, organization, and action never before available. We have the means, as well as the need and the right, to bridge the geographic and cultural barriers that have for so long divided us and to bring forth cultures and institutions that cultivate and reward our higher nature. Do we have the will? I believe we do. It is being expressed by growing millions of people working largely outside the institutions of Empire.

The propagandists of Empire tell us that we are by nature a flawed species incapable of caring and cooperation, that we would destroy ourselves but for Empire's controlling, organizing hand. Recent findings from science tell a different and more enabling story: a desire to cooperate and serve is hardwired into the human brain.[1]

Born to Care and Cooperate

Scientists who use advanced imaging technology to study brain function report that the healthy human brain is wired to reward caring, cooperation, and service. Merely thinking about another person experiencing harm triggers the same reaction in our brain as that of a mother who sees distress on her baby's face.

Conversely, the act of cooperation and generosity triggers the brain's pleasure center to release the same hormone that's released when we eat chocolate or engage in good sex. In addition to producing a sense of bliss, it benefits our health by boosting our immune system, reducing our heart rate, and preparing us to approach and soothe. Positive emotions such as compassion produce similar benefits.

By contrast, negative emotions suppress our immune system, increase our heart rate, and prepare us to fight or flee.

These findings are consistent with the pleasure that most of us experience being a member of an effective team or extending an uncompensated helping hand to another being.

It is entirely logical. If our brains were not wired for life in community, our species would have expired long ago. We have an instinctual desire to protect the group, including its weakest and most vulnerable members — its children. Behavior contrary to this positive norm is an indicator of social and psychological dysfunction. Caring, cooperation, and service are both the healthy norm and wonderful tonics — and they are free.

Traversing the Path from "Me" to "We"

Psychologists who study the developmental pathways of the individual consciousness observe that, over a lifetime, those who enjoy the requisite emotional support traverse a pathway from the narcissistic, undifferentiated magical consciousness of the newborn to the fully mature, inclusive, and multidimensional spiritual consciousness of the wise elder. It is a journey from "me" to "we" that over a lifetime traverses from a my-group "we" to a human "we," to a living Earth "we," and ultimately to a cosmic "we."

The lower, more narcissistic, orders of consciousness are perfectly normal for young children, but they become sociopathic in adults and are easily encouraged and manipulated by advertisers and demagogues. Even more tragic for humanity, people who have been thwarted on the path to maturity are those most likely to engage in the ruthless competition for positions of unaccountable power. Moreover, imperial institutions implicitly recognize that these psychologically damaged individuals come with an imperialistic drive and values that well serve their purpose. We have suffered enormous harm from the imperial culture's celebration of the accomplishments of triumphant psychopaths and its promotion of them as the standard of human achievement.

The more mature consciousness recognizes that true liberty is not a license to act in disregard of others; rather, it necessarily comes with a responsibility to protect and serve the larger we. Doing the right thing comes naturally to the mature consciousness, which minimizes society's need for coercive restraint to prevent antisocial behavior. This commitment to personal responsibility and capacity for self-restraint is an essential foundation of a mature democracy, a caring community, and a real-wealth economy. It is one of society's most valuable real-wealth assets.

Strong, caring families and communities are not only essential to our physical health and happiness; their emotional support and stimulation facilitate the maturing of our emotional and moral consciousness and guide our children to mature, responsible adulthood. They are essential to the realization of our humanity and to the realization of true democracy, a real-wealth economy, and the world of our shared human dream.

THE WORLD OF OUR DREAMS

In 1992, I participated in the civil society portion of the Earth Summit in Rio de Janeiro, Brazil, where I was part of a gathering of some fifteen thousand people representing the vast variety of humanity's races, religions, nationalities, and languages. It was at the time the largest and most diverse global gathering in human history. Our discussions centered on defining and committing ourselves to the vision of the world we would create together.

These discussions were chaotic and often contentious. But at one point it hit me like a bolt of lightning. Despite our differences, we all wanted the same thing: healthy, happy children, families, and communities living in peace and cooperation in healthy natural environments. Out of our conversations emerged an articulation of our shared dream of a world in which people and nature live in dynamic, creative, cooperative, and balanced relationships. The Earth Charter,[2] which is the product of a continuation of this discussion, calls it Earth Community, a community of life.

The Vision We Share

I've lived in a lot of places with starkly different cultures: Ethiopia, Nicaragua, Indonesia, the Philippines, California, Massachusetts, Florida, Virginia, Washington State, and a New York City apartment on Union Square between Madison Avenue and Wall Street. The latter provided an inspirational setting for writing *When Corporations Rule the World*. As I reflect back on this experience, I realize that we humans are a lot more alike than we generally realize. Most of us want to breathe clean air and drink clean water. We want tasty, nutritious food uncontaminated with toxins. We want meaningful work, a living wage, and security in our old age. We want a say in the decisions our government makes. We want world peace.

As Rabbi Michael Lerner, the editor of *Tikkun* magazine, observes,

> The great spiritual-religious wisdom traditions of the world have all taught some variant of this message: The deepest human pleasures come from living in a world

based on justice, peace, love, generosity, kindness, and celebration of the universe and service to the ultimate moral law of the universe (whether learned through revelation or through reason).[3]

That should not be surprising. The knowledge is wired into our human brain. The amazing part of our current human situation is that the world we must now create is the world that all but the most psychologically deranged human beings want — and it is within our grasp.

This recognition of our common dream helps answer the question, What is real wealth? The deepest truths seem so obvious once we discover them. Real wealth is a healthy, fulfilling life; healthy, happy children; loving families; and a caring community within a beautiful, healthy natural environment. It is a fulfilling means of livelihood that affirms our inherent worth and service. It is a peaceful world. These are the things of real value, and their presence or absence is the only truly valid measure of economic performance.

Getting the Indicators Right

We intuitively recognize real wealth when we experience it, but because in its most precious forms it is not available for purchase or sale, its value cannot be readily reduced to a monetary equivalent. Economists largely ignore such issues and assess economic performance by growth in gross domestic product, a measure of the market value of economic output, which they treat as a proxy for human well-being. Since GDP tells us little or nothing about what is most essential to our happiness and well-being, this has led to a terrible distortion of human priorities.

Human health and well-being depend on a great many things that do have market value: food, housing, transportation, education, health care, and many other essentials of a healthy life. These, however, are but means to other ends. Their real value is a function of their contribution to improving human and natural health and vitality.

Note, for example, that the food component of the GDP makes no distinction between healthy and unhealthy food or between wholesome food consumed by a malnourished child and junk food consumed by a compulsive eater. An increase in the market value of food consumed, which increases the GDP, often coincides with a decline in well-being.

Or take transportation. An increase in expenditures on transportation, even adjusting for energy-price inflation, may simply mean people are spending more time stalled in traffic jams — hardly an improvement in well-being.

The GDP can be rising in the face of simultaneous epidemics of child obesity and starvation. It can be rising in the face of disintegrating families and a vanishing middle class, increasing prison populations, rising unemployment, the disruption of community, collapsing environmental systems, the hollowing out of domestic manufacturing capabilities, failing schools, growing trade deficits, and costly but senseless foreign wars.

You probably noticed that these are not hypothetical examples. Vision of Humanity compiles an annual Global Peace Index[4] based on qualitative and quantitative indicators compiled from respected sources, covering both internal factors such as crime and prison populations and external factors such as the number of external conflicts fought. In 2009, the United States ranked 83 out of 144 countries.

Since the mid-twentieth century, most nations have been managing their economies to maximize the economic cost of whatever level of health and happiness — high or low — they enjoy. In the face of the current economic carnage, politicians point to a rising GDP and tell us with a straight face that the economic fundamentals are sound. Yet, as the examples demonstrate, the GDP is best treated as a measure of the cost, not the benefit, of economic activity.

Why in the world would we seek to maximize economic costs rather than the benefits we really want? Perhaps it has something to do with the fact that Wall Street corporations profit from almost all forms of economic activity, whether they're harmful or not, and the Wall Street demand for interest on every dollar in circulation means that the market value of economic output must grow or the financial system will crash, as explained in chapter 7. It turns out that we do it all for Wall Street.

NAVIGATING THE TURNING

Think of the work at hand as navigating a great turning from a money-serving Wall Street phantom-wealth economy to a life-serving Main Street real-wealth economy. In the larger picture, it is a turn from Empire to Earth Community, from an era of domination to an era of partnership.

My wise friend and colleague Puanani Burgess tells the story of Nainoa Thompson, a Native Hawaiian navigator who learned and practiced the ancient Polynesian art of navigating to previously unvisited islands thousands of miles beyond the horizon. In the distant past, that ability guided the first Tahitian settlers to Hawaii.

Nainoa made his first solo voyage from Hawaii to Tahiti in 1976 using this ancient practice. As Puanani tells the story,

> Nainoa Thompson was taught by the master navigator from the Satawal Island in Micronesia, Mau Pialug, to navigate without instruments, using his native way-finding skills to guide the Hawaiian double-hulled canoe Hokule'a on a Hawai'i-Tahiti voyage of more than 2,200 miles.

As part of Nainoa's training process, Mau would take him to a lookout on Oʻahu, where he could see the islands of Molokaʻi, Maui and Lanaʻi. Mau would tell him, "Look beyond the horizon, so that you can see the island you are going to. Especially because you have never been there before, you have to see that island in your mind, or else you can never get there."

That ability — no, courage — to see something you have never seen before is an important part of navigating to the Earth Community that we all long for. Our ability to see it, describe it, share that vision is critical to making it real.

Like the navigators of the Pacific Ocean, the navigators of the Great Turning will require the gifts of mind as well as the heart of someone with the qualities of humility, leadership, courage, and kindness. When we think the journey is hard and impossible, I remember that we made the journey then and now.[5]

▶•◆•◆•◀

Beyond our varied races, religions, nationalities, and languages, we humans share a collective dream of a world of healthy, happy children, families, communities, and natural environments joined in peace and cooperation. The greatest barrier to achieving this world is the fabricated belief that we are by nature incapable of cooperating in the common good.

The institutions of the Wall Street economy not only champion a perverse morality by celebrating and rewarding the qualities of individualism, materialism, greed, and violence characteristic of our lower nature but also actively suppress our realization of the qualities of caring and compassion of our higher nature. These institutions are a collective choice and creation of those whose life experience has thwarted the development of these higher-order capacities. They are not our collective destiny.

It is within the means of the more functional majority to make a conscious collective choice to bring forth a New Economy that champions a positive morality and that cultivates and rewards our distinctive human capacity for cooperation and reason in service to all.

Those who join in the work of navigating a great turning from a Wall Street phantom-wealth economy to a Main Street real-wealth economy embark on a bold and courageous journey to a destination beyond the horizon of our immediate experience.

CHAPTER 11

▶•◆•◆•◀

AT HOME ON A LIVING EARTH

The wise and virtuous man is at all times willing that his own private interest should be sacrificed to the public interest of his own particular order or society.

ADAM SMITH

There's a general tendency to presume people just act for short-term profit. But anyone who knows about small-town businesses and how people in a community relate to one another realizes that many of those decisions are not just for profit and that humans do try to organize and solve problems.

ELINOR OSTROM, WINNER OF THE 2009 NOBEL MEMORIAL PRIZE IN ECONOMICS

Adam Smith believed that our mature human nature is to be caring and responsible and to serve the greater interest of the community. Elinor Ostrom, the first woman to win the Nobel Prize in economics, and the first economist of either gender to win that prize for work on cooperation, notes that people engage in cooperative problem solving every day within their local communities.

We must now bring this caring and cooperative aspect of our nature to the fore, accept responsibility for our relationship with Earth's biosphere, and restructure the institutions of the economy accordingly.

THE COOPERATION IMPERATIVE

Scientists are in nearly universal agreement that to avoid driving Earth's system of climate regulation into irrevocable collapse, we must achieve at least an 80 percent reduction in

BIOSPHERE

The term *biosphere* was coined by geologist Eduard Suess in 1875 to refer to "the place on Earth's surface where life dwells." It is Earth's narrow zone of life, the global ecosystem comprising all of Earth's regional and local ecosystems.

The idea that this zone of life is properly understood as a living, self-organizing superorganism traces back to a lecture in 1789 by James Hutton, considered the father of geology. This idea was more recently popularized as the Gaia hypothesis by James Lovelock.[1]

global greenhouse gas emissions by no later than 2050, and possibly sooner. Given the disproportionate responsibility of the United States for the existing emissions, doing our share will require a reduction closer to 90 percent. Meeting these goals will require unprecedented human cooperation and a sharing of resources at all levels of society, from the local to the global.

Even if we are able to significantly reduce greenhouse gas emissions, we face the prospect of significant, possibly permanent, disruptions of food production due to climate changes, collapsing fisheries, water shortages, and the loss of topsoil. Meeting this challenge will require unprecedented cooperation.

Meanwhile, even the most optimistic estimates project a growth in the human population of at least a billion people between now and 2050. If we do not act to voluntarily and responsibly reduce our numbers, nature will do it for us through the Malthusian solutions of plague, famine, and violence.

Neither phantom-wealth money nor any technology remotely within reach is going to change this grim equation. Nor can we look to Wall Street to figure out what will. Wall Street excels at increasing aggregate human demand, does even better at increasing inequality, prefers investment in phantom wealth to investment in real wealth, and loves population growth as a source of cheap labor and potential market expansion.

If you were a fan of the original *Star Trek* TV series, as I was, perhaps you can hear Captain Kirk calling Scotty in engineering in the aftermath of a narrow escape from a Klingon attack. "Kirk to Scotty, give me a quick status report on life support." "Aye, Captain. It's looking bad." "Scotty, shut down all nonessential systems immediately and transfer all available resources to life support." Need I note that Wall Street plays the role of the Klingons in this dramatization?

AWAKENING FROM AN ILLUSION

We humans have been living an illusion that our world is an open frontier of endless resources free for the taking and have organized our economies accordingly. Assuming ourselves separate from nature, we have too often attacked or sought to destroy or subdue her as though she were our enemy.

We are awakening to the reality that we inhabit a wondrous but finite living planet and that our lives are inseparably interlinked with all of Earth's species. We must learn to live by the biosphere's rules and restructure our economic systems accordingly, which presents an epic test of our human capacity for creative innovation, collective choice, and self-organization.

As we consider the transformation ahead, we must recognize that our individual choices are constrained by collective

FROM MAXIMIZING FLOWS
TO MAXIMIZING STOCKS

In his classic essay "The Economics of the Coming Spaceship Earth," Kenneth Boulding observed that the illusion that we live on an open frontier of limitless resources has led us to manage our economy to maximize GDP, a measure of the *flow* of materials and services through our economy.[2]

On an open frontier, resources are abundant. If such abundance is equally available to all, anyone who complains that another man's fortune comes at the expense of his own is properly dismissed as too lazy or ignorant to take advantage of readily available opportunities. Anyone who applies this same logic on a spaceship is delusional.

Earth's frontier closed for humans sometime during the 1970s, when our consumption of Earth's natural regenerative resources exceeded the limits of what Earth could sustain and many natural systems began to collapse. Thus, our reality has changed and so too must our ways of thinking and doing business.

Astronauts hurtling through space understand that their well-being depends on secure and adequate *stocks* of oxygen, fuel, food, water, and other essentials. Minimizing flows and recycling everything is essential to their long-term well-being. Because nothing can be replaced, nothing can be wasted. Consuming faster than stocks regenerate is actively suicidal.

The frontier is no more. Now we must live by Earth's rules or die.

societal choices beyond our individual control. For example, when Fran and I lived in the heart of New York City, we had no need of a car and chose not to have one, because everything we needed was within easy walking distance or was readily accessible by efficient public transportation.

In most U.S. cities, and certainly most suburban or rural locations, the layout of our built spaces combines with the lack of public transportation to create a powerful incentive for households to buy and maintain at least one car. This happens to be a lack of choice that works well for the Wall Street corporations that make and sell automobiles. The story of how General Motors successfully killed the streetcar as a once widely available public transportation option is well documented.[3]

Contrary to capitalism's claim that unregulated markets maximize consumer choice, Wall Street corporations go to great lengths to limit our choices to those most profitable for themselves. One of the more telling examples is Wall Street's drive to create an unregulated, borderless economy in which goods and money move freely at the discretion of global corporations that operate beyond the reach of accountability to any government.

WHY WALL STREET GLOBALIZED THE ECONOMY

The elimination of national borders as barriers to the expansion of corporate control of world markets and resources didn't happen as a result of some inexorable law of nature. It came about over a period of some thirty years through the relentless effort of Wall Street interests using every political tool at their disposal to remove legal barriers to their expansion.

Wall Street did not expend all this effort to improve the health of people and the biosphere. It figured out that its ability to generate profits would be best served by a system that maximized each locality's dependence on distant resources and markets.

Create Dependence

Take the system by which we produce, process, transport, and market our food. A farmers' market where local producers and consumers gather to engage in direct exchange offers many benefits from a community perspective. The food is fresh, the energy costs of transport are minimal, the personal exchanges enhance community ties, farmers can adapt rapidly to changing local preferences and conditions, and the local economy is cushioned from food shocks elsewhere in the world.

Wall Street has a different perspective. It observes this scene and says in effect:

> What's the profit here? We need a global food system in which producers in Chile depend on customers in New York and vice versa. Then both are dependent on us to serve as middleman. We can monopolize global markets, set prices for both producers and consumers, and force producers either to buy our seeds, fertilizers, and insecticides at whatever price we choose or to lose their market access. The greater our success in convincing local producers that they will have higher profits, and local consumers that they will have greater selection at low prices when everything is traded globally, the more they will depend on us as intermediaries, the greater will be our hold on people's lives everywhere, and the more profit we can extract.

When the world's agricultural land is organized on the model of industrial monocropping, both producers and consumers depend on the global agricultural conglomerates for their survival. Until a crisis strikes, few notice that the resulting increase in global food interdependence increases the real costs of food production and reduces food security for everyone. This in turn creates lucrative opportunities for Wall Street speculators who profit from volatile commodity prices as a weather disruption on one side of the world creates food shortages on the other.

If the United States decides to convert its corn crop to ethanol, the price of tortillas in Mexico shoots through the roof. One nation may decide that it is more profitable to pave over its farmland and import food from a place where labor and land are cheaper. A nation may see the folly of this choice only when the supplying country decides to do the same or faces a bad harvest and shuts off its exports in favor of feeding its own people. Corporations that control global markets then profit from the frantic bidding up of prices by countries desperate to avoid the rebellion of a hungry population.

Such a system is also folly from a biological standpoint. The resilience of economic and biological systems is a function of local diversity and self-reliance. The less diverse and self-reliant the local system, the greater is its dependence on resources and decisions over which the people affected have no influence. In the case of the economy, this works to the benefit of global corporations, not the local communities that depend on choices made by those corporations without consideration for community interests or preferences.

Furthermore, shipping massive quantities of food around the world breaches natural ecosystem barriers and introduces alien predators against which ecosystems on the receiving end have no defense. In addition, monoculture cropping is particularly vulnerable to invasive pests or a change in weather conditions.

Eliminate Local Options

A thriving Main Street economy comprising locally owned, community-oriented enterprises is essential to the creation of a sense of community and place. Wall Street, however, has political clout, which it uses shamelessly to promote public policies that favor its corporations and investors at the expense of local enterprises and ownership.

Local stores that have served their communities for generations are driven out of business by subsidized corporate box stores. Local manufacturers find themselves competing with foreign producers that pay their workers pennies an hour and freely discharge toxic pollutants into the air and water.

As local businesses close their doors, wages fall, once-thriving Main Streets that served as centers of community life are abandoned, and ugly, auto-dependent strip malls, box stores, and shopping centers dominate the countryside. The disruption of community life and the loss of natural beauty and biologically productive open space come at an enormous but largely unacknowledged cost in lost social and environmental capital and increased physical and mental stress.

We must now seize this pivotal moment in our collective history to recognize that we are in fact part of Earth's biosphere and transform our economies accordingly.

LIFE AS TEACHER AND PARTNER

Earth's biosphere is segmented into countless self-organizing ecosystems, each exquisitely adapted to its particular place on Earth to optimize the sustainable use of locally available resources in service to life. It involves a highly sophisticated and complex fractal structure of nested, self-reliant, progressively smaller ecosystems.[4]

Our task is to reorganize our human economies to function

as locally self-reliant subsystems of our local ecosystems. This requires segmenting the borderless global economy into a planetary system of interlinked, self-reliant regional economies, each rooted in a community of place and organized to optimize the lives of all who live within its borders.

These economies will trade their surplus with their neighbors in return for that which they cannot reasonably produce for themselves. Most needs, however, will be met by local production using local resources in the manner of local ecosystems. As each local economy limits its population growth and eliminates wasteful and destructive resource use to bring itself into balance with its place on Earth, global GDP will shrink, overall human well-being will increase, and we humans will come into balance with Earth's biosphere.

Organizing ourselves to partner with the biosphere properly begins with identifying the biosphere's underlying organizing principles. These principles are a product of an extraordinary 3.5-billion-year evolutionary experience

FRACTALS IN NATURE

A fractal is a geometric figure in which each part has the same statistical character as the whole, which means that similar patterns recur at progressively smaller scales. Fractal structures are ubiquitous in nature. I sense that they have much to teach us about organizing human economies that will function in balanced, creative relationship to nature at all system levels, from the household to the bioregion to the global biosphere. A Web search on *fractals in nature* yields a wealth of photos and videos that illustrate the concept and stir the imagination.

ORGANIZING PRINCIPLES OF HEALTHY LIVING SYSTEMS

1. Self-organize into dynamic, inclusive, self-reliant communities of place.
2. Balance individual and community needs and interest.
3. Practice frugality and reciprocity.
4. Reward cooperation.
5. Optimize the sustainable capture and use of energy and matter by adapting to the specific details of the microenvironment.
6. Form and manage permeable boundaries.
7. Cultivate diversity and share knowledge.

through which life has learned to optimize its potential on a varied and finite Earth. This experience has much to teach us about what we must do to prosper in balanced relationship with the whole of Earth's web of life.

Cooperative Self-Organization

Since our early turn to dominator systems of organization, we humans have been inclined to see life as a brutal competitive struggle for food, sex, and survival, perhaps to justify our imperial brutality to one another. Although life's competitive elements contribute to its dynamism, competition is only a subtext to the larger story of life's extraordinary capacity for cooperative self-organization.

The secret to life's success is found in the trillions upon trillions of cells, organisms, and communities of organisms engaged in an exquisite dance of continuous exchange with their living neighbors. Each maintains its own identity and health while contributing to the life of the whole. Each balances its own needs with the needs of the larger community. Biologists at the cutting edge of their field now tell us that the species that prosper over the longer term are not the most brutal and competitive, but rather are those that find a niche in which they meet their own needs in ways that simultaneously serve the needs of others and contribute to the life of the whole.

In its continuous exchange, life is both frugal and reciprocal. The waste of one species is the food of another in constant and pervasive processes of recycling and reuse.

Because life thrives on diversity and depends on continuous exchange, living beings can exist only in community. An individual organism cannot survive in isolation from other organisms or in a monoculture exclusive to its own species. The greater the diversity of the bio-community and the greater the cooperation among its diverse species, the greater the community's resilience in times of crisis, its potential for creativity in the pursuit of new possibilities, and its capacity to adapt to diverse and changing local conditions.

Self-Reliant Local Adaptation

This capacity for self-organization supports a constant process of adaptation to the intricate features of Earth's distinctive physical microenvironments, using nature's fractal structure of nested subsystems. Each subsystem is able to optimize the capture, sharing, use, and storage of available energy and material resources, both for itself and as its contribution to the needs of the larger system of which it is a part, all the way down to the microscopic level. Because of this fractal structure, each ecosystem level up to and including the biosphere is local everywhere within its boundaries, which is the key to the ability of all system levels to be both adaptive and resilient.

Local self-reliance in each microsystem's food and energy capture and production maximizes security and stability both locally and globally. A disturbance in one part of the system is readily absorbed and contained locally, instead of disrupting the whole system. Local self-reliance also forces each local system to balance its consumption and reproduction with local resource availability, thus maintaining balance in the system as a whole.

Managed Boundaries

Living systems have learned to form permeable membranes at every level of organization — the cell, the organ, the multicelled organism, and the multispecies ecosystem. At each of these levels, from the individual cell to the ecosystem, the living entity must capture energy from its environment and then maintain it in an active state of continuous flows within itself and with its neighbors. The membrane is also the entity's defense against parasitic predators that would sup on its energies while offering no compensating service in return.

If the membrane is breached, the continuously flowing embodied energy that sustains the organism's internal structures mixes with the energy of its environment, and it dies. It also dies, however, if the membrane becomes impermeable, thus isolating the entity and cutting off its needed energy exchange with its neighbors. Managed boundaries are not only essential to life's good health but are essential to its very existence.

We must learn to apply these principles of cooperative self-organization, self-reliant local adaptation, and managed boundaries to our own economic systems as our planetary crises force us to recognize that we must play by Earth's rules.

A community that organizes its economy around locally

rooted businesses that rely primary on local resources to meet its needs is unlikely to find its economy devastated because a large corporation decides to outsource its production and close the local factory on which the town depends. It is less likely to suffer a loss of its markets because of some sudden shift in the global terms of trade. And it faces less risk from invasive species.

▶•◆•◆•◀

We humans are awakening to the reality that we are living beings who inhabit a finite living Earth to whose ways we must now adapt by creating economies that mimic the biosphere's fractal structure and capacity for self-reliant local adaptation through cooperative self-organization.

The transition to an economy suited to the realities of life on a living Earth poses a significant creative challenge. It also presents an epic opportunity to get our priorities right, express our human capacity for creative innovation, and actualize humanity's long-shared dream of a world of universal peace and prosperity.

CHAPTER 12

►•◆•◆•◄

NEW VISION, NEW PRIORITIES

We cannot manage the scale, complexity and dynamics
of the 21st Century with the tools of the 20th. We are at a
turning point in world history where new ideas, new values, new strategies and new institutional arrangements are
needed. We must find the vision, the leadership, and the
creativity to collaborate in developing constructive solutions to offer a decent future to present and succeeding
generations.

R. MARTIN LEES, THE CLUB OF ROME

There is no place on an already overstressed living Earth
for war, speculation in phantom wealth, advertising to
encourage people to consume beyond their means and needs,
paving over or otherwise taking productive land out of service, depleting or contaminating water reserves, or engaging
in gratuitous displays of material excess. Yet a major portion
of the current GDP is derived from or dependent on these
activities. On a living Earth these are acts of suicidal insanity
that of necessity must be strongly discouraged or prohibited.

We can and must reallocate to more beneficial pursuits
the resources these undesirable activities expropriate.

The current massive misallocation of resources is the arti-
fact of a belief that human prosperity is maximized by unrestrained global competition for resources, markets, and money
to increase the consumption of whatever goods and services
generate the greatest private profit. This is the underlying
theory around which the institutions of the corporate-led

151

global economy have been organized. The result is military conflicts worldwide; a global race to the bottom on wages, benefits, and environmental standards; and unregulated financial markets that produce prosperity for the few, misery for the many, and insecurity for all.

As elaborated in the previous chapter, the path to true and secure economic prosperity is through global cooperation in a race to the top for the healthiest people, families, communities, and natural systems. The supporting economic system will allocate the sustainable product of the biosphere to maximize the well-being of people and nature rather than the profitability of Wall Street corporations.

INSTITUTIONAL SYSTEMS FOR A NEW ECONOMY

Although I'm sometimes called an economist because I write and speak about economic issues, the discipline for which I received my academic training is organizational systems design. I view the economy through that lens.

As a Harvard Business School professor in the early 1970s, I taught the art of structuring human relationships in corporations to maximize profit. Partly, that involves getting the incentives right; it also involves culture, authority, communication flows, and a host of other influences subject to management intervention.

The same intellectual tools can be used to design the institutional structures of societies either to consolidate the power and privilege of the ruling elites or to share power and facilitate creative, democratic self-organization to enhance a community's well-being. These are essential tools for a fully developed science of applied ecology.

To create a global human system that supports the sharing of power to optimize human and natural health and well-being, we must first be able to see it in our collective human mind, just as the ancient South Pacific mariner saw in his mind the otherwise unknown distant island that was the object of his journey.

We seek systems of values and institutions that support self-organization toward three defining conditions. Defining these values and institutions can help us visualize the future we seek.

Three Defining System Conditions

A *system condition* refers to the equilibrium state toward which a healthy, resilient system self-corrects in the aftermath of a disturbance.

The institutional system of the old economy lacks the ability to self-correct, not only because its most powerful decision makers are insulated from the social and environmental consequences of their decisions but also because their definition of system health and success is itself fatally flawed. They take the rate at which their financial-asset accounts are growing as the measure of success and allocate resources accordingly, wholly unmindful of any connection between their decisions and rising unemployment, family and community breakdowns, collapsing fisheries, and melting glaciers.

They are most exuberant about the economy's performance when a financial bubble is rapidly inflating, a condition of disequilibrium, and respond by feeding the bubble, a path to certain system collapse.

The Keynesian economist John Kenneth Galbraith called this self-destructive predisposition "irrational exuberance" and demonstrated that it is the condition toward which capitalist systems have consistently self-organized for more than 360 years, with no apparent ability to self-correct or learn from experience.[1]

For a human system to self-correct, it must provide negative feedback to the decision makers when they make choices that threaten the system's health. This means the group that reaps the rewards must also bear the costs.

The New Economy goal is to create a resilient system of economic institutions, values, and relationships that dynamically self-correct toward a healthy condition of ecological balance, equitable distribution, and living democracy. Let's take a closer look at each of these system conditions.

1. ECOLOGICAL BALANCE: To avoid the tragedy of leaving a ruined world to our children and grandchildren, we humans must reduce our aggregate consumption to bring it into balance with the regenerative capacity of Earth's biosphere. In the past hundred years, we humans have achieved a technological mastery beyond the imagination of previous generations. Yet, lacking the wisdom of place and community that is the heritage of many indigenous peoples, the cultures we call mainstream have lost their way — forgetting the human place in nature and our dependence on the web of planetary life.

2. EQUITABLE DISTRIBUTION: Social justice and fairness are foundational underpinnings of a good society. When wealth and income are highly concentrated, the majority of people are denied basic opportunities for personal and social development. A growing body of research suggests that societies that share wealth and work equitably among all their members enjoy greater physical and emotional health, stronger families and communities, less violence, and healthier natural environments. They also are more democratic and more resilient in the face of crisis. This is not a coincidence. A significant wealth disparity creates severe psychological and emotional stress and insecurity even for those at the top. Sharing prosperity brings greater health and happiness for all.[2]

3. LIVING DEMOCRACY: Living democracy manifests the ultimate ideal of popular sovereignty — government of the people, by the people, for the people. It is the very opposite of corporatocracy and plutocracy — government by the few with wealth. Most concretely, living democracy is a daily practice of civic engagement through which popular sovereignty finds expression as part of the essential fabric of community life. It celebrates and affirms diversity, cooperation, and local decision making within a framework of individual rights, community responsibility, democratically determined rules, and mutual accountability. Because it supports active community engagement rather than passive dependence on elected officials too easily controlled by elite interests, it is a step beyond representative democracy in the transition to full citizen sovereignty. *Economic democracy*, defined as broad participation in the ownership of productive assets, is an essential foundation of both living democracy and equitable distribution.

The biosphere embodies the natural equivalents of these three system conditions. As we restructure our human economies to support these conditions, they will increasingly mimic and integrate with the biosphere's structures and processes.

The New Economy as a Living Economy

I use the terms *living economy, real-wealth economy*, and *New Economy* interchangeably. All three refer to economic systems that mimic the organization of healthy ecosystems, as outlined in the previous chapter. The measure of a living economy's wealth is the vital creative life energy actively embodied in its people, relationships, and natural environment.

Living economies self-organize within a framework of market rules. They are rooted locally everywhere, designed to balance the need for stability with a capacity for creative adaptation to local microenvironments, and structured to be locally self-reliant in meeting most of their energy and other resource needs. Individual enterprises are human-scale and locally owned. Decision-making power is distributed among the community's members in their multiple roles as producers, consumers, and citizens.

The culture of a living economy recognizes the mutual responsibility of individuals to meet their own needs in ways that contribute to the well-being of the whole and thereby to their own well-being. Business enterprises are expected to do the same. Profit is recognized as a means of doing business, not its sole or primary purpose.

Note that this is exactly the opposite of the perverse and illogical old-economy claim that the well-being of the society is optimized when each individual competes for maximum personal advantage.

Protecting the Community Interest

As with any living system, the structure of a living economy is defined primarily by its internal flows of life energy. In a human system, the life energy flows through the joyful non-monetary exchanges of trust and caring that build the social fabric, or social capital, of a vital, cohesive community. I've concluded from my experience with the Business Alliance for Local Living Economies that one of the most important assets of a living-economy leader is a flair for organizing great street parties.

Absent an active, managed energy exchange, life does not exist, which is why life exists only in communities defined and bounded by managed permeable membranes. To function as a healthy living organism, a human community must have a sense of its own identity and a shared commitment to investing in the human, social, and natural capital crucial to its vitality and capacity to serve its members. To make such investments, it must control its economic resources and have the means to protect the products of its investment from rapacious predators that make no beneficial contribution to their creation.

This does not mean shutting out the world. Every living community depends for its continued vitality on a continuing exchange beyond the boundaries defined by its permeable membrane. Vital living economies exchange their surplus goods and services for the surplus goods and services of their neighbors and freely share ideas, technology, and culture in a spirit of respect for the needs and values of one another. Formal communities form democratic governments through which they determine the rules by which they will live and choose leaders to represent the community's interests in defining and negotiating its relationships with other communities.

The global confrontation between the rights of corporations and the rights of people and communities is largely a conflict of boundaries. The corporation, as represented by its top managers, says in effect,

> It is my right and responsibility to protect the legal boundary that defines my private interests and resources. No one has the right to infringe on my liberty by taking my property, telling me how to use it, or interfering with my right to do business wherever I choose.

The community, as represented by its government, says,

> It is our right and responsibility to protect the geographic boundaries that define the private and public interests and resources of those who live within these boundaries. Furthermore, we have a collective right to use the human, social, and natural capital that we create, protect, and preserve in ways that maximize our individual and collective well-being as we choose to define it. Others are

> welcome to participate in our economy, but only so long as they honor our rules and values. Corporations formed outside our jurisdiction by and for people who are not part of our community have no inherent right to do business here, but may be welcome if they provide us with benefits we cannot organize to provide for ourselves.

These are inherently conflicting rights defined by inherently conflicting boundaries.

When a living community seeks to protect its boundaries and assets, Wall Street corporations cry "protectionism" and in the name of "market freedom" (read: freedom for the market's most powerful players) demand open access to expropriate community wealth that they had no part in creating.

The Wall Street position is based on the bogus argument that there is no public interest beyond the simple aggregation of private interests and that conflicts between private interests are properly resolved through free market competition.

As we have noted, the life of any individual organism depends on the health of the living community on which its own existence depends. This creates an inherent public interest in maintaining the health and coherence of the living community and the underlying resource base on which its continued well-being depends.

By any rational reckoning, the collective rights of a geographically defined living community trump the presumed rights of a legally defined aggregation of property that comes only to expropriate community wealth in the manner of a predatory invasive species.

Collective Choices

The existing economic system did not arise as the result of some immutable natural force. It was created by a small clique of corporate power brokers and free market fundamentalists who reshaped the rules of the national and international economy so that they could reap a greater share of the rewards of economic activity while passing more of the costs to others. From their perspective, it has been a splendid success.

For the rest of us, the current system provides a powerful demonstration of why, in our role as citizens, we need to become more savvy about issues of institutional design. It should now be clear why an unregulated, borderless global economy controlled by gigantic transnational corporations that recognize no allegiance to people or place and that mimic the behavior of a cancer is harmful to our health.

Wall Street, of course, claims that any departure from business as usual will impose unbearable sacrifice. We are not supposed to notice the extensive opportunities at hand to improve the quality of our lives by rolling back wasteful and destructive forms of consumption. The following are a few of the more obvious examples of such opportunities.

SENSIBLE RESOURCE ALLOCATION

Reallocating resources from harmful or wasteful uses to beneficial ones is a foundational priority of the New Economy agenda. For example, we can and must

- renounce war as an instrument of foreign policy and dismantle the military establishment;
- reorganize and retrofit our built spaces to roll back urban sprawl, reduce auto dependence, increase energy efficiency, strengthen community, and reclaim and restore forests, agriculture, and wild spaces; and
- eliminate the advertising pollution of public spaces and the promotion of compulsive consumption of harmful or wasteful products, and reallocate these communications resources to education and community media.

Those are just three of the many opportunities to reduce the aggregate human burden on Earth while simultaneously improving the health and happiness of everyone.

Redefine National Security

Of all the misallocations of crucial resources, the military-industrial complex represents the most obvious and egregious.

Our most certain security threats come from human-induced climate chaos and the related food insecurity, economic dependence on oil, declining supplies of clean freshwater, extreme inequality and disintegration of the social fabric, catastrophic health care costs, and an unstable financial system. Our primary national security commitment has been to maintain an outsized military establishment, to engage in foreign wars that create more terrorists who threaten our security, and to construct new prisons more likely to transform minor offenders into hardened criminals than to contribute to their rehabilitation. Our future depends on a dramatic reallocation of resources to deal with both terrorism and crime in more intelligent and less costly ways while giving greater priority to real and immediate security threats we have too long ignored.

It is both stupid and unconscionable that we in the United States devote more than half of the federal government's discretionary budget to the military — an amount roughly equal to the combined spending of all other national governments[3] — to the neglect of education, health, infrastructure, environmental, and other needs. Yet our primary military threats come from from a handful of terrorists armed with little more than a willingness to die for their cause.

A recent report by the Rand Corporation, a Pentagon-funded think tank, concluded that terrorist movements of the past forty years have been defeated primarily by economic and political, rather than military, measures. It was hardly news.[4]

Students of military science have long known that using conventional military force against an unconventional enemy that blends into the civilian population is futile and counterproductive. The inevitable collateral damage of a military approach spreads outrage, strengthens resistance, and accelerates the recruitment of new combatants. The leading proponents and primary beneficiaries of such foolish and costly nonsense are, of course, Wall Street corporations.

We would have a lot fewer foreign enemies if we depended less on expropriating other people's resources to support wasteful and destructive consumption, engaged in fewer foreign wars, and scaled back our global military presence. We would do far better to renounce war as an instrument of foreign policy, limit the U.S. military to a predominantly civilian National Guard home defense force, à la Switzerland and Costa Rica, and redirect the human and material resources thus freed up to addressing our real security threats.

Make Buildings Green and Roll Back Sprawl

Low-density urban sprawl has many disadvantages. It consumes prime agricultural and forest lands, reduces food security, increases infrastructure costs, reduces aquifer regeneration, creates auto dependence, increases dependence on foreign oil, increases pollution, and undermines community. Rational transportation policies and the reconfiguration of our physical space to bring home, work, school, shopping, and recreation into close proximity can eliminate the need for most private vehicles; recover land needed for agriculture, forests, and natural habitat; and help restore the relationships of community essential to human well-being and happiness.

The construction and maintenance of buildings accounts for a major portion of U.S. energy use. To meet our target of a 90 percent reduction in greenhouse gas emissions, all new construction will need to meet the *living building* standard, which requires that buildings be at minimum environmentally neutral and ideally make a net positive contribution to energy production and to clean air and water. We also will need an ambitious program aimed at retrofitting existing homes and buildings to these new standards.

It may turn out to be a blessing that much of our national transportation and public infrastructure is in an advanced state of decay due to decades of neglect. The disintegrating system in place is based on an outdated transportation and land-use model. Since we must rebuild, it makes sense to rebuild on a model that promotes energy efficiency, uses renewable-energy sources, supports community, and reduces auto dependence.

Once the transition is complete, the GDP will decline. Security and the quality of life will improve.

Limit Advertising and Expand Public Service Media

The proper role of business in living economies is to provide Earth-friendly products and services in response to human needs, not to create artificial wants. Advertising beyond informing the public of the availability and features of products and services is contrary to the public interest. To simply ban advertising, however, would raise complex constitutional free speech issues.

There is no constitutional barrier, however, to requiring that the costs of advertising beyond providing basic information on product availability and specifications come from after-tax revenues, the same as other forms of speech. The same, of course, would apply to corporate expenditures for political advertising and lobbying.

Nor is there legitimate reason to give Wall Street free use of one of our most valuable public resources: the broadcast spectrum. The airwaves are a public commons properly used to serve the public interest. Allowing a few private media corporations to monopolize this resource to generate revenue from advertising makes no sense.

Independent public and community radio and TV stations representing a diverse range of perspectives should receive substantial preference over absentee Wall Street owners in the allocation of the broadcast spectrum.

▶•◆•◆•◀

The institutional design for a New Economy will support systemic self-organization toward ecological balance, equitable distribution, and living democracy. This requires a cultural and institutional transformation to shift the economic system's defining value from money to life, its locus of economic decision making from global corporations and financial markets to local communities, its defining dynamic from competition to cooperation, and its primary purpose from increasing the financial fortunes of the few to building the living-community wealth of everyone.

The transition will be far from painless, particularly for those employed by institutions of the old economy, such as most Wall Street financial houses, that have no place in a New Economy. Wall Street's self-inflicted implosion has already begun the transition by eliminating many old-economy jobs.

Fortunately for everyone, essential New Economy investments — for example, to reindustrialize on a new green model — will create far more jobs than will be lost as the Wall Street economy winds down.

Done properly, there will be ample meaningful, fairly compensated work for everyone, including Wall Street refugees and those presently denied access to any means of creating a meaningful livelihood. Former Wall Street workers who find it difficult to adjust to a fair compensation package might consider taking a course on the joy and practice of voluntary simplicity.

Living economies can come into being only through self-organizing, bottom-up processes of learning and emergence. Overcoming the barriers erected by Wall Street is an epic challenge. Fortunately, the cultural transformation required to align our cultural stories with our higher human nature and our shared vision of the world we want is under way. The institutional transformation is also under way, building on the foundation of what remains of Main Street economies.

Let us now turn to the question of what we can do to accelerate the process.

PART IV

A LIVING-ECONOMY AGENDA

▶•◆•◆•◀

The life-serving market system we want and the life-destructive capitalist system we have feature very different structures and operate by very different rules. A healthy market system is designed to facilitate the beneficial self-organizing exchange of goods and services in response to people's self-defined needs. The capitalist system, by contrast, is designed to concentrate economic power to support the expropriation of wealth for the exclusive private benefit of the system's most powerful players.

The rules formulated and enforced by government ultimately favor one or the other of these competing systems. The tension between them defines the political struggle of our time. Government makes the rules that determine the economy's structure and priorities. Its choices commonly favor Wall Street capitalism over Main Street markets, because Wall Street controls the money and the media that drive Washington politics. The public rarely hears about options supportive of a healthy Main Street market system, and such options do not find their way into the platforms of the major political parties.

To shift the political balance, we the people must articulate a compelling and holistic New Economy policy agenda for a planetary system of market-based Main Street living economies, bring it to the forefront of public attention, and compel the major political parties to make it a centerpiece of their legislative agendas. The three chapters of part IV provide an initial framework and identify focal points for strategic intervention.

Note that the focus here is on the substance of the legislative and administrative action needed from government. Mobilization strategies are addressed in part V.

Chapter 13, "Seven Points of Intervention," presents a seven-point policy agenda for liberating Main Street and banishing the Wall Street phantom-wealth casino to the dustbin of history.

Chapter 14, "What About My . . . ?" reveals how the financial "services" promoted by Wall Street are organized and managed to con the buyer. It then outlines public agendas for addressing the need for consumer credit, mortgage, insurance, retirement, and equity financing in ways that are at once more effective and more fair.

Chapter 15, "A Presidential Declaration of Independence from Wall Street I Hope I May One Day Hear," provides a synthesis of the New Economy policy agenda in the form and style of a presidential economic policy address. It also sets a political marker for civil society. We will know we are at a breakthrough point on a path to success when we have created a political context that compels a sitting U.S. president and other heads of state to deliver the equivalent of this address.

CHAPTER 13

▶•◆•◆•◀

SEVEN POINTS OF INTERVENTION

Life or money: that is our choice. The current Wall Street system serves only money. Our task is to replace it with a New Economy system that serves life.

In this chapter, I identify seven critical system-intervention clusters around which citizen action can mobilize to hasten the dying of the old and the birthing of the new.[1] The order in which the intervention points are presented defines a hierarchy of sorts, in that each item on the list provides a foundation for those that follow.

Living-wealth indicators provide the basic reframing of the New Economy's purpose and values. That reframing becomes the basis for reorganizing the money system, which in turn creates a more favorable context for sharing wealth, making the transition to living enterprises, and restoring democracy and markets by breaking up big corporations. All of the above come together in local living economies organized as subsystems of their local ecosystems. New global rules create the necessary overarching legal framework to secure local democracy and prevent global corporations from stifling the development of local living economies by monopolizing economic resources and political power.

A logical sequencing of the intervention clusters is helpful in seeing the essential relationships among them. As a practical matter, of course, it is necessary and appropriate that grassroots groups work simultaneously on each cluster — which they are indeed doing. Let's take a closer look at the interventions.

LIVING-WEALTH INDICATORS

THE GOAL: *Replace financial indicators with indicators of human- and natural-systems health as the basis for evaluating economic performance. We get what we measure, so let's measure what we want.*

Children are society's most vulnerable members. If you know the rates of infant mortality, child poverty, childhood malnutrition, teenage crime, and out-of-wedlock pregnancies, you have a remarkably clear picture of a society's state of health. Other suitable indicators of human health include longevity and life satisfaction.

Indicators of social health include high school graduation rates, the percentage of jobs that pay a living wage with benefits, the unemployment rate among people seeking a paid job, average commuting times, attendance at farmers' markets, and involvement in community service.

For natural systems, air quality, rates of soil runoff, biodiversity, the amount of CO_2 in the atmosphere, and the size of fragile fish, bird, and frog populations are excellent indicators.

Once we adopt such indicators as the basis for evaluating economic performance, our national economic priorities will shift dramatically from a focus on money to a focus on life. We will see more clearly the benefits of reallocating real-wealth resources from the military to health care and environmental rejuvenation, from prisons to rehabilitation, from automobiles to public transportation, from mining to recycling, from suburban sprawl to compact communities, from advertising to education, and from financial speculation to financing local entrepreneurship.

SEVEN INTERVENTION CLUSTERS

Living-wealth indicators: Replace financial indicators with indicators of human- and natural-systems health as the basis for evaluating economic performance.

Living-wealth money system: Redesign the money system to direct the flow of money to productive Main Street businesses rather than to Wall Street speculators.

Shared prosperity: Redistribute income and ownership to achieve a more equitable distribution of power and real wealth.

Living enterprises: Redefine the purpose of the enterprise from making money to serving community needs, and favor enterprise forms that support this purpose.

Real democracy/real markets: Free both the market and democracy from corporate domination by breaking up concentrations of economic power and limiting political participation to real people.

Local living economies: Create a planetary system of coherent, self-reliant local economies that function as subsystems of their local ecosystems.

Global rules: Restructure global rules and institutions to support all of the above.

One of my favorite living-wealth indicators is the Happy Planet Index, created by the New Economics Foundation in London,[2] which is based on purely nonfinancial indicators.

The numerator is a composite of two indicators: life expectancy, which is a simple objective measure of physical health, and life satisfaction or happiness, which is a subjective proxy for mental health. The denominator is the ecological footprint, an indicator of the economy's per capita environmental burden.

$$\text{Happy Planet Index} \quad = \quad \frac{\text{Life Satisfaction} \times \text{Life Expectancy}}{\text{Ecological Footprint}}$$

The result is an indicator of the ecological efficiency with which a society's economy is producing a given level of physical and emotional well-being. The results demonstrate that it is possible to live long, happy lives with a relatively small environmental impact.

The highest-scoring nation is Costa Rica, where people report much higher levels of satisfaction than Americans and live slightly longer but have an ecological footprint less than a quarter of that of the United States. The United States is 114 on the list, and our rank declined between 1990 and 1995. We could be far happier and healthier at a far lower environmental cost if we chose to base our economic choices on social and environmental, rather than financial, indicators.

Because GDP is best understood as the economic cost of achieving a given level of well-being, we may wish to retain it as a measure of the economic costs we seek to reduce. Thus, instead of our current quest for ways to grow our GDP, we would look for ways to shrink it.

LIVING-WEALTH MONEY SYSTEM

THE GOAL: *Redesign the money system to direct the flow of money to productive Main Street businesses rather than to Wall Street speculators. Real resources follow the money, so design the financial system to put the money where it will produce the greatest living-wealth benefit.*

The money system is to the modern economic system what the circulatory system is to the body. Where blood flows freely, the body's cells flourish. Where blood flow is restricted, they become anemic and may die. The design of society's money system institutions likewise determines which people, localities, and enterprises will have the opportunity to thrive and which will perish or struggle for survival.

Official money can be created by banks lending it into existence or by governments spending it into existence.

In our current system, most new money is created by private for-profit banks when they issue loans based on their assessment of risk and profitability. In recent years this has meant lavishing credit on speculation, housing bubbles, and consumer credit and withholding it from productive enterprises. As set out in chapter 2, this is exactly the opposite of what a sound money system would do. There are three issues to be addressed: (1) the structure of the banking system, (2) the respective roles of banks and government in money creation, and (3) money supply oversight and management. Let's take them one at a time.

The banking system can be structured to favor large Wall Street banks or small community banks. The ownership can be for-profit or nonprofit. Nonprofit banks can be governed by a self-perpetuating board, organized as cooperatives, or owned by a state or local government. Priorities of the individual banks will vary accordingly. Private banks will favor their profits. Cooperative banks will favor their member interests. Government-owned banks will favor public purposes. There is nothing radical about a nonprofit bank. Cooperative banking has a long history in the United States and elsewhere.[3]

A New Rules Project study has confirmed exactly what we might expect.[4] The smaller the bank, the greater the portion of its loans that goes to Main Street businesses. Because we want to favor a system that gives priority to funding productive Main Street business, it makes sense for the federal government to take over failed Wall Street banks, break them up, and restructure their local branches as individual community banks, savings and loans, or credit unions. To encourage the community banks to give priority to community interests over private profit, some or all might be organized as non-profits or cooperatives. Perhaps some might be owned by state and local governments.

This process can be advanced further by legislating limits on bank size, taking antitrust actions to break up large banks, and implementing regulations and tax penalties that render banking conglomerates unprofitable.

Under a real-wealth banking system, the federal government would continue to insure the deposits of member institutions, as is now the case. But they would do so only on acceptance of strict reserve- and equity-ratio requirements. It is appropriate that local banks retain the capacity to issue credit equivalent to some modest multiple of their total equity and deposits, as this allows them to increase or shrink the local money supply in response to changing community needs and opportunities.

Now let's look at the question of the respective roles of government and banks in creating the overall money supply. In a living-wealth money system, banks and the federal government would share the functions of money creation and allocation. As corporations and wealthy individuals have used their political leverage to significantly lower their taxes, the federal government has experienced a growing fiscal deficit that it makes up by borrowing money at interest from these same corporations and wealthy individuals, effectively shifting the burden to less affluent taxpayers. Chapter 9 described the example of Wall Street banks relending money to the government at 3 percent that they borrowed from the Federal Reserve at nearly zero interest. This, in effect, means that middle- and lower-income taxpayers are incurring future liabilities to cover the deficit created by lowering the tax rate for corporations and wealthy individuals, the bailout money paid to these same corporations to cover their speculative losses and, in turn, the losses of their wealthy clients.

This makes sense only to the bottom lines of private bankers. The federal government should be taxing corporations and wealthy individuals at a rate commensurate with their ability to pay and the public benefits they receive. If the federal government still needs credit to cover essential expenses, or to invest in productive public infrastructure such as public transportation systems, it can and should make the necessary accounting entry itself, avoid the subsidy to Wall Street, and save taxpayers a great deal of money.

This brings us to money-supply management, which must equitably serve both public and private needs. That means it is inherently a federal government responsibility, although the authority currently resides with the Federal Reserve. The Fed professes to be a federal agency and is so listed in the government's organization chart. It operates, however, beyond meaningful public oversight and generally acts in the best interests of Wall Street bankers — which rarely coincide with the public interest.

The Fed is properly brought under the general supervision of Congress and the Treasury Department and its operations rendered publicly transparent and subject to audit. A restructured Fed would have the tools to adjust the flows of both private and public money as required to support productive investment, local employment, and environmental balance while minimizing wage and asset inflation.

So what of the Wall Street casino? Let would-be gamblers go to Vegas, where the games are regulated.

The ideal way to deal with a malignant cancer is to cut off its blood supply. Similarly, the best way to deal with financial speculators is to cut off their money supply through appropriate taxes and regulatory actions that render illegal or unprofitable outsized banks, financial speculation, predatory lending, financial fraud, and the shadow banking system of unregulated hedge funds and private equity funds.

SHARED PROSPERITY

THE GOAL: *Redistribute income and ownership to achieve a more equitable distribution of power and real wealth. We all enjoy greater health, happiness, security, and social solidarity when wealth is equitably shared.*

Globally, nearly a billion people struggle to survive on less than a dollar a day, while fifty private investment fund managers each average nearly $2 million a day. In the United States,

- The wealthiest 1 percent of the country's households hold a third of all private assets, more than the bottom 95 percent of households combined
- The top 1 percent of households received 9 percent of the country's total income in 1976; by 2007, that figure had increased to 23.5 percent[5]

Contrary to the claims of market fundamentalists, unregulated markets do not fairly reward everyone willing to work commensurate with their ability and contribution.

Among the world's thirty richest countries, the United States has the greatest wealth disparity. According to the social epidemiologist Richard Wilkinson, that disparity explains why "the USA has the highest homicide rates, the highest teenage pregnancy rates, the highest rates of imprisonment, and comes about 28th in the international league table of life expectancy."[6] These are all negative consequences of the social and mental stress associated with extreme inequality.

On an environmentally stressed planet, the destructive

effects of extreme wealth disparity cannot be resolved merely by expanding the economy to bring up the bottom. Redistribution is essential. When income and ownership are equitably distributed, the health of everybody — even the rich — improves. The market allocates more efficiently in response to the needs of the many rather than the wants of the few.

Appropriate corrective actions include the following:

- Instituting income and social services policies that assure every person access to a basic means of living, while favoring those who produce real value through productive work — for example, teachers, entrepreneurs, factory and service workers, family farmers, agricultural laborers, doctors, and hospital attendants

- Implementing progressive taxation and public spending policies that continuously recycle wealth from those at the top, who have far more than they need, to those at the bottom, who lack access to the basic essentials of a secure and fulfilling life

- Eliminating payroll and income taxes on incomes below $200,000 a year and replacing them with resource-extraction fees at the point of extraction and pollution fees at the point of release, along with stiff luxury taxes on items of personal extravagance such as outsized personal yachts and private jet aircraft

- Minimizing the class divide through policies that encourage every person to engage in productive work *and* to share in the benefits and responsibilities of ownership in order to advance employee ownership, much as government advanced broad participation in home-ownership following World War II

- Supporting regional land-use policies for multistrata, compact development, and preventing geographic divisions by class and race and between affluent and blighted neighborhoods

- Requiring any corporation that decides to sell or close a local plant to give the workers or other interests in the affected community an option to buy the assets on preferential terms

LIVING ENTERPRISES

THE GOAL: *Redefine the purpose of the enterprise from making money to serving community needs, and favor enterprise forms that support this purpose.*

A living enterprise is human-scale. It has preferably fewer than a hundred employees and rarely more than five hundred, and it organizes around communities of people rather than pools of money. A smaller size means less need for hierarchy and bureaucratic control. That, in turn, supports innovation, teamwork, worker satisfaction, and ethical practice. The stronger the sense of community within the enterprise, the greater the firm's contribution to strengthening the social fabric of the larger community it serves.

Markets are more efficient, innovative, and responsive to a diversity of needs when served by many small firms. When workers are owners, the conflict between workers and owners disappears, individuals have a stronger sense of ownership in their community, and democracy is more robust.

Global corporations get the vast bulk of media attention, and in the minds of many, they define the business sector. The vast majority of business enterprises, however, are human-scale, rooted in the communities they serve, and mindful of community needs and values.

In its ideal form, the living enterprise seeks to provide a fair and balanced return to all its stakeholders — including safe, meaningful family-wage jobs for its employees; good service and useful, safe, high-quality products for its customers; and a healthy social and natural environment for the community in which it is located. Owners who are engaged in the enterprise as managers, workers, customers, or suppliers secure the firm's relationship to the community and receive a living return that includes the benefits of life in a healthy and prosperous community with a vibrant natural environment.

Living enterprises may be organized as consumer cooperatives, worker-owned corporations, community corporations, partnerships, nonprofits, family businesses, and simple sole proprietorships — all of which involve rooted, engaged ownership. An enterprise that is publicly traded or owned by a Wall Street private equity fund is captive to Wall Street financial values and priorities, which are antithetical to the values and priorities of a living enterprise.

Contrary to the claims of market fundamentalists, there is no reason that all enterprises should be for-profit. There are many needs — health insurance, banking, electricity, and water among them — that may be best served by community-owned, nonprofit, or cooperative enterprises.

Where the nature of the work requires greater aggregations of skills and capital, individual living enterprises may come together to form larger alliances that still maintain the principles of human-scale organization and community-rooted ownership. Well-known examples include the Mondragón Cooperatives in Spain, the Organic Valley dairy co-op in the United States, local manufacturing networks located throughout the world, and purchasing and branding cooperatives owned by member stores, such as Ace Hardware and True Value.

In what could prove to be a breakthrough initiative for the U.S. labor movement, the United Steelworkers union signed an agreement in October 2009 with Mondragón International, an arm of the Mondragón Cooperatives in the Basque region of Spain, to draw on Mondragón's expertise in cooperative worker ownership. If unions are to have a future, it will center on worker ownership, and this seems a promising model.[7]

REAL MARKETS/REAL DEMOCRACY

THE GOAL: *Free both the market and democracy from corporate domination by breaking up concentrations of economic power, getting big money out of politics, making corporations pay their own way, and reserving Bill of Rights protections for people.*

Real democracy and real markets go hand in hand. Both are accountable and responsible to the people they serve. Both are free from domination by Wall Street corporations that operate as governments unto themselves, organize their internal economies as private fiefdoms, and pass the outsized costs of their centralized command-and-control structures onto the public in the form of social, environmental, and taxpayer subsidies.

Events following the Wall Street meltdown significantly raised public awareness of the Wall Street–Washington political axis and its pernicious consequences for democracy and the market economy. It is a defining issue. For so long as we continue to allow big money to make the rules and set our priorities as a nation, we will continue to bear the consequences of stagnant wages, wasteful consumption, unaffordable health care, climate chaos, and all the other phantom-wealth casino-economy ills.

Wall Street interests lobby relentlessly against rules that protect democracy, such as those that would limit their ability to influence elections and legislation. Similarly, they lobby against rules that protect the market, such as those that would limit the size of individual enterprises, support an equitable distribution of income and ownership, or require corporations to internalize their social and environmental costs. Wall Street also lobbies against any public program that does not direct lucrative public subsidies or contracts to private corporations. The unrelenting objective is to expand corporate monopoly control of resources, markets, money, technology, knowledge, and information.

Democracy is supposed to provide a political forum in which people come together on an equal footing with one another to determine by mutual agreement the rules by which they will live. The market similarly is supposed to provide an economic forum in which people come together on an equal footing to exchange goods, services, and resources based on their individual needs and preferences.

When the essential condition of equal footing is met, the combination of democratic rule making and market exchange gives every person a voice in how society allocates the resources available to it. When a corporation that accepts no allegiance to the community or its interests takes control of both the political forum and the market forum, both democracy and the market lose all but symbolic meaning.

The corporation's governing framework has evolved primarily through a patchwork of federal and state court decisions favoring the interests of concentrated private capital. Great care went into writing and amending the U.S. Constitution as a governing framework for the organization of political power. As a society, we have never taken on the task of debating and crafting a governing framework for the organization of economic power. Both are essential to a functioning democracy and healthy markets.[8]

Some basic principles would seem to be self-evident. Because all corporations are created by public action, they properly function as quasi-public bodies accountable to the communities in which they operate. Whatever wealth they create is the collective product of contributions by managers, workers, customers, suppliers, and communities, without which the investments of absentee owners would be worthless. That wealth is therefore properly shared among those who contributed to its creation.

Size, ownership, and rights are all relevant to this discussion. Initiatives to break up and restructure the ownership of oversized corporations are foundational. Rigorous antitrust enforcement can break up concentrations of corporate power and give employees or the communities in which they live first option to purchase the divested units.

Employees and communities should have the option in bankruptcy proceedings of paying off creditors at a discounted rate and taking possession of the corporation's remaining assets. Rules governing company pension funds might allow employees to use them to purchase the assets, and voting control, of the firms that employ them. The rules governing employee stock ownership plans need to be revised to assure real worker control.

A corporation's workers, managers, and investors all properly enjoy the protections of the U.S. Bill of Rights. The corporation itself should not. If a constitutional amendment is needed to communicate that message to the Supreme Court, then so be it.

Other measures to support a transition to real democracy and real markets include

- levying a progressive tax on corporate profits and assets to create an incentive to voluntarily break up monopolistic concentrations of corporate power;

- introducing proportional representation and instant runoff voting to open meaningful space for third parties in elections;

- eliminating public subsidies for private-benefit corporations;

- establishing rules to assure that corporations bear the

full social and environmental costs of their operations and imposing fees on those that do not; and

- requiring that all corporate charters clearly specify the public purpose the corporation is chartered to serve and revoking the charters of corporations that do not comply.

LOCAL LIVING ECONOMIES

THE GOAL: *Create a planetary system of coherent, self-reliant local economies that function as dynamic, life-nurturing subsystems of their local ecosystems.*

When economies are local and self-reliant, people have more control over their lives and enjoy the full benefit of their labor and investments. When communities focus on sustaining themselves using their own resources rather than appropriating the resources of others, they give more attention to living within their environmental means.

When people know they and their children will be living with the social and environmental consequences of their business decisions, they have a compelling reason to take the health of the community and the natural environment into consideration.

All the many elements of the New Economy come together at the level of the bioregion: the living-wealth indicators and money system; policies that support the sharing of resources; living enterprises; real markets; and real democracy. All of these are supported by the new global rules discussed in the next section.

To advance local living economies, we need to nurture the growth and interlinking of living enterprises to form the building blocks of prosperous, resilient bioregional economies supportive of ecological balance, equitable distribution, and living democracy. We must reorient land-use patterns and transportation systems; retrofit buildings; concentrate populations in walkable, energy-efficient, multistrata communities; and rebuild local productive capacities based on closed-loop production and consumption models to reduce long-distance shipping, eliminate waste, and increase energy efficiency. We also must implement regional living-wealth indicators to track our progress toward zero waste and self-reliance in food, energy, water, and other essentials of daily life.

The decay of our public physical infrastructure creates an opportunity to reshape land-use and transportation patterns as we rebuild. The decimation of our industrial capacity allows us to reindustrialize on a new model of green technology, functional durability, and regionalized, closed-loop, zero-emissions product cycles.

Striving for local self-reliance does not mean closing one's borders. It does mean recognizing that every healthy living organism depends on a protective membrane that is essential to maintaining its integrity. The single cell has the cell wall. The animal has its skin, the tree its bark, the ecosystem its topographic and climatic barriers, and the biosphere Earth's atmosphere.

The fair and balanced exchange of surpluses among regional economies is integral to the New Economy vision, as is the free sharing of information and technical knowledge. Trade, however, is never a priority in itself, and there is no assumption that more trade is necessarily better.

These basic ideas are spurring local living-economy initiatives around the world that are interlinking living enterprises to form the essential building blocks of diversified, self-reliant local economies. A local food and agriculture building block, for example, typically includes a region's farmers, ranchers, and fishers as well as food processors, food transporters, farmers' markets, restaurants, food retailers, and food-serving institutions such as schools and hospitals, among others.[9]

There are far too many elements to these many initiatives to offer details. You can find more information on real-life initiatives on the Web sites of the American Independent Business Alliance (amiba.net), the Business Alliance for Local Living Economies (livingeconomies.org), the New Rules Project (newrules.org), and *YES! Magazine* (yesmagazine.org).

GLOBAL RULES

THE GOAL: *Create a system of global rules and institutions that support living-wealth indicators and money systems, shared prosperity, living enterprises, real democracy, and local living economies.*

Over the past thirty years, corporate interests have aggressively crafted global rules and institutions that in effect give global corporations a protected right to do business in whatever country they choose while restricting the right of a government to intervene to protect the interests of its own people, communities, and natural systems.

Some international trade and investment agreements even go so far as to give corporations the right to sue a government if they lose expected profits as the result of a regulation that protects the health of a community's people and natural systems. They also require governments to vigorously protect corporate intellectual property rights, thus impairing the international sharing of information and technical knowledge.

Such rules put the rights of corporations ahead of the rights of people and even the rights and responsibilities of government. They give private for-profit global corporations virtual control over local economic priorities, free from accountability to the people affected.

Recall that the larger New Economy goal is a planetary economic system that self-organizes toward three system conditions: ecological sustainability, equitable distribution, and living democracy. To achieve these three conditions, each bioregion must have substantial control of its economic priorities and resources. There is little place in such a system for global corporations that command internal economies larger than that of most countries and accept no responsibility for the common good.

To achieve a New Economy world that works for all, the right to economic self-determination of nations and peoples must trump the assumed rights of any transnational corporation. Appropriate global rules will limit the rights and size of individual corporations, support balanced trade, set fair commodity prices, and internalize the true cost of goods and services in market prices — all in line with sound market principles. They will further recognize the right of nations and communities to determine with whom they will trade and whom they will invite to invest in their economies and on what terms.

The struggle over global rules is in essence a struggle between corporate power and people power, between capitalism and democracy, to determine who will rule. To tip the balance in favor of democracy, international trade agreements will need to be rewritten and global institutions like the World Trade Organization, the World Bank, and the International Monetary Fund, which are organized to advance the old economy, will need to be dismantled and replaced by institutions designed to serve the new.

➤•◆•◆•◄

The seven critical intervention clusters outlined in this chapter are intended to replace an inherently unstable system moving toward collapse with a more stable system that maintains equilibrium around three system conditions we defined earlier as ecological balance, equitable distribution, and living democracy.

These intervention clusters are focal points for mobilizing citizen action to achieve the needed cultural and institutional transformation. Successful action will shift the system's defining value from money to life, its defining purpose from the creation of phantom wealth to the creation of real wealth, and its locus of power from corporations to people and from global to local.

This is an ambitious agenda. We will address the *how* question in greater depth in part V. First, however, I want to address a few questions I suspect may be weighing heavily on your mind: If we really shut down Wall Street, what happens to my credit card? mortgage? retirement? insurance? These are good questions, to which we now turn.

CHAPTER 14

▶•◆•◆•◀

WHAT ABOUT MY...?

A confidence trick or confidence game ... is an attempt
to defraud a person or group by gaining their confidence.
The victim is known as the mark, the trickster is called
a confidence man, con man, confidence trickster, or con
artist, and any accomplices are known as shills. Confidence
men exploit human characteristics such as greed and dis-
honesty, and have victimized individuals from all walks
of life.

WIKIPEDIA, "CONFIDENCE TRICK"

In my experience, the first reaction of most people to the
call to shut down Wall Street is one of jubilant enthusi-
asm — a measure of the public outrage at Wall Street excesses.
The second reaction is, "But what about my 401(k) retirement account?" The same question might be raised about
our credit cards, mortgages, and medical, homeowners, and
auto insurance.

In fact, the Wall Street way of dealing with each of these is
a scam. Wall Street doesn't develop its business plans to meet
our needs; it develops its plans to place us in a position of
dependence on Wall Street products that afford it the greatest opportunity to profit at our expense.

There are better ways to meet each of the needs that Wall
Street offerings address. To understand the options, we must
step back to identify the real need we are trying to satisfy and
then explore what the alternatives might be to the Wall Street
product.

186

This chapter is about that exploration. Along the way, we will come to recognize the ways in which Wall Street has succeeded in limiting our options to those that generate the greatest profit for itself. In each instance, we will find that we will be better served by options that Wall Street has denied us or hopes we will not discover.

In short, we are the marks in a sophisticated Wall Street con game that depends on our buying into the illusion that phantom wealth is somehow real.

PHANTOM WEALTH IS ONLY PHANTOM WEALTH

To understand what we are up against, we must revisit the distinction between phantom wealth and real wealth. Phantom wealth is bogus, a product of illusion and fantasies of effortless luxury that are expertly cultivated by highly skilled professional propagandists funded by Wall Street with billions of advertising dollars. To get the picture on the fantasy, thumb through any business magazine and look at the images and promises in the ads for Wall Street investment houses. These ads are part of what in con slang is called setting up the mark.

Setting Up the Mark

I grumble every time I hear business reporters on the evening news refer to stock market results by saying, "Today, investors [did this or that]." It is another example of setting up the mark by manipulating the language to make the marks believe that they are making a serious, solid investment rather than betting on a crapshoot. Gambling in Vegas is more honest. There you don't "invest" in the roulette wheel. You place a bet on the ball. On Wall Street, bets on the movement of prices of pieces of paper are called investments to make them sound real and productive.

Real investors commit funds and entrepreneurial energy to creating and growing businesses. People who buy and sell pieces of paper in hopes of making unearned gains on price movements are engaging in speculation, otherwise known as gambling, and those who hold the bets and distribute the winnings are bookies or dealers. Simply using honest language would help to distinguish between real investors creating real wealth and speculators creating phantom wealth with financial games.

The con is so massive and sophisticated that even many of its most important inside players do not recognize themselves as accomplices in a fraud. They buy into the Edmunds fallacy described in chapter 2, believe they are creating real wealth, and convince themselves, in the memorable words of Goldman Sachs CEO Lloyd Blankfein, that they are "doing God's work."

Four Wall Street Cons

Boil it down to the basics and you see that Wall Street is in the business of operating four sophisticated, large-scale confidence games.

- COUNTERFEITING: It creates facsimiles of official money for private gain unrelated to anything of real value — facsimiles otherwise known as phantom wealth.

- SECURITIES FRAUD: Selling shares in asset bubbles that are maintained solely by the constant inflow of new money is, in effect, a Ponzi scheme.

- REVERSE INSURANCE FRAUD: Insurance fraud by common definition occurs when the insured deceives the insurer. In reverse insurance fraud, the insurer deceives the insured. In Wall Street practice this involves collecting premiums to cover risks the insurer lacks adequate reserves to cover and then refusing to pay legitimate claims.

- PREDATORY LENDING: Using a combination of extortion, fraud, deceptive promises, and usury, predatory lenders lure the desperate into perpetual debt at exorbitant interest rates.

Given Wall Street's hold on lawmakers, these may all be perfectly legal, but phantom wealth is still phantom wealth, and a con is still a con.

In three-card monte the dealer shuffles the cards so fast you can't follow them, and talks even faster. Complex derivatives are a fast shuffle that makes it virtually impossible to follow the connection to any real value.

What makes the Wall Street con so much better for the dealers than a typical street-level three-card monte con is that Wall Street dealers are able to bet on their own game using other people's money and then manipulate the market outcome in their own favor, just as the monte dealer manipulates the shuffle.

Some Wall Street observers suggest that the big players like Goldman Sachs have the ability to use their capacity for microsecond trading to move markets at will, both to extract speculative earnings and to send a warning message to politicians who propose actions they want to kill.[1] They further rig the game by rewarding themselves with huge bonuses when they win and taking billions in taxpayer bailouts when they lose. It sure beats being a dealer on the street or in Vegas.

Unfortunately, no magic wand can convert the phantom-wealth expectations created by Wall Street to the real wealth we must have to meet our retirement needs for real food, shelter, and medical care; treat our ailments; or make us whole after a fire or collision. In the real world, there is no way to fulfill the promise of the mythic dream that Wall Street has so skillfully cultivated. These needs can be met only by people and organizations engaged in producing real-wealth goods and services.

Using taxpayer money to make good on false promises — that is, to make whole those whom Wall Street has defrauded — only shifts the burden from those who once had enough money to play the Wall Street game onto those who did not play.

Here is what we can do as part of the economic restructuring outlined in chapter 13.

RECOVER THE LOOT AND SHUT DOWN THE TABLE

We can start by recovering from the Wall Street con men what we can of their unearned phantom loot and encouraging them to take up honest work by rendering their schemes against society either illegal or unprofitable. Here are a few suggestions:

1. Legislate an outright prohibition against selling, insuring, or borrowing against an asset not actually owned by the seller or issuing any security not backed by a real asset. With a little investigation, competent regulators can surely come up with a longer list, but you get the idea — and yes, these are all common Wall Street practices that generate substantial quantities of phantom wealth, distort markets, and create instability.

2. Place strict limits on how much a financial institution can borrow in order to buy a property, and establish reserve and capital requirements for institutions in the business of selling insurance of any kind.

3. Regulate bond-rating agencies and impose strict penalties for fraudulent ratings.

4. Impose a small financial-speculation tax of a penny on every $4 spent on the purchase and sale of financial instruments such as stocks, bonds, foreign currencies,

and derivatives. This would have no consequential impact on real investors making long-term investments in real businesses and assets. But it would discourage extremely short-term speculation and arbitraging (the simultaneous purchase and sale of the same asset in different markets to profit from fleeting minuscule price differences).[2]

5. End the preferential tax treatment of hedge fund manager compensation. Currently, an obscure tax loophole allows hedge fund managers to report their billion-dollar compensation packages as capital gains, taxed at only 15 percent, whereas the wages of real workers are taxed at much higher rates.

6. Assess a significant surcharge on short-term capital gains to make many forms of speculation unprofitable, stabilize financial markets, and lengthen the investment horizon without penalizing real investors. The capital gains surtax on profit from the sale of an asset held less than an hour should be 100 percent. For assets held less than a week, it might be as high as 80 percent, perhaps falling to 50 percent on assets held more than a week but less than six months.

Opponents will claim that such taxes will stifle financial innovation. Good. That is the intention. We should not be providing incentives to financial predators to come up with ever more innovative forms of theft.

FREE THE DEBT SLAVES

Debt slavery is an ancient institution that traces back to the beginning of Empire. In earlier times, it was more explicit and visible, because it was more personal. The hapless borrower became the bonded servant or slave of the lender — a condition that prevails today in many low-income countries. In the contemporary United States, it is more systemic and less personal.

Indentured service, a condition in which servants are not at liberty to negotiate the terms of their labor or leave their masters, played a major role in the economic history of the United States.

At the time of the settling of the North American continent, land in Europe was scarce and its ownership concentrated. Surplus labor kept wages low and unemployment high. Tales of America's vast fertile lands and great wealth free for the taking stirred the imagination of Europeans of all classes, but especially the poor and starving whose homelands afforded them neither land nor employment.

Those unable to pay for passage to the New World agreed to commit to a period of indentured service to whomever was willing, on their arrival, to pay their debt to the ship captain who provided passage. Many a young woman voluntarily became the wife of whatever man paid the captain's fee. Once married, a woman and all she owned, acquired, or produced became the property of her husband. The status of an indentured servant differed from that of an outright slave mainly in having a promised date of release.

Following the Civil War, blacks were technically free, but whites owned the land and controlled the jobs on which blacks depended for survival. Continuing the imperial pattern, the rights of owners continued to trump the rights of workers as the moneylenders stepped in for the kill. Blatantly unfair sharecropper arrangements forced blacks into debts that became an instrument of bondage only one step removed from an outright return to slavery.

In the period following World War II, full employment and high wages for working people, combined with high taxes for the rich, created the celebrated American middle class. For a historically brief period, debt slavery became a relatively rare condition, at least for whites. Then, as Wall Street fundamentalists gained control, they weakened unions and outsourced jobs to create a downward pressure on wages while increasing the use of sophisticated advertising to promote ever more extravagant lifestyles and the use of credit card debt to finance them.

As wages continued to fall relative to the cost of living, Wall Street promoted credit card and mortgage debt as the solution. Some people responded out of sheer desperation to put food on the table. Innocents simply bought into Wall Street's enticements to consume now, pay later. People were soon locked into ever-growing debt they could never repay, and Wall Street's take from whatever pittance they were able to earn increased, as did the total share of income going to those who lived off Wall Street profits relative to those who did honest work. Thanks to Wall Street's control of the political system, this kind of indentured servitude is not only mostly legal but also is enforced by a legal system that favors the rights of property over the rights of people.

In a related move, Wall Street pressed for tax breaks for the rich and an expansion in military spending. The government began running up record deficits. To make up for the lost tax revenues, the government borrowed from the rich what it had formerly raised from them in taxes — much as working people were borrowing from the rich to make up for inadequate wages. Government also became a debt slave to Wall Street.

When Wall Street got in trouble, Washington, suffering from what we might call battered-slave syndrome, responded with a bailout paid for with money it borrowed from Wall Street courtesy of the Federal Reserve.

Regulating the abusive slave masters to reduce fraud and place limits on their excesses seems a positive step within the established frame. It reduces the deception and the pain of the indebted. On the downside, it lends a patina of legitimacy to Wall Street and helps deflect the public outrage that might otherwise provide political support for a more serious system transformation.

The proper goal is not to make debt slavery safer and more comfortable. It is to eliminate such slavery by raising the wages of working people and the taxes of the moneylenders while rethinking our approach to meeting a variety of needs to which Wall Street offers itself as the solution.

RETHINKING HOW WE DEAL WITH REAL FINANCIAL NEEDS

Money may be nothing but a number, but survival in a modern society is impossible without it. There are, however, better ways to deal with our very real financial needs than those presently offered by Wall Street.

Let us look at alternatives for consumer credit, home mortgages, insurance, retirement, and equity investments. Be forewarned that what follows is not a self-help primer on managing your money and securing your retirement. Rather, it is a primer on why the options available won't meet your needs and what we need to do as a society to change that.

Consumer Credit

Credit and debit cards have two distinct functions: clearing transactions and providing an open line of credit. The use of debit and credit cards to clear transactions is a straightforward and beneficial service if properly regulated and transparent. The use of either as an open line of credit, particularly to pay for current consumption, is an enticement to debt slavery and an instrument of predatory lending.

To maintain the convenience of paying with plastic as a substitute for writing checks, New Economy community banks, savings and loan associations, and credit unions can form a transaction-clearing system owned cooperatively by its member institutions. The largely nonprofit system can operate as a transparent and publicly accountable regulated public utility.

Financing for large durable purchases such as a home, car, or major appliance can be arranged on a case-by-case basis with a local bank, savings and loan, credit union, or even the local merchant from which the purchase is made.

In my youth, I worked for a time in the credit department of my dad's music and appliance store. My dad loved making money, but that love was always second to the commitment at the core of his identity to provide reliable products and services to the people of the community in which we lived. In my experience, this is typical of small-business owners who have strong community roots.

At what by current standards was a very modest interest rate, we offered a one- to three-year payment plan for major purchases such as a piano or refrigerator that would serve for many years. We retained title to the merchandise until all payments were received, and our primary recourse was to repossess if the buyer defaulted. If customers who demonstrated good faith ran into temporary difficulty from an illness or business downturn, we noted this on the accounts and generally worked out some arrangement that would allow them to keep the merchandise and pay as they were able. There were no penalties or special fees.

We financed this service with a commercial line of credit from our local bank, secured by our customer accounts receivable — promises to pay from people we knew and on whose future business we depended. We made the decisions and carried the risk. It was an arrangement that encouraged responsible decision making on all sides.

The solution to wages inadequate to provide for daily needs is not easier, cheaper, or fairer credit; it is to restore living-wage jobs, tax the rich to provide a floor of essential public services, and reduce household expenses by restoring the household as a unit of production.

We restore living-wage jobs by rolling back ill-conceived trade policies that encourage the international outsourcing of jobs and the suppression of wages, by raising the minimum wage, and by generally making the provision of living-wage jobs for all who seek them an economic policy priority.

We restore basic public services by taxing the rich commensurate with the benefits they have received from society and by rolling back wasteful government expenditures on military adventurism and corporate subsidies.

We restore household production by reorganizing our lives so we devote less time to paid employment and more to undertaking many of the things at home that we have outsourced to the money economy, such as gardening, food processing, meal production, lawn care, handyman tasks, entertainment, and child care.

The restoration of household production has received a major boost from an economic downturn that leaves many people with more time than money. Others, particularly youth, are pioneering this path by choice and discovering how to do it in ways that are both highly fulfilling and consistent with an appropriate commitment to balanced gender roles and work sharing. I'm a fan of Shannon Hayes's *Radical Homemakers: Reclaiming Domesticity from a Consumer Culture*,[3] which shares the stories of these modern pioneers and the lessons of their experience.

To sum it up, the appropriate cure for systemic debt slavery is a New Economy.

Home Mortgages

The purpose of a mortgage is to finance homeownership, not to create a foundation for loan pyramids, fuel speculation, and inflate a housing bubble. The idea that the inflation of housing prices is creating wealth is only one of many phantom-wealth fictions. It may increase the relative advantage of homeowners over renters, but escalating home prices create a growing barrier to first-time homeownership. And using one's home as a substitute for a paying job to support current consumption is a path to serfdom.

The goal of broad participation in responsible homeownership is best advanced by increasing job security, raising wages, and maintaining stable housing prices. We also can create a system of responsible mortgage lending, much like the one we once had.

That system consisted of local financial institutions, primarily member-owned savings and loan associations, that served as repositories for local savings and issued mortgages to homebuyers with the backing and strict supervision of various federal agencies. It worked well until deregulation of the financial system broke down the carefully calibrated division of responsibilities among local financial institutions and opened the door to increasingly risky and predatory behavior.

It is time to restore a system of well-regulated community banking to serve a variety of community needs for legitimate and responsible financing, including homeownership.

Insurance

Insurance involves an arrangement by which a group of individuals join a risk pool to guarantee one another against individual ruin from a catastrophic illness, fire, or other random, unavoidable event.

There are three basic approaches to organizing an insurance pool.

1. PRIVATE NONPROFIT: A number of people or institutions voluntarily form a mutual insurance association that pools the risks for certain disasters or life events, such as fire, flood, or disability. Each member of the pool

takes on the roles of both insurer and insured in a community-based mutual security arrangement grounded in cooperation, caring, and sharing. Any excess in premiums collected over the cost of the claims paid plus appropriate reserves is returned to the policyholders. Often identified by the word *mutual* in the name, as in Mutual of Omaha, this type of association was once the most common way of organizing insurance services.

2. GOVERNMENT: A government insurance program such as Social Security or Medicare organizes and manages a mutual pooling of risk on a national scale. Coverage is mandatory, which assures universal coverage, spreads the risk over a large number of people, and minimizes the costs of recruitment and administration.

3. PRIVATE FOR-PROFIT: A private, profit-seeking individual or entity offers to insure against specified risks in return for a fee. This creates a sharp divergence between the roles and interests of the insurer and insured. Both, of course, would prefer to avoid a loss, but the insurer wants to maximize fees and minimize the payment of claims, whereas the insured wants the opposite. This conflict of interest encourages the insurer to exclude those in greatest need and to find excuses to reject legitimate claims. It also carries high overhead costs to cover dividends to shareholders, executive bonuses, marketing campaigns, claims processing, and disputes over denied payments. The results can be disastrous, as is the case with the U.S. private health insurance industry.

Generally, the private nonprofit and government options provide the strongest and most socially efficient risk-sharing solution. The least satisfactory from a community perspective is a noncompetitive, private for-profit system.

Attempting to create a system that involves competition between a mix of nonprofit and unregulated for-profit providers creates an inherently destructive dynamic. Nonprofit providers are committed to providing everyone with affordable care; for-profit providers are concerned only with maximizing profits. If not prevented by government regulation, the for-profits will cherry-pick the pool of insurance buyers by offering lower rates than the nonprofit — but only to the young and healthy who are the least likely to need expensive care.

This leaves the sick and elderly to nonprofit providers. To raise the premiums on their narrowed customer pool sufficiently to cover the claims would place those premiums out of reach of any but the richest members of society, who have no need of such insurance in the first place.

The nonprofit thus either stops covering those in evident need and competes with the for-profit for the low-risk population or is forced into bankruptcy. Either way, those with the greatest need go without care. This is exactly what happened in the case of health insurance in the United States, and it did in some wonderful nonprofit providers.[4]

There is a deeper problem that no form of insurance risk pooling can resolve on its own. Many previously insurable risks are escalating out of control for reasons that lead back to a dysfunctional economic system.

Health care costs are an example. Part of the reason for their escalation can be traced to price gouging by pharmaceutical companies, the practice of defensive medicine driven by the fear of lawsuits, and aggressive end-of-life care that may at best extend life by a few months. Possible solutions include encouraging greater competition among pharmaceutical makers by limiting patent protection, reforming the tort system to distinguish between defensible questions of judgment and true malpractice, and expanding coverage for hospice care. Action on these issues falls more to government than to either nonprofit or for-profit insurance providers.

If we look further upstream, we find causes that fall

entirely outside the province of health care institutions. These include the toxic contamination of our air, water, and soil; heavy advertising of junk food rich in salt and sugar; and sedentary lifestyles devoted to watching TV and playing video games. We could be healthier and achieve enormous health care savings by increasing the availability of nutritious food to inner-city residents, banning junk food from schools, lowering the amounts of sugar and salt allowed in processed foods, improving food labels, and levying a fee on junk food advertising to cover related health care costs and public education programs. We also could provide easy access to home and neighborhood primary health care (as Cuba, for example, does) and lay out public spaces in ways that encourage walking and bicycling.

We need a similar approach to reducing the impact of catastrophic weather events, which are almost certain to increase. We must deal with the cause by reducing carbon emissions while at the same time investing in remediation actions such as improving levees, removing brush, changing land-use patterns, and revising building codes.

Above all, we must keep in mind that our best insurance when tragedy does strike is a strong and resilient community that mobilizes quickly for mutual assistance. Building strong, equitable, and resilient communities brings us back to the seven critical system interventions outlined in the previous chapter.

Again, the look upstream brings us back to the need for a New Economy.

Retirement

So what about retirement and our dependence on our 401(k)s to provide support in our elder years? Here we encounter perhaps the most cunning and diabolical element of the Wall Street con. We are lured into placing our retirement funds with Wall Street investment houses by an impossible and carefully cultivated dream of ten to twenty years of secure and effortless retirement luxury. After our money is in Wall Street hands, we have a stake in political decisions favorable to Wall Street interests — and in believing and perpetuating Wall Street's phantom-wealth lies. The prospect that Wall Street is interested only in its own commissions and is gambling away our money on phantom-wealth Ponzi schemes that cannot be sustained and would not in any event fulfill the promise is too frightening to consider, because society offers us few alternatives for dealing with retirement.

Recall the Malaysian forestry minister mentioned in chapter 2 who wanted to cut down all the trees and put the money in the bank to earn interest. Debates about individual retirement accounts and putting Social Security money in an interest-bearing "lockbox" are based on the same phantom-wealth fallacy.

Retirees cannot eat money. They need real food, shelter, medical care, clothing, recreation, and other goods and services — all of which must be produced and provided by working people at the time the retirees' needs are presented.

In the real world, retirement is necessarily a contract between retirees and the working people who agree to devote a portion of the fruits of their labor to providing for the retirees' needs. The threat facing future retirees is not insufficient money — which government can easily create with an accounting entry — it's demographics.

In 1935, when the newly signed Social Security bill set the retirement age at sixty-five, males at birth had a life expectancy of sixty years. The average person was dead at sixty-five. Life expectancy rose to seventy-four by 2005 and is expected to grow to eighty-five by the end of this century. The accepted retirement age, however, has stayed almost the same, creating an increasingly impossible expectation that those of working age (from around twenty to sixty-five) will reduce their own consumption relative to the value of what they produce, sufficient to support extended vacations of ten to twenty years' duration for a rapidly growing population of folks over sixty-five.

In 1960, there were five working people per retiree. Because of longer life spans and the greater percentage of people reaching retirement age, that ratio was 3.3 to 1 in 2004 and, unless the retirement age changes dramatically, will be down to 2 to 1 by 2040.[5] At some point, working people struggling to keep their children fed and clothed will say, "Enough already." Whether we assume that they will be compensated by money from Social Security taxes or phantom-wealth returns created from nothing by Wall Street is a technicality. Either way the burden is unsustainable.

Another conceptual flaw is the Wall Street argument that private investment accounts are a proper retirement solution. We have no idea how long we will live or what our end-of-life medical needs will be. I might have died in an accident or suffered a lethal heart attack the day before I reach sixty-five, in which case I would have needed no retirement account at all. Or I might live to 105 and spend my final years in intensive care, in which case I might need a retirement account in the millions of dollars. Most people fall somewhere in between, but no one knows what his or her individual need will be.

Retirement is not an individual savings issue; it is an insurance issue that requires a pooling of risk and an intergenerational contract. The basic design of Social Security is sound on both these counts so long as the ratio of retirees to workers does not become so high as to place an unbearable burden on the working generations. This issue can be resolved only by changing our expectations regarding the appropriate retirement age.

The larger society can and should manage Social Security as a universal insurance pool to provide for the care of the physically and mentally incapacitated of any age, but it has neither the means nor the moral obligation to guarantee any able bodied person a ten- to thirty- or forty-year fully funded vacation. Most of us need to remain active contributors to the real-wealth economy for as long as we are able.

A major shift in our thinking is required to recognize that the truly satisfying life is one of creative engagement. If we organize societies to make work fulfilling and engaging, then it becomes a source of self-fulfillment for everyone, including those of us in our elder years. So we are back again to the New Economy.

This brings us to another question that may already have occurred to you. If we eliminate Wall Street, how will we provide equity funding for productive enterprises?

WHAT YOU AREN'T SUPPOSED TO KNOW ABOUT THE STOCK MARKET

According to the corporate-ethics guru Marjorie Kelly, the public sale of newly issued corporate common stock in 1999 netted $106 billion. That was the only money from stock sales that went to the issuing corporation. It was less than 1 percent of the $20.4 trillion in corporate shares traded in that same year.

Even more surprising, Federal Reserve data reveal that during the twenty years from 1981 to 2000, the overall net flow of money to corporations from stock sales was a *negative* $540 billion, meaning that the corporations spent more money from their treasuries to buy back their own shares than they raised by selling new shares.[6]

One might wonder why corporate management would use company money to buy back its own shares rather than use it either to pay dividends to shareholders or to invest in new productive capacity.

The effect of such purchases is to inflate the price of the stock, which defenders of the practice point out serves shareholder interests. Another answer is offered by the independent market observer and author Thornton Parker. Using Federal Reserve statistics, Parker found that from 1982 to 2008, the largest net sellers of corporate stocks were households — to the tune of $5,082 billion, or just over $5 trillion. Corporations during this same period were net buyers by $737 billion.[7]

At first blush, it makes no sense. The presumed function of share markets is to facilitate the purchase of corporate shares by households to raise money for productive corporate investments. Corporations should be net sellers and households should be net buyers.

Parker provides a telling explanation. When corporate executives sell the shares they receive as part of their compensation packages, the proceeds go to them, not to the corporation, and therefore count as household sales. The data thus suggest that since the 1980s, the function of the public share markets has been to fund the private fortunes of corporate executives who took a major portion of their compensation in newly issued shares.

Ownership, as discussed in chapter 13, should be in the hands of people who have a stake in the long-term health of the enterprise and the community and ecosystem in which it is located. Rather than turn our retirement savings over to Wall Street con artists, we will do much better as individuals and as a society to favor direct, long-term investments by individuals in companies of which they have personal knowledge. An owner who needs to cash out his or her shares can sell them to another owner, a new stakeholder, or even the company itself in a private transaction.

▶•◆•◆•◀

Wall Street operates a sophisticated con game that leaves us dependent on a series of scams that it presents to us as financial services essential to our well-being. By pushing down wages relative to the cost of living, Wall Street makes us ever more dependent on consumer credit and borrowing against our home equity. The greater our desperation, the higher it pushes fees and interest rates. It collects our insurance premiums in exchange for promises of payment in the event of a personal disaster that it has no intention of keeping.

It entices us to put our savings in the care of professionally managed phantom-wealth funds with fantasies of a luxurious ten- to twenty-year work-free vacation at the end of our lives that would place an impossible burden on the working population. It would have us believe that when we buy shares of stock on Wall Street exchanges we are providing investment funds for companies to expand productive output, when in fact we are mostly converting our personal financial assets to the personal financial assets of Wall Street privateers.

Daily expenditures should be covered by living family wages. Insurance is best provided by nonprofit insurance pools managed for the benefit of their participants. Old-age security depends on an intergenerational contract. Savings should flow to real investment in real productive enterprises and infrastructure.

As we shall see in part V, the leadership for change will not come from within the Wall Street–Washington axis. It will come from a powerful citizen movement that reframes the public debate and the political context. The movement will know it is on a path to success when a sitting president issues a Declaration of Independence from Wall Street and outlines a New Economy agenda.

CHAPTER 15

►·◆·◆·◄

A PRESIDENTIAL DECLARATION OF INDEPENDENCE FROM WALL STREET I HOPE I MAY ONE DAY HEAR

In a February 2010 interview with *BusinessWeek*, President Obama sought to reassure corporate America that he was on their team. "We are pro-growth. We are fierce advocates of a thriving, dynamic free market. But we do think that there have to be some rules of the road."[1]

These words were less reassuring for those of us looking for signs that there is a New Economy vision lurking in our visionary president's mind. Rules of the road are essential to prevent crashes, but if the road ends at the edge of a cliff and is populated by gas-guzzling SUVs with jammed accelerators and defective brakes, then rules to order the flow of traffic are not sufficient.

During the 2008 presidential campaign, the soaring rhetoric of candidate Obama led many of us to hope he would be the kind of president who would build a new road that skirts the cliff and populate it with safer, more efficient, and maneuverable vehicles.

During the heat of candidate Obama's campaign, I drafted the economic address to the nation that I hoped he might give early in his administration as part of a commitment to deliver on his promise of change. It provided an overview of the New Economy agenda in the format of a presidential address in candidate Obama's style.

Even if President Obama overcomes the disappointment of those who were hoping for a build-a-new-road president and wins a second term, it now seems unlikely that we will hear from him anything resembling the following speech — unless a shift in the political context compels it.

The speech, in this updated and expanded version, thus becomes a marker for the political dimension of the task now before civil society. We must create a political context that makes the U.S. president — and other heads of state the world over — feel compelled to give such an address as their declaration of national independence from Wall Street and its global counterparts — and to follow through on its commitments.

Here is the address.[2]

Fellow Citizens:

My administration came to office with a mandate for bold action to deal with the evident failure of our most powerful economic institutions. They have crippled our economy; burdened our federal, state, and local governments with debilitating debts; divided us into the profligate and the desperate; corrupted our political institutions; and threatened the destruction of the natural environment on which our very lives depend.

After the September 2008 financial crash, the U.S. government stepped in to save Wall Street's biggest institutions with massive public bailouts. The banks took this taxpayer money and used it to pay executive bonuses, issue stockholder dividends, finance acquisitions, play speculative games, and fight even modest reforms. They did virtually nothing to get the economy going again by funding productive, job-creating enterprises or giving relief to desperate homeowners with underwater mortgages.

It is time to face up to the fact that the Wall Street institutions now in place are creations of a failed economic ideology that says if government favors the financial interests of the rich to the disregard of all else, everyone will benefit and the nation will prosper. A thirty-year experiment with the trickle-down economic policies promoted by this ideology has demonstrated that it works well in the short term for fat-cat Wall Street bankers who manipulate the financial system to make money without the burden of contributing to the production of anything of real value.

This creates unearned phantom-wealth claims over the real wealth produced by people on Main Street who are doing honest, productive work and making honest, productive investments. Wall Street calls the creation of phantom wealth financial innovation. I call it theft. It is legal only because Wall Street has the money to buy the votes of politicians to make it legal.

We now live with the devastating consequences of Wall Street's ill-conceived social engineering experiment: a disappearing American middle class and a crumbling physical infrastructure; failing schools; millions without health care; dependence on imported goods, food, and energy, and even essential military hardware. At the same time, it has increased our burden on Earth's living systems and created an often-violent competition between the world's peoples and nations for Earth's remaining resources.

Wall Street is so corrupt that its major players no longer trust one another. The result is a credit freeze that starves legitimate Main Street businesses of the money they need to pay their workers and suppliers. Pouring still more taxpayer money into corrupted institutions hasn't, and won't, fix the fundamental problem.

This is not a broken system in need of a fix. It is a failed system that must be replaced with a new system based on the lessons of our experience.

Corrective action begins with a recognition that our economic crisis is, at its core, a moral crisis. Our economic institutions and rules, even the indicators by which we measure economic performance, consistently place financial values ahead of life values. They are brilliantly effective at making money for rich people. We have tried our experiment in unrestrained greed and individualism. Our children, families, communities, and the natural systems of Earth are paying an intolerable price.

We have no more time or resources to devote to fixing a system based on false values and a discredited ideology devoted primarily to creating phantom wealth. We must now come together to create the institutions of a new economy based on a values-based pragmatism that recognizes a simple truth: if the world is to work for any of us, it must work for all of us.

We have been measuring economic performance against GDP, or gross domestic product, which essentially measures the rate at which money and resources are flowing through the economy on their way to our overflowing garbage dumps. Let us henceforth measure economic performance by the indicators of what we really want: the health and well-being of our children, families, communities, and the natural environment.

I call on faith, education, and other civic organizations to launch a national conversation to identify the indicators of human and natural health against which we might properly assess our economic performance. It is time to take seriously what we now know about the essential importance of equity, caring communities, and the vitality, diversity, and resilience of nature to our overall physical and mental health and well-being.

The GDP is actually a measure of the cost of producing a given level of human and natural health and well-being. Any business that sought to maximize its costs, which is in effect how we have managed our economy, would soon go bankrupt — and indeed our relentless commitment to growing GDP at all costs has brought our nation to the edge of financial, as well as moral, bankruptcy. We will henceforth strive to grow the things we really want, while seeking to reduce the cost in money and natural resources.

No government on its own can resolve the problems facing our nation, but together we can and will resolve them. I call on every American to join with me in rebuilding our nation by acting to strengthen our families and our communities; to restore our natural environment; to secure the future of our children; and to reestablish our leadership position and reputation in the community of nations.

Like a healthy ecosystem, a healthy twenty-first-century economy must have strong local roots and maximize the beneficial capture, storage, sharing, and use of local energy, water, and mineral resources. That is what we must seek to achieve, community by community, all across this nation, by unleashing the creative energies of our people and our local governments, businesses, and civic organizations.

Previous administrations favored Wall Street, but the policies of this administration henceforth will favor the people and businesses of Main Street — people who are working to rebuild our local communities, restore the middle class, and bring our natural environment back to health. Together we can actualize the founding ideals of our nation as we restore the health of our nation and its economy.

- We will strive for local and national food independence by rebuilding our local food systems based on family farms and environmentally friendly farming methods that rebuild the soil, maximize yields per acre, minimize the use of toxic chemicals, and create opportunities for the many young people who are returning to the land.

- We will strive for local and national energy independence by supporting local entrepreneurs who are creating and growing businesses to retrofit our buildings and develop and apply renewable-energy technologies.

- It is a basic principle of market theory that trade relations between nations should be balanced. So-called free trade agreements based on the misguided ideology of market fundamentalism have hollowed out our national industrial capacity, mortgaged our future to foreign creditors, and created global financial instability. We will take steps to assure that our future trade relations are balanced and fair, return manufacturing jobs to America, rebuild our manufacturing capacity on an environmentally sound closed-loop manufacturing model, and learn to live within our own means.

- We will rebuild our national infrastructure around a model of walkable, bicycle-friendly communities with efficient public transportation to conserve energy, nurture the relationships of community, and recover our agricultural and forest lands.

- A strong middle-class society is an American ideal. Our past embodiment of that ideal made us the envy of the world. We will act to restore that ideal by rebalancing the distribution of wealth. Necessary and appropriate steps will be taken to assure access by every person to high-quality health care, education, and other essential services, and to restore progressive taxation, as well as progressive wage and benefit rules, to protect working people. These policies are familiar to older Americans because they are the policies that created the middle class, the policies with which many Americans grew up. They were abandoned by ideological extremists to the detriment of all. We will restore them, with appropriate adaptation to current circumstances.

- We will seek to create a true ownership society in which all people have the opportunity to own their own homes and to have an ownership stake in the enterprises on which their livelihoods depend. Our economic policies will favor responsible ownership of local enterprises by people who have a stake in the health of their own communities and economies. The possibilities include locally owned family businesses, cooperatives, and the many other forms of community- and worker-owned enterprises.

My administration will act at the national level to support your efforts to advance these objectives at the local level by engaging in a fundamental reordering of our national priorities.

Because the world can no longer afford war, the foreign policy of this administration will be crafted to build cooperation among people and nations in order to eliminate terrorism and its underlying causes; resolve conflicts through peaceful diplomacy; roll back military spending and demilitarize the economies of all nations; restore environmental health; and increase economic stability.

We will work to replace a global system of economic competition with a global system of economic cooperation based on the sharing of beneficial technology and the right of the people of each nation to own and control their own economic resources to meet their needs for food, energy, shelter, education, health care, and other basic needs. We will work to protect the rights and health of working people and the environment everywhere.

An unprecedented concentration of power in transnational corporations that owe no allegiance to any nation, place, or public purpose undermines democracy, distorts economic priorities, and contributes to a socially destructive concentration of wealth. Corporate charters give a group of private investors a special legal right to aggregate and concentrate economic power under unified management.

The only reason for a government to grant such a charter is to enable a corporation to serve a well-defined public purpose under strict rules of public accountability. I am appointing a commission to recommend legislation that redefines the corporate charter so that each corporation's public purpose is specified in its charter and periodically subject to public review.

There will be no more no-strings government bailouts of failed banks or other corporations during my administration. Any for-profit corporation that is too big to fail is too big to exist. We will institute vigorous antitrust enforcement to break up excessive concentrations of economic power and restore market discipline. When no individual company is so big that its failure can bring down the whole economy, there will be no need for bailouts.

Because absentee ownership invites irresponsibility, we will create incentives for publicly traded corporations to break themselves up into their component units and to convert to responsible ownership by their workers, customers, or small investors in the communities in which they are located.

Through a public legal process, we will withdraw the charter from, and force the dissolution of, any corporation that consistently fails to obey the law and fulfill a legitimate public purpose.

There is no place in a life-serving twenty-first-century economy for financial speculation, predatory lending, or institutions that exist primarily to engage in these illegitimate practices.

We will act to render Wall Street's casino-like operations unprofitable. We will impose a speculation tax, require responsible capital ratios, and impose a surcharge on short-term capital gains. We will make it illegal for people and corporations to sell or insure assets that they do not own or in which they do not have a direct material interest. We will prohibit financial institutions from trading for their own accounts securities they sell to the public. The brainpower and computing capacity now devoted to trading electronic documents in speculative financial markets will be put to work solving real social and environmental problems and financing life-serving Main Street enterprises that create living-wage green jobs.

To meet the financial needs of the new twenty-first-century Main Street economy, we will reverse the process of mergers and acquisitions that created the current concentration of banking power. We will restore the previous system of federally regulated, locally owned and managed community banks that fulfill the classic textbook banking function of serving as financial intermediaries between local people looking to secure a modest interest return on their savings and local people who need a loan to buy a home or finance a business. Many of the individual banks will be organized as nonprofit cooperatives. Some may be owned by state and local governments. The new system will operate as a well-regulated public utility to assure that money flows to where it is needed to address the self-defined needs of people and communities.

And last, but not least, we will implement an orderly process of monetary reform. Most people believe that our government creates money. That is a fiction. Private banks create virtually all the money in circulation when they issue a loan at interest. The money is created by making a simple accounting entry with a few computer keystrokes. That is all money really is, an accounting entry.

Many years ago, our government gave private banks the exclusive power to create money through the issuance of debt. This means that someone has borrowed and is paying interest to a private bank for virtually every dollar in circulation. The more our economy expands, the greater the debt owed to the bankers who create with mere accounting entries the money essential to economic exchange.

This makes banking a very profitable business, but it creates inherent economic instability as credit expands and contracts. Furthermore, because banks create only the principal loaned, but not the interest, the debt-money system creates an imperative for perpetual economic expansion to generate new loans so that sufficient money will be available to allow borrowers to pay the interest — unless interest payments flow right back into the community.

In the current system, when banks receive the savings and interest payments of honest working people, they are less likely to invest those payments in productive enterprises than to put the money into play in the global casino, creating inherent instability and assuring that as a nation we will continue to be mired in ever-growing debt. Locally owned community banks, particularly those organized as nonprofits, are more likely to charge modest interest rates and assure that interest payments immediately recycle back into the community.

U.S. household mortgage and credit card debt stood at $13.8 trillion in 2007, roughly the equivalent of the total 2007 GDP, and much of it was subject to usurious interest rates. The federal debt inherited from the previous administration stood at $5.1 trillion in 2007, even before the Wall Street bailout, and it cost taxpayers $406 billion a year in interest alone, the third-largest item in the federal budget after defense and income transfers like Social Security. That debt has since more than doubled, with a commensurate increase in our federal interest burden.

This debt hamstrings our government and places an intolerable burden on American families that undermines physical and mental health and family stability. It also creates a massive ongoing transfer of wealth from the substantial majority of households that are net borrowers to the tiny minority of households that are net lenders. This engenders a form of class warfare that has become a serious threat to the security of America's working families. One answer is to assure that jobs pay a family wage sufficient to allow families to live comfortably.

There is another serious consequence of giving control of our money supply to Wall Street. When Wall Street banks stop making the accounting entries needed to fund Main Street, the real-wealth economy collapses, even though we have willing, skilled workers and must still meet the needs of our families, maintain the nation's physical infrastructure, and protect our natural resources. The economy stops solely because banks are not making the necessary accounting entries to allow real businesses to function. We cannot allow the moral corruption of Wall Street to bring down our entire economy, indeed our entire nation.

Money-supply management is currently the responsibility of the Federal Reserve. Even though we call it the "Federal" Reserve, it operates independently from accountability to any public body and is largely captive to the interests of Wall Street's biggest banks. It secretly buys up toxic securities from Wall Street financial institutions on unknown terms and with no public accountability, and it issues credit to the same institutions to buy U.S. Treasuries at interest rates that guarantee them an effortless profit. All the while it adamantly rejects congressional calls for a public audit.

I have instructed the treasury secretary to take immediate action to assume control of the Federal Reserve and restructure it to function as a publicly transparent federal agency accountable to the president and the Congress. The new federalized Federal Reserve will have a mandate to stabilize the money supply, contain housing and stock market bubbles, discourage speculation, and assure the availability of credit to eligible Main Street borrowers, on fair and affordable terms.

In conjunction with the newly federalized Federal Reserve, the secretary of the treasury will begin an orderly process of converting to a banking system composed of independent, locally owned community banks and raising reserve requirements to assure that all banks maintain sufficient capital to cover foreseeable obligations. The treasury secretary will also initiate an orderly, long-term process of monetizing the federal debt to reduce the interest that taxpayers pay for money that private banks created with an accounting entry, which can just as well be made directly by the U.S. Treasury.

In the future, we will look to the Fed to issue interest-free credit to the U.S. government as approved by the Fed and the U.S. Congress and as needed for investment in productive human, physical, and natural capital to build the physical and social infrastructure of a twenty-first-century economy consistent with full employment and price stability.

We will recommit ourselves to the founding ideals of this great nation, focus on our possibilities, and liberate ourselves from the failed ideas and institutions of Wall Street. Together we can create a stronger, better nation that secures a fulfilling life for every person and honors the premise of the Declaration of Independence that every individual is endowed with an unalienable right to life, liberty, and the pursuit of happiness.

PART V

NAVIGATING UNCHARTED WATERS

▶◆•◆•◀

Barack Obama was swept into the U.S. presidency on a promise of change. On the economic front, he pushed through a stimulus package, but his efforts to rein in Wall Street have been tepid and sporadic at best. This is due only in part to Wall Street's political power. More relevant to the theme of this book is the extent to which actualizing the New Economy vision outlined here requires navigating uncharted waters. The available charts and instruments with which the current ship's officers are familiar are all carryovers from the old economy.

For President Obama or any future president to provide the leadership we need, we not only must generate popular demand from below that is too powerful to ignore but also must produce the required charts, navigational instruments, and senior officers familiar with their use.

Our current situation as a nation and a species has instructive parallels to that of the early American settlers who mobilized to win their independence from a distant king. There was no model for the democratic processes and institutions to which their rebellion led. They learned and advanced the arts of political democracy through invention and practice as they set in motion the historic process of dismantling the institutions of Empire while simultaneously creating the institutions of a new nation.

The process they initiated remains unfinished. We the people of our time must mobilize to carry the process forward by learning and advancing the arts of economic democracy as we declare our independence from Wall Street in both word and deed.

The power of popular movements resides in their ability to act on three fronts. They must:

1. Challenge and change the cultural stories that frame the collective life of the society

2. Create new cultural and institutional realities from the bottom up in the communities where the members live

3. Use the power of their numbers to demand that politicians change the rules to favor real markets and real democracy

Although they work below the media radar, millions of people are engaged on each of these fronts, which is a reassuring cause for hope.

The four chapters of part V address the challenge before us. There is no magic-bullet solution to a human crisis five thousand years in the making. The needed changes touch on nearly every aspect of society and our individual lives.

Chapter 16, "When the People Lead, the Leaders Will Follow," spells out why leadership for deep change necessarily depends on popular action and identifies parallels between the self-organizing resistance movements of the earlier colonists who achieved their independence from British rule and we, the subject colonists of our day, who through our actions are declaring our independence from Wall Street.

Chapter 17, "A Visionary President Meets Realpolitik," identifies the reasons President Obama did not — indeed, could not — capitalize on the Wall Street crash to move forward a New Economy agenda, and spells out what we as citizens must do to create a political context that makes such action politically imperative.

Chapter 18, "Change the Story, Change the Future," examines how culture shapes individual and collective behavior and how social movements can use the power of authentic cultural stories to turn the course of history.

Chapter 19, "Learning to Live, Living to Learn," frames the threefold strategy by which millions of people are living the New Economy into being through a process of learning by doing. It then outlines the contributions needed from media, education, religion, and the arts and provides guidance for people from all walks of life who seek to contribute.

The book closes with an epilogue that presents "The View from 2084" of the world we may yet leave to our grandchildren if we succeed — a world defined not so much by dazzling new technologies as by the opportunities it offers for meaningful fulfillment.

CHAPTER 16

►•◆•◆•◄

WHEN THE PEOPLE LEAD, THE LEADERS WILL FOLLOW

There is a tendency to think that what we see in the present moment will continue. We forget how often we have been astonished by the sudden crumbling of institutions, by extraordinary changes in people's thoughts, by unexpected eruptions of rebellion against tyrannies, by the quick collapse of systems of power that seemed invincible.

HOWARD ZINN

It is time to stop trying to fix what can't and shouldn't be fixed, declare national and global independence from Wall Street, and get on with building the New Economy and the new institutions required to serve its financial needs.

Judging from the record to date, we cannot expect the leadership to come from either Congress or the Obama administration. As demonstrated all too clearly by the events both before and after the financial crash, Washington operates as a wholly owned Wall Street subsidiary. This can and must change, but it will happen only as an engaged citizenry mobilizes to demand it.

The idea of ordinary citizens being able to free democracy and the market from the grip of the Wall Street–Washington axis would seem a naive fantasy if not for the fact that we live in a unique historical time in which seemingly impossible transformations of unjust and deeply destructive relationships

WITNESS TO HISTORY

My belief that an economic restructuring of the magnitude I am proposing is possible reflects my experience with the transformative power of social movements.

In my early youth, I rode a bus in Miami in which "colored" people were confined to the last rows. It was beyond imagination that I would live to witness whites weeping tears of joy over the landslide election of a black president.

Fran, my wife, was warned by her father when she went off to college that if her grades were too high, no man would marry her. She had a straight-A average when I met her. I married her anyway—a smart choice, as it turned out—but assumed without question that she would follow me without complaint and subordinate her career to mine. Years later, she was the primary wage earner and I happily and productively followed her path from the United States to Asia and back again, fashioning my career to fit hers.

In 1994, when I was writing *When Corporations Rule the World*, corporations were acting with impunity to circumvent democracy and consolidate their power, using trade agreements to rewrite the rules of global commerce. There was little public awareness that trade agreements were an issue, and seemingly little interest in them. In 1999, a historic Seattle protest brought the powerful World Trade Organization to its knees in a shock from which it never recovered.

of power can and do occur on a global scale with heartening speed and regularity.

IMPOSSIBLE TRANSFORMATIONS

An advantage of reaching my elder years in this historically unique time is that I have experienced many such transformations and have seen, sometimes firsthand, how committed groups shape and accelerate them. My lifetime has spanned the liberation of India from rule by the powerful British Empire, the collapse of the Soviet Union and the dismantling of the Berlin Wall, the end of apartheid in South Africa, and the People Power Revolution that brought down the Marcos dictatorship in the Philippines. All came quickly and were achieved through largely peaceful means.

From my vantage point as an Air Force officer assigned to the Office of the Secretary of Defense in the Pentagon as the Vietnam War began to wind down, I witnessed the beginning of the defeat of the world's most powerful military, by decidedly violent means, by an ill-equipped, ragtag army of Vietnamese peasants. From that experience I learned that attempting to resist the will of a determined people is futile, no matter how many guns and how much money you have at your disposal.

I have also been witness to the dramatic changes wrought by the great social movements of the latter half of the twentieth century, including the civil rights, women's, and environmental movements.

GLOBALIZED PEOPLE POWER

Most of all, my sense of our human potential to choose our future through conscious collective action comes from my involvement in the resistance against corporate globalization that gave birth to global civil society. The organized resistance began with a few small conversations in the early 1990s. It announced itself to the world with the historic Seattle protest against the World Trade Organization in 1999. It mobilized millions of people in subsequent protests wherever corporate elites met with national political leaders and bureaucrats to negotiate away the people's rights,[1] and it stalled Wall Street's free trade juggernaut. It is the leading edge of the emerging New Economy movement.

From the beginning, the defining issue has been democracy, not trade, and the demonstrations have given a visible face to the confrontation between the opposing forces of globalized people power and globalized corporate power.

Democracy was also the underlying issue when more than ten million people mobilized on February 15, 2003, to protest the anticipated U.S. invasion of Iraq. Made possible by the Internet, this protest was the largest, most inclusive, and most global expression of public opinion in human history. A *New York Times* article dubbed it the second global superpower.[2]

Chapters 6 and 8 placed the resistance against Wall Street colonization of the U.S. and global economies in the historical context of a larger human struggle against the violence, domination, and exploitation of five thousand years of Empire. The civil rights, women's, and environmental movements are all expressions of this struggle. Each of these has contributed to the foundation on which the emerging New Economy movement and its drive to true democracy is building.

Because economic democracy and political democracy necessarily go hand in hand, the New Economy movement is an essential leading edge of this next phase in the larger human struggle to liberate ourselves from cultural and institutional chains of our own making. It bears striking and informative resemblance to the experience nearly two and a half centuries ago of the early American colonists who launched this epic experiment when they rebelled against the predatory excesses of a distant king.

As we saw in chapter 8, what became the American Revolution began not with the founding fathers but with the self-organization of an engaged citizenry. The founding fathers assumed the leadership and issued a formal declaration of independence only after it was clear that events would otherwise sweep them away.

Wall Street is a formidable foe, but so was Britain. At the time of the rebellion, it was the most powerful empire on Earth. Fortunately, the advantage in any such struggle ultimately lies with a motivated and organized citizenry.

TWO EPIC MOMENTS IN THE GREAT DEMOCRATIC EXPERIMENT

The parallels between the independence movement that liberated thirteen colonies on the east coast of what is now the United States and the efforts of those seeking independence from Wall Street are both revealing and instructive:

As the economies of Britain's thirteen colonies on the eastern seaboard of North America began to grow in their production of real wealth, their prosperity attracted the attention of the British Crown, which sought to increase its share of that wealth through new taxes and the grant of a tea monopoly to the East India Company, in which the king held a financial interest.

In the years following World War II, the policies of the Roosevelt New Deal created a prosperous middle class and flourishing Main Street businesses growing the real wealth of their local communities. Main Street's prosperity attracted the attention of Wall Street, which gradually asserted its economic and political power to increase its share. It charged Main Street usurious interest rates and fees; asserted monopoly control of intellectual property rights, markets, money, and natural resources; and accelerated the creation of phantom wealth that enlarged Wall Street's claims against the real wealth of the rest of society.

As the threat to their liberty and prosperity became evident, the colonists mobilized in resistance to the British Crown. Some colonists formed local resistance groups, with names such as Sons of Liberty, Regulators, Associators, and Liberty Boys, to engage in acts of noncooperation such as refusing to purchase and use the tax stamps that the Crown demanded be applied to all colonial commercial and legal papers, newspapers, pamphlets, and almanacs.

The New England merchant class given to slave trading and piracy had no reservations about evading import taxes by adding smuggling to their business portfolios. When the Crown decided to assert its authority over the Massachusetts Supreme Court by paying its judges directly from the royal treasury, the people responded by refusing to serve as jurors under the judges.

Other colonists formed Committees of Correspondence, groups of citizens engaged in sharing ideas and information through regularized exchanges of letters carried by ship and horseback. These committees linked elements of diverse citizen movements in common cause across the colonial borders that had long kept them divided.

As the threat to their liberty and prosperity became clear, the people began mobilizing in resistance to Wall Street. They formed organizations with names like Art and Revolution, Direct Action Network, Indigenous Environmental Network, the Institute for Local Self-Reliance, the International Forum on Globalization, National Farm Workers

Association, Public Citizen, Rainforest Action Network, the Ruckus Society, and United for a Fair Economy. They organized Internet forums to engage in sharing ideas and information and to unite movements in common cause, reaching out even across the national borders that had long kept them divided. In alliance with similar groups in other nations, they mobilized millions in global demonstrations that regularly disrupted the international meetings in which the rich and powerful gathered to circumvent democracy, rewrite the rules of commerce to remove restrictions on the consolidation of corporate power, and negotiate their division of the spoils.

The colonists also undertook initiatives aimed at getting control of economic life through local production. They boycotted British goods and subjected merchants who failed to honor the boycott to public humiliation. Artisans and laborers refused to participate in building military fortifications for the British. Women played a particularly crucial role by organizing Daughters of Liberty committees to produce substitutes for imported products.

Local Main Street businesses, workers, and consumers undertook initiatives aimed at getting control of economic life through local production and the patronage of local business. They organized farmers' markets, food co-ops, "local first" campaigns, local investment funds and credit unions, and consumer boycotts of big-box stores and the products of corporations that harm the environment and pay substandard wages. Local businesses formed national alliances like the American Independent Business Alliance, the Business Alliance for Local Living Economies, and Transition Towns. Local chambers of commerce disaffiliated from the corporate-dominated national Chamber of Commerce and joined these new alliances. New organizations like Americans for Financial Reform, the New Economy Network, the New Economy Working Group, and a New Way Forward formed to mobilize popular support for new rules to break up the big banks and hold financial institutions accountable to the public interest.

You get the picture.

A TRIBUTE TO HUMAN POSSIBILITY

Both of these historic resistance movements demonstrate the enormous and often-unnoted human capacity to organize in causes larger than the self-interest of any given individual. They accomplished everything reported here without establishment leadership, support, or sanction. There were many organizations, but the movement that brought them together had no organization charts and no central budgets. There were only thousands of leaders — millions, in the case of global civil society.

The organizing accomplishments of the colonists are all the more remarkable given their inauspicious circumstances. They had neither motor vehicles nor any form of electronic communication. Their speediest means of communication was a rider on a fast horse.

The colonists who pulled it off were themselves a generally scruffy and unruly lot unburdened by an excess of formal education. The earliest colonial settlements were operated as privately owned company estates ruled by overseers accountable to British investors. Many of the subsequent settlements were organized as parishes ruled as theocracies by preachers who taught that democracy is contrary to the will of God.

Many settlers were misfits and criminals forcibly shipped from England by a government eager to be rid of them, debtors escaping their debts, and rogues who came to seek their fortune by any means. The colonial economies depended on slaves and bonded labor, and the family structure placed women in a condition of indentured servitude. The lands the colonies occupied were acquired by genocide, and their social structures embodied deep racial and class divisions.

Precious little beyond a shared antipathy to British taxes and corporate monopolies bound the people together. Nothing in their experience hinted at their potential to organize a radically democratic self-organizing social movement. Yet organize they did. Through dialogue and participation in acts of resistance, they awakened to possibilities long denied, mobilized to walk away from their king, and created a new political reality that changed the course of human history. In the process, they invented the arts of democracy through their practice.

The historian Roger Wilkins named the decade preceding the Declaration of Independence the most important in U.S. history. In addition to drawing attention to the reality that we learn democracy only through its practice, his words are a guide to those who would ask in our time, "What can I do?"

> The stunning achievements of the 1765–1775 period were not only instances of resistance to specific obnoxious acts of the British government but also key stages in the development of a continental revolutionary consciousness and impulse toward self-government, as well as the creation of the rudimentary instruments to carry out those purposes. . . .
>
> All of the practices and arts of politics were deployed in that fruitful decade. The colonists paid careful attention to public affairs. They spent time alone exploring and honing their opinions on important issues by reading history and philosophy as well as the latest correspondence, dispatches, and political tracts. They thought hard about what was occurring and consulted

with others in order to inform and sharpen their views. They became involved in local and colonial politics by standing for office and putting forward proposals for action. When necessary — when, for example, colonial legislatures were disbanded, or when new instruments for protest and self-governance were required — they crafted appropriate new mechanisms. But most of all they thought, talked, debated, listened to one another, wrote, and created in ever-widening circles. All the while, their activities were fraught with great personal, political, and financial risk.[3]

The experiences that birthed the phenomenon of global civil society have had the same quality and serve the same ends, but on a far greater scale, with far greater diversity. And they are supported by far more advanced communication technologies. They hint at our possibilities for creative, radically democratic self-organization far beyond any historical experience, now that modern communications technologies have obliterated the barriers of geography.

►•◆•◆•◄

In many respects, our situation bears a striking resemblance to that of the early American colonists who refused to accept the authority of a distant British monarch and his rapacious appointees and chartered corporations. Through word and deed they created a political imperative to which the political leaders we call the founding fathers were compelled to respond by issuing a Declaration of Independence and raising an army. The founding fathers acted, however, only after the people had mobilized and a self-organized popular rebellion was well established. Once the people led, the leaders followed.

Yet ours is a moment of history like no other. The confrontation with planetary limits creates the imperative for a new ethic of sharing and cooperation on a global scale. The unprecedented opportunities for cross-cultural contact and immersion made possible by global travel are opening the human consciousness to previously unrecognized possibilities. Breakthroughs in communications technology have erased geographic barriers to make possible the nearly instant global spread of ideas and information.

Together these historic developments are unleashing a new phase in the great human experiment in democratic self-governance. The mobilizing political force demanding and driving the transition to democracy invariably and inevitably comes from those who bear the injustice of exclusion by imperial institutions that serve only the few. The resistance to this democratizing force comes from those who enjoy the privilege that imperial institutions afford them and from those who find comfort in the promise of certainty and security these institutions make to those whose acquiescence they seek.

Would-be reformers who work within the halls of power, no matter how sincere their intention, face nearly insurmountable constraints. Their inside influence depends on the power afforded them by the very institutions they seek to transform. If they overtly threaten the power of those institutions, they will be cast out from the positions on which their influence depends. This is a fundamental dilemma for those who would transform the system from within.

The case of President Obama is instructive.

CHAPTER 17

▶•◆•◆•◀

A VISIONARY PRESIDENT MEETS REALPOLITIK

The basic facts of President Obama's first year in office are well known. Given what he inherited — a devastated economy, record national and foreign debts, a mounting budget deficit, two expensive and unwinnable wars of occupation, Wall Street's corrupting hold on Washington politics, and a take-no-prisoners far-right opposition in Congress — he merits high marks.

His continuation of the Bush administration's bank bailout prevented total financial collapse, and his stimulus package slowed the loss of jobs. He has attempted to moderate Wall Street bonuses, speculation, and credit card rip-offs. He has greatly improved America's international image. He has recognized that global climate change is real and put it on the agenda for action. He has strengthened the ability of Americans to challenge discriminatory pay and increased health insurance for children of working-class families. He has put on hold new trade agreements that sell out public interests to corporate interests. He is winding down the war in Iraq. He pushed through much-needed health care reform legislation in the face of ruthless, unified opposition from those who believe they will gain political points if they cause his administration to fail.

Compared with where we might now be on any of these issues under a McCain-Palin administration, President Obama deserves our admiration and gratitude as a nation. Yet, compared with many of the hopes raised by his campaign and the urgent need for deep economic transformation, his administration and the Democratic Party majority in Congress have fallen far short.

LIMITS TO TRANSFORMATIONAL LEADERSHIP

Although our hopes for, and expectations of, President Obama on the New Economy front were consistent with his campaign rhetoric, they were unrealistic from the beginning.

- We underestimated Wall Street's political power.
- We overlooked Barack Obama's personal predisposition to avoid political confrontation in favor of bringing people together in search of common ground.
- We failed to appreciate the significance of the absence of an articulated and widely supported New Economy economic model that could provide an alternative framework to that offered by market fundamentalists and Keynesians.

Wall Street's Political Power

For more than forty years, Wall Street corporations have been aggressively tightening their hold on Washington politics to push their program of deregulation and privatization. They control the money and the media in a money-driven political system. Wall Street banks and investment houses, Goldman Sachs first among them, were candidate Obama's biggest campaign contributors. During the campaign Robert Rubin, once cochair of Goldman Sachs and more recently chair of Citigroup, was one of his most influential advisers.

Obama brought in former treasury secretary Larry Summers to be his top White House economic adviser and chose

Timothy Geithner, former head of the New York Federal Reserve and close associate of the heads of Wall Street's biggest banks,[1] to be his treasury secretary. Rubin, Summers, and Geithner bear significant individual and collective responsibility for the policies that led to the meltdown, as does Ben Bernanke, whom Obama kept on as Federal Reserve chair.

Among other qualities, Barack Obama is a political pragmatist. He did what he needed to do to win the election and trusted in his own ability to bring competing factions together to advance a shared vision of American possibility after taking office. Once elected, he staffed key positions with competent people who knew the system and were skilled in its ways.

Leadership to curb establishment power and excess rarely comes from within the establishment. Even when an armed revolution inserts new leaders into the institutions that the revolution sought to dismantle, the new leaders generally replicate the patterns of domination and abuse of those they displaced. They quickly learn that their ability to shape events depends on maintaining the power of the institutions they sought to transform and now head.

Recall that before Al Gore became vice president in the Clinton administration in 1992, he wrote *Earth in the Balance,* which presented a passionate plea to make environmental sustainability the organizing principle of public policy. Many of us hoped that he would use the powers of the vice presidency to make this a priority of U.S. domestic and foreign policy. Instead, he shamelessly campaigned for the North American Free Trade Agreement, which weakened environmental protections. As the chief U.S. negotiator at the Kyoto climate change summit in 1997, he demanded loopholes that contributed to gutting the final document. After leaving office in 2000 to return to private life, he rediscovered his environmental passion and became one of the world's most influential voices calling for action on global climate change.

Presidents may be as different as Bush and Obama in their experience, ability, values, and political alliances, but the system has its own logic that creates enormous barriers to change from within, even by those at the pinnacles of power. That is why the leadership to transform our economic system must come from millions of committed people organizing as citizens to create a compelling people-power counterforce to Wall Street's money.

A Nonconfrontational Leadership Style

Black men do not get ahead in a white world by being confrontational. They get ahead by gaining the trust and confidence of whites through building a reputation for being wise, competent, nonconfrontational bridge builders. Being biracial, growing up in multiple cultures, organizing competing factions in Chicago ghettos, excelling at Harvard Law School, and serving as president of the prestigious *Harvard Law Review*, Barack Obama mastered the arts of bridge building and nonconfrontational leadership.

No-Drama Obama keeps his cool almost to a fault, takes a problem-solving approach to each issue, assumes the good faith of the participants, and looks for win-win solutions. This style has been a key to his extraordinary accomplishments and served him well during the election.

Unfortunately, U.S. presidents face a divisive Washington political system that puts winning ahead of problem solving. It is owned by Wall Street interests that see no need to compromise and will by any means resist political initiatives that do not give them new rights or provide them with new subsidies.

Attempting to engage in good-faith problem solving or negotiation when the necessary actions require stripping Wall Street of its political power, public subsidies, and its ability to create phantom-wealth fortunes is a futile exercise.

The times require the kind of hard-knuckle, head-knocking realpolitik that is neither Obama's style nor his forte. He got his baptism by fire in this regard to achieve an extraordinary victory on health care. Perhaps it will prove to be a positive start.

President Obama is a fast learner and the most able and sympathetic president we are likely to get in a long time. For him or any other president to stand up and confront the beast, however, we the people must create the necessary political imperative and cover.

The Lack of an Articulated New Economy Model

Two established schools of economic thought frame the public debate regarding appropriate responses to the economic crash: market fundamentalism and Keynesianism.

Market fundamentalism is also known as the Chicago School because of the influence of a group of economists led by Milton Friedman at the University of Chicago. More ideology than science, market fundamentalism calls for privatizing public assets and services, leaving resource-allocation decisions exclusively to market forces, and limiting government's role to enforcing contracts and protecting property rights. This school has prevailed for more than thirty years and provided the intellectual justification for the deregulation that enabled the reckless and unaccountable concentration of economic power and crashed the economy.

Keynesian economics is the only school of thought that offers a recognized counter to the Chicago School in policy circles. According to Keynesianism, optimal economic function depends on government intervention. It asserts that the aggregate demand created by households, businesses, and government is the most important driving force in the market and that only government can manage that demand to create and maintain price stability.

When the financial markets crashed, some market

fundamentalists called for subjecting failing banks to market discipline by letting them fail. Keynesian pragmatists, however, recognized that given their size and interlinking derivatives contracts, this would crash the whole economy and thereby extract an intolerable price from the innocent as well as the guilty.

President Obama staffed his key economic positions with Wall Street insiders who have market fundamentalist sentiments, but they lean toward Keynesianism in that they recognize the need for government intervention to stimulate demand and keep money flowing in times of economic downturn. So they picked up seamlessly on the bank bailout from where the Bush administration left off. Unlike the Bush administration, however, Obama's economic team quickly added economic stimulus money to keep people working, to provide unemployment payments for the majority of those who weren't, and to create new green jobs — far better choices than allowing the money system to collapse entirely and a big improvement on the Bush administration's bank-bailout-only response.

Keynesians, however, still share the market fundamentalist obsession with GDP growth as the defining economic objective and true measure of economic performance, take institutions as a given rather than a policy choice, and make no distinction between phantom wealth and real wealth. In short, their guiding intellectual frame includes none of these essential elements of the New Economy. The options on the screen of the economists who defined the options available to President Obama were limited to those that fit the frame of one of the two prevailing schools of economics.

Under a New Economy frame, the goal vis-à-vis Wall Street would have been to transform the money system from a phantom-wealth system to a living real-wealth system (see chapter 13). They would have taken over failing banks, negotiated financial settlements with creditors at steeply discounted prices, shut down operations engaged in derivative scams and speculation, and restructured depository banking operations to spin off individual units as independent, locally owned community banks, mostly organized as nonprofits or cooperatives.

Obviously, restructuring the banking system takes more time than simply pouring in cheap money at the top in the hope that credit will start flowing again — which it didn't. Instead, the taxpayer money was diverted to bonuses, dividends, takeovers, and the purchase of Treasury bonds the government had sold to fund the bailout. This money would have had far more positive effect if Wall Street had been forced to absorb its losses and the government had instead flowed the money into the economy at the bottom, where it could have kept people working and in their homes. How different things might now be!

With a New Economy frame, the federal government would also have placed the Federal Reserve under government supervision and used its facilities to support a restructuring of the financial system and provide interest-free financing for a greatly expanded Main Street stimulus program.

Such a dramatic departure from business as usual, however, would have required a team of strong leaders working from a shared framework understood and embraced by a major segment of the public. Tragically, the education and experience of our leaders — including President Obama — and the general public have been limited to economic models that are either actively destructive or seriously limited.

Most of the New Economy ideas have been around for a long time. However, no established school of economic thought has emerged to pull them together into a coherent holistic framework taught and promoted as a basis for legislative and administrative action by government. Ecological economics is making an essential contribution to creating economic models that incorporate a strong ecological perspective, but it has done little to develop an institutional analysis or to translate its models into frameworks for institutional restructuring.

There is a field of institutional economics, but its members mostly work within what is essentially a market fundamentalist frame with a focus on transaction costs. Political economists, who generally bring a larger perspective, tend to be sidelined because of political economy's historical association with Marxism. Moreover, their primary interest tends to be in studying economic ideologies as phenomena to be explained rather than as sources of practical policy guidance.

Again, it remains to the institutions of global civil society to articulate and popularize a sound and compelling New Economy policy framework that includes a strong institutional component. The New Economics Foundation in London has been engaging New Economy policy issues for many years. As discussed elsewhere, a number of new groups have formed since September 2008 to carry forward this work, including the New Economy Working Group, the New Economy Network, the New Economics Institute, and the American Sustainable Business Council. Among the existing schools of economics, ecological economics is probably best positioned to take the leadership on the academic side. I hope that it may yet rise to this challenge.

THE UNDERLYING GRASSROOTS CONSENSUS

Political divisions among grassroots organizations tend to obscure an almost universal sense of having been betrayed by distant institutions that act contrary to society's interests. The Wall Street bailout is a particular focus of outrage. Taking money from struggling taxpayers in order to give it to Wall Street bankers so they could pay themselves bonuses for crashing the economy spurred outrage across the political spectrum. The Supreme Court decision in *Citizens United v. the Federal Election Commission*, which gave corporations carte blanche to buy elections, added to the nonpartisan outrage. Follow-up polls reported that the Supreme Court's decision was opposed by 80 percent of Americans, including 76, 81, and 85 percent of Republicans, Independents, and Democrats, respectively — a truly extraordinary consensus in this time of political division.[2]

The Wall Street–Washington Axis

The primary division among the outraged would appear to be between conservatives, who focus their anger on government, and liberals, who focus it on Wall Street. The debate about whether to blame government or Wall Street obscures the real issue, which is the undemocratic, elitist alliance between big business and big government so dramatically exposed by post-crash events.

Whether the blame lies more with Wall Street or with Washington is largely beside the point. The problem can be resolved only by citizen action at both ends of the axis to break up Wall Street financial institutions, get big money out of politics, democratize the economy, and hold Washington politicians accountable to the popular will.

The sense that Wall Street and Washington are running out of control in pursuit of agendas contrary to the interests of ordinary people is the basis for a powerful political realignment supportive of a New Economy agenda of institutional transformation to root both economic and political power in people and community.

The more important division appears to be more psychological than ideological, as reflected by the more visible distinctions between the Tea Party and the Coffee Party. Both have launched political movements in response to the outrage generated by the Wall Street–Washington axis. Their look and emotional tone, however, could scarcely be more different.

The nearly all-white Tea Party appeals to the negative emotions of fear and anger and mobilizes primarily around outraged opposition to Washington. Many of the placards and slogans favored by its members in demonstrations are blatantly racist.

Yet despite the strong streak of antigovernment libertarianism, the Tea Party is no friend of Wall Street. One of its major complaints against Washington is that it bailed out Wall Street banks rather than letting them fail. The sidebar on the About Us page of its Web site featured several decidedly anti–Wall Street jokes, including[3]

- What is the only difference between Wall Street and the Monopoly game? Wall Street controls all the "Get Out of Jail Free" cards.
- The U.S. has made a new weapon that destroys people but keeps the buildings standing. It's called the stock market.
- CEO – Chief Embezzlement Officer
- CFO – Corporate Fraud Officer

The Tea Party has no more love for Wall Street than it has for Washington.

By contrast, the multiracial and multicultural Coffee Party appeals to the positive emotions of love and hope and mobilizes around calls to engage in positive problem solving. According to its Web site, it "demand[s] a government that responds to the needs of the majority of its citizens as expressed by our votes and by our voices, *NOT corporate interests as expressed by misleading advertisements and campaign contributions*" (emphasis in the original). [4]

A Focal Point for Mobilization

These two parties define the most salient political division of our time: one appealing to anger and confrontation; the other, to love and problem solving. Both start from a nearly identical concern that a Wall Street–Washington axis has stolen our money and country and denied us our rights. Each has its distinctive strengths and limitations; they differ mainly in how they seek resolution.

Unless accompanied by positive problem solving, rage is blind, easily manipulated by hate mongers, and rarely contributes to positive solutions.

On the other hand, love and problem solving alone are unlikely to be effective when there is no potential resolution that can simultaneously fulfill Wall Street's unquenchable thirst for unearned profits and obscene bonuses, achieve a just distribution of material wealth, and bring humans into balance with the biosphere. Such a resolution will require determined resistance combined with hardball negotiation while those who share a commitment to good-faith problem solving engage in a search for real solutions — rather as President Obama finally grabbed the political ball and ran health care reform through Congress.

Three objects of public outrage cut across the political spectrum and provide potential for building a broadly based political alliance devoted to confronting and stripping the Wall Street–Washington axis of its power:

1. The no-strings Washington bailout of too-big-to-fail Wall Street banks

2. The *Citizens United* Supreme Court decision that freed corporations from crucial restraints on their ability to buy elections

3. The corrupting influence that corporate money, perks,

and the revolving door between Congress and lobbying firms exert on legislation and attempts at regulation

▸•◆•◆•◂

Until there is a serious shift in public policy toward the New Economy framework, the gap between the economic fortunes of Wall Street and those of Main Street will endure. This will assure that the window of opportunity for broadly based political organizing remains open indefinitely. The initiative, however, lies with us, not with President Obama.

His options are limited by the realities of Wall Street's hold on the Washington political establishment, his personal style, the lack of established support for a recognized New Economy economic model, and the perennial contradiction facing those who seek to transform the institutions that are the source of their authority. He can provide leadership toward a New Economy agenda only when we the people create the political imperative for him to do so.

This may not be so difficult as it first appears. Despite our political divisions, we have a nearly universal national consensus on a major issue: the illegitimate alliance of government and corporate power that mocks the democracy we thought we had and strips all but the richest among us of a political voice. The Wall Street–Washington axis presents a powerful unifying focus for mobilizing to create a new political context.

►•◆•◆•◄

CHAPTER 18

CHANGE THE STORY, CHANGE THE FUTURE

Whoever tells the stories of a nation need not care who
makes its laws.

ATTRIBUTED TO ANDREW FLETCHER,
SCOTTISH PATRIOT (1653–1716)

The greatest barrier to the economic transformation we
seek is not corrupt politicians, greedy CEOs, or even the
destructive institutions discussed in previous pages. It is a
flawed cultural story that misinforms our collective understanding of our nature and possibilities as humans and of the
world we inhabit.

STORY POWER

Some years ago the Filipino activist-philosopher Nicanor
Perlas shared with me the insight that each of the three primary institutional sectors has a distinctive competence in
institutional power. The distinctive power of government is
coercion. The distinctive power of business is financial. The
distinctive power of civil society is cultural.

As a civil society, we lack the police and military powers of
the state and the financial power of business. Our advantage
lies with the power of authentic moral values communicated
through authentic cultural stories.

This simple frame helped me see the extent to which the global citizen resistance against the use of multilateral trade agreements centered on a contest between competing stories. According to the story fabricated and promoted as the prevailing conventional wisdom by Wall Street interests:

> The elimination of barriers to the free flow of trade and investment through multilateral trade agreements is bringing universal peace, prosperity, and democracy to all the world's peoples and nations.

Wow, that sounds wonderful. But something was amiss on the ground.

An initially small group of citizen activists from around the world began meeting to share their experiences with the actual outcomes of these agreements. They found a consistent pattern of results wholly contrary to the corporate story. They organized to break the silence and spread the real story:

> Multilateral trade agreements are freeing global corporations from restrictions on their ability to exploit workers, ignore community interests, circumvent democracy, pollute the environment, and expropriate the resources of poor countries, with devastating consequences for people, community, democracy, and nature.

The civil society story trumped the corporate story, even though corporations controlled the money and the media, for the simple reason that it was true. This awareness changed the political context of corporate-sponsored international trade negotiations and brought them to a near standstill.

That insight regarding the pivotal nature of framing stories led me to see the much larger story at stake in the struggle between global people power and the axis of Wall

Street's financial power and Washington's coercive power. Here is one version:

> Competition is a law of nature, the foundation of all progress, and has been the key to human success since the beginning of time. Consistent with nature's way, it is our human nature to be violent, greedy, and individualistic competitors. It is all to the good, and there is no alternative.
>
> The invisible hand of the unregulated free market channels our competitive energy in ways that increase efficiency, drive innovation, and optimize the allocation of resources to maximize society's wealth and thereby the well-being of all. We have two civic duties: to consume and to seek the maximum financial return on our investment as our contribution to maximizing the growth of the economy, which is the measure of our progress and prosperity as a society.
>
> Beware of socialists who want to strip away your freedoms and kill the engine of prosperity by taxing your income and requiring corporations to sacrifice a margin of their profit in the name of some supposed higher public purpose, such as a more equitable distribution of wealth. The only public interest is the aggregation of private interests. You are the best judge of how to spend your money to your greatest private benefit.
>
> Far from being a problem, inequality is essential to social order and prosperity. It creates wealthy individuals who are able to bear the risks of investing in the creation of jobs and a working class motivated by economic insecurity to work hard at those jobs at a globally competitive wage—thus creating the rising tide that lifts all boats. If a few get rich, instead of condemning them out of envy, celebrate their good fortune, because as the rich get

> richer, wealth trickles down and we all get richer. In America, anyone can succeed who applies himself. Failure is a sign of incompetence or a flawed character.

We hear elements of this story so often they run through our heads as a constant refrain telling us that the world of our dreams isn't possible.

The genius of this debilitating story is that it becomes self-affirming. Our media bombard us with stories of violence, greed, and individualism promoted and rewarded by corrupt economic institutions. These institutions appoint power-driven personalities to their highest positions and then celebrate their political and financial success, promoting them to society as role models. When this perversion goes unchallenged in public forums, most people simply accept at face value the message that such individuals do indeed represent the best of our human nature, instead of recognizing them as pathological exceptions to the healthier human norm.

We humans can be conditioned to believe some weird things. To understand how this happens and to resist such manipulation, it is helpful to understand the nature and role of culture in social organization.

CULTURE AS A FOUNDATION OF COMMUNITY LIFE AND SOCIAL CONTROL

Culture is the system of beliefs, values, perceptions, and social relations that encodes the shared learning of a particular human group that is essential to its orderly social function. As a culture's defining stories change through shared learning, its collective behavior realigns accordingly — the subject of the next chapter.

The processes by which culture shapes our perceptions and behavior occur mostly at an unconscious level. It rarely occurs to us to ask whether the reality we perceive through the lens of the culture within which we grow up is the "true" reality. We take for granted that it is.

For five thousand years, successful imperial rulers have recognized that their power rests on their ability to fabricate cultural stories that evoke fear, alienation, learned helplessness, and the individual's dependence on the imperial power of a strong ruler.

The falsified culture induces a kind of cultural trance in which we are conditioned to deny our inherent human capacity for responsible self-direction, sharing, and cooperation that is an essential foundation of democratic self-rule. The falsified stories create an emotional bond between the ruled and their rulers while alienating the ruled from one another and the living Earth, eroding relations of mutual self-help, and reducing the ruled to a state of resigned dependence.

Corporate advertisers and public relations propagandists have mastered and professionalized the arts of such cultural manipulation, particularly through corporate-controlled mass media. They would have us base our individual identity on the corporate logos we wear, the branded products we consume, the corporation for which we work, and the Wall Street–funded political party to which we belong.

Awakening Cultural Consciousness

Cultural manipulation becomes less effective as an instrument of social control as more of us become familiar with cultures distinctly different from our own. Such experiences awake our consciousness to the reality that culture is a social construct subject to choice and falsification.

In the United States, the process of awakening received a significant boost from the civil rights movement in the 1950s and '60s as millions of people awakened to the reality that relations between races are defined by cultural codes that have little to do with reality.

After people learned to recognize the difference between reality and an unexamined belief system in reference to race relations, it became easier to see similar distortions in the cultural codes that defined the relations between men and women, people and the environment, heterosexuals and homosexuals, and people and corporations.[1] The civil rights

A COUNCIL OF STORYTELLERS

One of the most important contributions one can make to movement building is to organize forums in which small groups of people regularly gather to share their stories and build the relationships of mutual trust and understanding that make effective teamwork possible even in times of extreme stress.

Much of my appreciation for the power of such spaces comes from my participation in the formation and early work of the International Forum on Globalization. The IFG grew out of a meeting in 1994 of a few dozen of the world's most dedicated activists engaged in one way or another with what Wall Street interests were calling "globalization."

We came from many different countries with widely different experiences, talents, and takes on what globalization meant. Through the sharing of our respective experiences and insights, we were able to discern the big-picture story of what the globalization that Wall Street corporations had in mind was really about, and we crafted a common language for communicating it beyond our circle.

movement thus prepared the way for the social movements that followed.

Globally, a rapid increase in international travel, exchange, and communication has exposed millions of people to sometimes unsettling, usually enriching encounters with cultures that initially seem exotic and perhaps uncomfortable but quickly come to seem normal and natural.

That experience has enabled many of us to see our own

Through our sharing, we developed genuine affection for one another and came to know, respect, and trust our differences, which allowed us to work in common cause across great geographic distances with brief e-mails as our only form of communication between face-to-face meetings.

Sometimes we acted as a group to hold teach-ins, issue joint statements, or coauthor papers and books. Smaller clusters shared resources to advance particular campaigns. Mostly we worked with and through our respective back-home constituencies, communicating our particular take on the big-picture story in meetings and through public presentations, publications, and media interviews.

Individual seeds of a new understanding were planted in many places. They germinated, took root, and grew to produce new seeds that multiplied with extraordinary speed. Within a few years, a powerful global social force was unleashed in an effective challenge to one of Wall Street's most destructive agendas.

culture and the larger world in a new light. The experience of cultural awakening has become a contagious, liberating process on a global scale that involves hundreds of millions of people and transcends the barriers of race, class, and religion.

The awakened consciousness is relatively immune to the distorted cultural conditioning promoted by corporate media, advertising, and political demagogues. For those who share this experience, racism, sexism, homophobia, and consumerism are more easily seen for what they are — a justification for domination, exploitation, and violence against life.

As the awakening spreads, so too does the potential for rapid social learning based on the conscious examination and revision of prevailing cultural stories.

Story Power Trumps the Power of Guns and Money

Just as fabricated stories are an instrument of social control, so authentic stories are an instrument of liberation. As the fabricated story that there is no alternative to the capitalist system is replaced by the New Economy story that it is possible to create a world of strong communities and living economies, people begin organizing to make the new story a reality in the places where they live.

Corporations command the power of money. Governments command the coercive power of the police and military. The power of civil society is the power of authentic values and aspirations communicated through stories of possibility.

At first blush, pitting mere stories against the financial power of Wall Street's modern robber barons and the police and military power of the state would seem to be the fantasy of would-be martyrs. It is not, however, so naive as it might at first sound.

Despite appearances, civil society holds the upper hand against Empire. The power of authentic stories ultimately trumps all other forms of power, because these other forms of power depend on the stories that lend them a patina of legitimacy. Unlike the fabricated stories of Empire, the stories of authentic values and lessons of authentic cultures resonate with what we know in our being to be true.

The New Economy story that we humans are capable of creating a vibrant, peaceful, cooperative world bursting with life resonates deep within most people. Once that connection is made, the trance is broken and we are free to find a path to reclaim control of our lives and get on with living a beautiful world into being.

HOW STORIES CHANGE

Every great social movement begins with a set of ideas validated, internalized, and then shared and amplified through media, grassroots organizations, and thousands, even millions, of conversations. Those for whom a truth strikes a resonant chord, and who hear it acknowledged by others, share it with their own circles. The new story spreads out in ever-widening circles that connect and intermingle. A story of unrealized possibility gradually replaces the falsified story that there is no alternative to the status quo. The prevailing culture begins to shift, and the collective behavior of the society changes with it.

For the civil rights and women's movements, the old story said: *Women and people of color have no soul. Less than human, they have no natural rights. They can find fulfillment only through faithful service to their white male masters.* For the environmental movement, one version of the old story said: *Nature was given to man by God to do with as man pleases.* A secular version says: *Nature has no value beyond its market price and is properly used for whatever purpose generates the greatest financial return.*

A profound cultural shift took root in the decades between

1950 and 1980. It was an epic period of cultural awakening and social restructuring that began with the civil rights movement, which was born in part from the words and writing of W. E. B. DuBois, founder of the National Association for the Advancement of Colored People (NAACP), and was carried forward by others such as the Reverend Martin Luther King Jr. Communicated through books, periodicals, and speeches, the ideas of these and other leaders inspired and shaped countless conversations, particularly in black churches, about race and the possibilities of integration based on a full recognition of the inherent humanity of people of all races.

The vision of possibility gave birth to social and political upheavals in the American South during the 1950s and '60s. Thinkers, writers, and activists who embraced the idea of integration engaged in verbal combat with those who defended the status quo as legitimated by the old story. As the story of possibility gained currency, proponents engaged in nonviolent civil disobedience in the form of sit-ins in segregated facilities, which began to create a new reality and set the stage for political demands to replace laws that institutionalized the old story with laws that institutionalized the new.

In 1963, as the civil rights movement was gaining traction, Betty Friedan published *The Feminine Mystique*, calling attention to a vague dissatisfaction plaguing housewives. It touched a deep chord and became the focus of thousands of living room conversations in which women shared their own stories. These women had been raised on the story that the key to a woman's happiness was to find the right man, marry him, and devote her life to his service.

Prior to these conversations, the woman whose experience failed to conform to the prevailing cultural story was culturally conditioned to believe the failure was due to a flaw in her character that she should strive to correct. As women gathered and shared their personal stories, they affirmed the idea put forward by Friedan that the story was working for few, if any, women. This meant that the flaw lay not with themselves but with a false story. Those whom these discussions initially liberated lent their voices to a growing chorus telling a story of women's rights and abilities. Millions of women were soon spreading a new gender story that has unleashed the feminine as a powerful force for global transformation.

Many trace the origin of the modern environmental movement to Rachel Carson's *Silent Spring*, published in 1962. It, too, stimulated countless conversations about the human relationship to nature that began to challenge the old stories and build the foundation of a new social consensus. The challenge spread through media and academic programs.

The modern voluntary simplicity movement, which presents a frontal challenge to the story that material consumption is the key to personal happiness, represents an important thread in the emerging New Economy movement. It received early impetus from Duane Elgin's influential book, *Voluntary Simplicity: Toward a Way of Life That Is Outwardly Simple, Inwardly Rich*, first published in 1981. His ideas struck an immediate chord with people who shared their stories in countless conversations that affirmed the ancient religious teaching that we truly come alive as we moderate material consumption and gain control of our time to devote more of our lives to the things that bring true happiness, like nurturing the relationships of caring families and communities. Millions of people were liberated from the trance induced by corporate advertisers and were inspired to restructure their lives.

Our New Economy messages and conversations challenge a number of defining cultural stories, including those that would have us believe:

- The MYTH that it is our inherent human nature to be individualistic, materialistic, greedy, competitive, and violent

- The ILLUSION that we live on an open frontier of

endless resources that are free for the taking to grow the economy

- The BELIEF that money is wealth, money defines the value of life, making money is our highest human calling, and everything related to money is best left to the market

Previous chapters have pointed out that in fact:

- The human brain is wired to support creativity, cooperation, and life in community. That is our nature. The prevalence of materialism, greed, competition, and violence common in modern society is a symptom of severe cultural and institutional dysfunction

- We humans inhabit a wondrous but finite living planet with a self-organizing biosphere to which we must adapt our lives and economies

- Money, unrelated to the creation of anything of real value, is phantom wealth, an accounting chit that has no intrinsic value, indeed no existence outside the human mind. In a mature belief system, life is the true measure of value and money's only legitimate use is in life's service. An obsession with making money is a sign of psychological and social dysfunction. With proper rules, the market is an essential and beneficial partner of an active civil society and democratic government — each in its appropriate role. Absent proper rules it becomes a capitalist weapon of mass destruction

▶•◆•◆•◀

The human brain processes the massive flow of data from our senses through an interpretive lens by which it distinguishes the significant from the inconsequential and draws out its meaning, which in turn shapes our behavioral response. "This plant will kill you. That one is food."

The lens reflects both the individual learning of personal experience and the shared learning of the tribe communicated through its framing cultural stories. These stories, which the tribe's storytellers pass from generation to generation, shape our collective identity and allow us to act coherently as a group in the interest of all. "This is who we are, what we value, and how we behave."

The work of professional propagandists and advertisers is to use the mass media to displace the tribe's authentic cultural stories with fabricated stories that support behavior that serves the interests of their clients, whether it be to vote for a particular political candidate or to buy a particular product. They succeed by playing to raw, animal emotions of fear and anger that activate our brain's primitive reptilian core, unhampered by the conscious mind. This is the source of the demagogue's power.

The power of civil society is the power of authentic stories that appeal to the higher-order emotions of love and caring. These stories awaken our capacity for conscious, reasoned choice and are the basis of our human capacity for responsibility and cooperation in the interest of the whole. Authentic stories liberate the human consciousness, build immunity to cultural manipulation, and give us the courage and insight to see the future that is the objective of our voyage in search of ecological balance, equitable distribution, and living democracy.

CHAPTER 19

▶•◆•◆•◀

LEARNING TO LIVE, LIVING TO LEARN

Once an emergent phenomenon has appeared, it can't be changed by working backwards, by changing the local parts that gave birth to it. You can only change an emergent phenomenon by creating a countervailing force of greater strength. This means that the work of change is to start over, to organize new local efforts, connect them to each other, and know that their values and practices can emerge as something even stronger.

MARGARET J. WHEATLEY

Midway in my international development career I had a defining learning experience. I was engaging the question of what makes the difference between development initiatives that achieve sustained positive changes in people's lives and those that produce only fleeting, or even negative, changes. As I examined the experience of a number of successful interventions in different countries of Asia, the answer revealed itself.

In the unsuccessful initiatives, outside experts were brought in to prepare a detailed blueprint with clear rules, budgets, timelines, and benchmarks. A public or private bureaucracy then attempted to implement those plans through a top-down process of command and control. This was the practice for most official development projects, which have an impressive record of failure.

Successful initiatives, by contrast, arose from the bottom up through a thoughtful process of trial-and-error learning through doing, which gradually created a system of organized support through which the learning could be shared and others could be guided in replications. I learned later that others who had made similar discoveries called the process social learning: the process by which groups of people, and even whole societies, learn new ways of being and relating through a shared learning experience.

It all seemed so obvious once I saw it. Blueprints are useful for designing and constructing buildings and machines based on established mechanical principles in static settings. Social systems are living, complex, dynamic, and constantly evolving as they learn from shared experience. They self-organize around ideas and relationships. The organism, not the machine, provides the appropriate metaphor. The relevant knowledge resides not in the heads of outside experts but in the people who populate the system. The challenge is to help them recognize, organize, and use that knowledge in ever more effective ways.

A THREEFOLD SOCIAL LEARNING STRATEGY

Stories alone do not, of course, bring down the institutions of Empire or put in place the rules, relationships, and institutions of a New Economy. These must be lived into being from the bottom up through dynamic self-organizing social learning processes. Lessons from this experience then inform specific initiatives that demand changes in the rules that determine whose rights and interests the power of the state will protect and advance.

Through these social learning processes, people innovate, create, learn to relate in new ways, and share the lessons of their experience. Individual learning translates into community learning that translates into species learning.

The overall process has three primary elements. Through their varied initiatives, participants:

1. CHANGE THE DEFINING STORIES OF THE MAINSTREAM CULTURE. As was already discussed, every great transformational social movement begins with new ideas and conversations that challenge and ultimately change a prevailing cultural story. In the case of the New Economy, we must change the prevailing stories by which we understand the nature of wealth, the purpose of the economy, our relationship to a living Earth, and the possibilities of our human nature. Through public presentations, books, magazines, talk shows, and the Internet's many communications tools, millions of people are spreading stories of New Economy possibilities, in part through action, which inspires further discussion and new personal choices.

2. CREATE A NEW ECONOMIC REALITY FROM THE BOTTOM UP. Many of those who have been inspired by some aspect of the New Economy story are already engaged in initiatives that are building the foundation of strong local living economies. They are establishing and supporting locally owned human-scale businesses and family farms that create regional self-reliance in food, energy, and other basic essentials. They are moving their money to local banks and credit unions, retrofitting buildings for energy efficiency, and changing land-use policies to favor compact communities, reduce auto dependence, and reclaim agricultural and forest lands.

3. CHANGE THE RULES TO SUPPORT THE VALUES AND INSTITUTIONS OF THE EMERGENT NEW REALITY. The rules put in place by Wall Street lobbyists put the economic rights of global financiers and corporations

ahead of the economic rights of ordinary people, place-based communities, and even nations. As we change the story and build appropriate institutions from the bottom up, we gain the political traction needed to change the rules to support democratic self-determination at the lowest feasible level of systems organization.

Work on each of these elements is complementary and simultaneous. It necessarily begins with a story of unrealized possibility that serves as a guiding beacon for those who are working to create a new reality, which in turn creates practical new experience to guide those who are changing the rules.

Nothing communicates the new story as powerfully as successful on-the-ground demonstrations, particularly when they are on the scale of a town, city, or region. New stories and practical demonstrations build a political constituency to support rule changes that in turn accelerate the emergence of new demonstrations and further spread the story — leading ultimately to national- and global-scale change.

Recall that chapter 13 identified seven critical system interventions. Think of these as natural clusters of activity, each focused on a key system-change leverage point. In each instance, success requires the cooperative effort of many groups, some working on changing a defining story, others creating new on-the-ground realities, and others working to change relevant rules.

Take the Living Indicators cluster as an example. Change starts with changing the story about the purpose of the economy. Instead of growing GDP and inflating share prices, the economy's proper purpose is to support the healthy development and function of people, families, communities, and nature. Economic performance is properly assessed against these outcomes.

Many groups are engaged in communicating the new story by promoting living-indicator projects in their communities or by carrying out studies that compare the performance of regional and national economies against a variety of living indicators. Others are mobilizing political support for rules that direct national statistical bureaus to develop and report on new indicators and that require other government agencies to use them as the basis for assessing program performance and policy options.

Successful social movements are emergent, evolving, radically self-organizing, and involve the dedicated efforts of many people, each finding the role that best uses his or her gifts and passions. Social movements grow and evolve around framing ideas and mutually supportive relationships instead of through top-down direction. New ideas gain traction or not depending on their inherent appeal and utility. As individual groups find one another, new alliances may emerge or not, depending on what works for those involved in the moment. Some alliance are fleeting; others endure.

As a social movement develops, multiple sources of leadership are essential. Any individual or group that presumes to be the leader of the whole or aspires to organize a central coordinating body to impose order on the chaos does not understand the process.

A SUPPORTIVE INSTITUTIONAL INFRASTRUCTURE

Four professional fields bring specialized expertise to the work of defining and propagating the cultural stories by which we understand our nature and possibilities: the media, education, religion, and the arts. Call these the cultural worker professions. Collectively they shape and disseminate the framing cultural stories of the society, including those by which we collectively define the economy's proper purpose and structure.

Each of these fields is subject to co-optation by Wall Street in the service of money. Each can choose to contribute to our collective liberation by helping to shape and communicate the new stories, encourage participation in initiatives that are creating the new reality, facilitate the sharing of lessons, and build political support for changing the rules.

In many instances, the institutions that employ the majority of the members of each of these professional fields are structured and managed in the service of money. Professionals thus encumbered who make the choice to serve life must decide whether to stay with their institutions and work for transformation from within or leave to join those on the outside who are creating the institutions of the future.

Here are some of the issues and possibilities.

Media

The profit-driven, advertising-dependent communications model of the corporate media is ideally suited to serving Wall Street interests. The consolidation of the mass print and broadcast media under the control of corporate conglomerates has reduced much of the mainstream news reporting to inane, politically slanted commentary limited to the market fundamentalist economic frame favorable to Wall Street interests.

The other end of the media spectrum is anchored by the service-driven communications model of nonprofit independent media outlets that democratize media control and create a vast potential to hasten a global embrace of the life-affirming cultural values of Earth Community.

YES! Magazine, a nonprofit independent communications organization for which I serve as board chair, is an example of the potential of this model. The fact that *YES!* is thriving even at this time when many conventional media outlets are failing suggests that this is a viable model responding to an important felt need.

We all live in the midst of a communications revolution that is linking the world in a seamless web of communication and information. This capability can be used to strengthen elite control or to provide an open-access information commons in support of the social learning processes that are building the New Economy.

Advancing a turning from the autocratic corporate media model to the democratic independent media model is an essential priority for citizen initiatives and policy advocacy. Many civil society initiatives are already demonstrating the possibilities in community newspapers and radio stations, independent media centers, blogs, and podcasts.

Other citizen initiatives are working to reverse corporate media concentration, reclaim the communications frequency spectrum, and maintain the Internet as an open-access resource. Some of these initiatives are opening political deliberation to diverse voices and lively debate. Others are exposing the bias and banality of corporate media and demanding accountability.

Education

As Wall Street has rewritten the tax laws to absolve corporations of their civic responsibility to pay their fair share of taxes, cash-strapped public schools and universities have turned to corporations for sponsorships, curriculum materials, and research grants. This has given corporations undue influence over the underlying academic culture to the detriment of the critical intellectual inquiry and teaching we so badly need.

This is one of the many reasons why reinstating a progressive tax system for both individuals and corporations is a high priority for a New Economy policy agenda. Corporations are properly required to support our educational institutions through taxes rather than through gifts that compromise the integrity of those institutions and their ability to produce creative, innovative citizens with critical minds.

The capacity and desire to learn are inherent in our human nature. Subjecting our children and young adults to test-driven regimentation isolated from the life of community suppresses this capacity and desire and is a poor substitute for real learning experience. We need education that prepares our young people for life and leadership in the vibrant human communities of the new human era that it falls to them to live into being.

The narrow discipline-oriented institutions of higher learning face a particular challenge. To become relevant they must take the following steps:

- Take down the walls that separate them from the community and engage in helping communities build local economies that function in harmony with their local ecosystems

- Organize faculty and students into interdisciplinary teams to engage in the study and design of critical institutional systems

- Teach history as an examination of the large forces that have shaped our past in search of insights into how large-scale social change happens and how it may be shaped by organized human intervention to put ourselves on a positive path

- Replace departments of economics with departments of applied ecology that incorporate economics as a subdiscipline and bring institutional and ecological frameworks to the fore

- Feature human developmental psychology courses that explore how cultural and institutional experiences shape or impede our individual progress to a fully mature human consciousness

- Replace the machine metaphor with the living-organism metaphor as the defining intellectual frame

- Assure that the perspective of the new biologists who strive to understand life on its own terms has a strong presence in biology departments

Such innovations are most likely to come one faculty member, one department, one school or university at a time at the beginning, but they will quickly grow to critical mass as the relevance of the New Economy system frame becomes more evident.

Religion

The New Economy must be built on the foundation of a moral and spiritual awakening. Faith institutions have an essential role to play in advancing this awakening, as well as in bridging the class, race, and religious divides easily exploited by political powers that want to keep us dependent on the centralized power of the Wall Street–Washington axis.

Sermons and adult education programs can raise the moral issues relating to human responsibility for one another and the living Earth. They might begin by examining Wall Street culture and institutions from the perspective of the table in chapter 9 contrasting the seven deadly sins with the seven life-serving virtues. They might encourage people to share and examine their personal beliefs regarding the potential and limitations of our human nature and the implications for our prospect of achieving each of the seven interventions of the New Economy policy agenda outlined in chapter 13.

They can form partnerships with faith institutions that follow different traditions and minister to people from other races, ethnicities, and classes to share perspective on the profound moral choices at hand.

I am privileged to count among my friends and colleagues the three Seattle-based "interfaith amigos" — Rabbi Ted Falcon, Pastor Don Mackenzie, and Sheikh Jamal Rahman — who are modeling interfaith inquiry and inviting fellow searchers from the three Abrahamic faiths of Judaism, Christianity, and Islam to join in their dialogue.[1]

As with educational transformation, the transformation of our faith institutions begins one church, synagogue, temple, and mosque at a time, with the potential to build quickly toward critical mass as more faith institutions come to understand what is at stake and what transformational possibilities are at hand.

The Arts

Among the four groups of professionals named, artists are the most likely to self-identify as cultural workers. The best among them are truth tellers who have the ability to awaken our minds from the cultural trance that leads us to consume harmful products, play the mark in Wall Street con games, and support public policies contrary to our interests.

Talented artists can help us see beauty, meaning, and possibility in what we may otherwise experience only as mundane and fragmented. They can take us on a journey to a future no one has yet visited to experience possibilities we may not have imagined.

I came to a deep appreciation of the profound potential of this aspect of the artist's craft through my friendship with Raffi Cavoukian. I met Raffi only as an adult but have been captivated by the magical quality of his music and its ability to awaken within both children and adults a profound yet playful appreciation of the beauty and possibilities of life. I see the evidence of his influence in the life of each of the many young people I meet from among the millions who grew up on his music.

In the middle of many of my public presentations on the New Economy, I play his "No Wall Too Tall,"[2] which he originally recorded for the launch of *Agenda for a New Economy*. It gets the whole auditorium dancing and unleashes an amazingly inspiring energy.[3]

Artists can use their craft to befuddle our minds, justify evil, and entice us into self-destructive behavior, as demonstrated by the many talented artists in the employ of Wall Street institutions. These corporate artists use their talents to cloud our ability to see the harmful side of Wall Street products, the deceits of its financial scams, and the real interests served by its favored public policies and political candidates. They earn high salaries, work with clear goals, and have impressive financial resources at their command.

Independent artists, by contrast, are commonly unorganized and simply trying to make a modest living producing works of grace and beauty.

Our movement needs the contribution of millions of artists who use their powers of perception and representation to liberate our consciousness, as articulated by Milenko Matanovic in the *YES! Magazine* issue on Art and Community:

> The artist endeavors to perceive directly, without filters or notions.... In the process the artist becomes more aware of the assumptions and myths that govern the world and so gains the ability to discard the obsolete, empower the appropriate, and create the new.... Images of the future generated through the power of imagination are essential to the health of all cultures, for a society's vitality is lost once its capacity to imagine is gone.... Artists can be a culture's scouts, forging paths into the future.[4]

My Bainbridge Island friend and colleague Bill Cleveland is collecting and sharing stories of a growing group of independent artists who are engaging whole communities to discover their inner beauty and creative potential through artistic experience. These artists work with children and adults involved in programs of community beautification and cultural enrichment to stage public productions. People who never thought of themselves as actors express and explore stories of themselves and their community in ways that heal and inspire. This strengthens the community's sense of itself and its readiness to engage together in community building and the creation of vibrant local living economies.[5]

MAKING A DIFFERENCE

For the many millions of us working to create a better world, it is easy to feel discouraged by the seeming insignificance of even major successes relative to the scale of the problems we face as a nation and a species. Consumed by the details and challenges of our daily engagements, we may easily lose sight of the big picture of the powerful social dynamic to which our work is contributing.

Step back from time to time; take a breath, look out beyond the immediate horizon to bring that big picture back into perspective.[6] Reflect in awe and wonder at the power of the larger social dynamic to which your work contributes.

So how do you know whether your work is contributing to a big-picture outcome? If you can answer yes to any one of the following five questions, then be assured that it is.

- Does it help discredit a false cultural story fabricated to legitimize relationships of domination and exploitation and to replace it with a true story describing unrealized possibilities for growing the real wealth of healthy communities?

- Is it connecting others of the movement's millions of leaders who didn't previously know one another, helping them find common cause and build relationships of mutual trust that allow them to speak honestly from

WHAT CAN YOU DO?

The first step in making a personal contribution to creating the New Economy is to take control of your life and declare your independence from Wall Street by joining the voluntary simplicity movement and cutting back on unnecessary consumption. Beyond that, shop at local independent stores where possible and purchase locally made goods when available. Make the same choices as to where you work and invest to the extent feasible.

Pay with cash at local merchants to save them the credit card fee. Pay your credit card balance when due and avoid using your credit card as an open line of credit. Do your banking with an independent local community bank or credit union that will invest your money back in your community. Green America provides an excellent free guide called *Investing in Communities* (greenamericatoday.org/PDF/GuideInvestCommunities .pdf).

The second step is to join with others in initiatives that contribute to any one or all of the five activities mentioned under "Making a Difference" on pages 269–272. Engage in conversations about our cultural stories. Facilitate new connections. Create liberated public spaces. Demonstrate new possibilities. Many specific possibilities are mentioned in chapter 16 under the heading "Two Epic Moments in the Great Democratic Experiment." Link your local initiatives into their hearts and to know that they can call on one another for support when needed?

- Is it creating and expanding liberated social spaces in which people experience the freedom and support to

national networks through groups like the American Independent Business Alliance (amiba.net), the Business Alliance for Local Living Economies (livingeconomies. org), and Transition Towns (transitiontowns.org).

Above all, engage in conversations about the realities of Wall Street, the difference between phantom wealth and real wealth, and the nature and possibilities of the New Economy. Be aware that economic reporting and commentary in the corporate media usually reflect a Wall Street phantom-wealth perspective. Listen with a skeptical ear and practice identifying the underlying fallacies. Invite your friends and colleagues to do the same.

Join or form a Common Security Club for mutual education and support in dealing with the economic crisis (extremeinequality.org/?p=92). Consider inviting a group of friends or neighbors to discuss *Agenda for a New Economy.* You can find a group discussion guide at greatturning.org, along with links to other New Economy discussion resources.

For all of the above, plus a wealth of stories and resources helpful in tracking the larger movement to which your work contributes, subscribe to *YES! Magazine* and draw on the wealth of resources on its Web site, yesmagazine.org.

You can find other links to resources on the New Economy Working Group site, neweconomyworkinggroup .org.

experiment with living the creative, cooperative, self-organizing relationships of the new story they seek to bring into the larger culture?

- Is it providing a public demonstration of the possibilities of a real-wealth economy?

- Is it mobilizing support for a rule change that will shift the balance of power from the people and institutions of the Wall Street phantom-wealth economy to the people and institutions of living-wealth Main Street economies?

These are useful guidelines for setting both individual and group priorities. Bear in mind that in a systems-change undertaking of this magnitude, there is no magic bullet and no one is going to make it happen on their own, so don't be discouraged if the world looks much the same today despite your special and heroic effort yesterday. It took five thousand years to create the mess we are in today. It will take more than a few days to set it right.

▶•◆•◆•◀

We humans have made enormous progress in our technological mastery, but we fall far short in our mastery of ourselves and the potential of our human consciousness. Failing to identify the true sources of our happiness and well-being, we worship at the altar of money to the neglect of the altar of life. Failing to distinguish between money and real wealth, we embrace illusion as reality, and enslavement to the institutions of Wall Street as liberty.

The implosion of the Wall Street phantom-wealth economy exposes how effective we can be in creating cultures and institutions that cultivate and celebrate the most pathological possibilities of our human nature. Let the ugliness that the implosion has revealed serve as an inspiration to finally get it right.

Our defining gift as humans is our power to choose, including our power to choose our collective future. It is a gift that comes with a corresponding moral responsibility to use that power in ways that work to the benefit of all people and the whole of life. Using that gift to best effect requires constant learning. Life is is our curriculum, and our assignment of the moment is to learn to live by the rules of the biosphere — which itself continues to learn and evolve. Learning is so embedded in the fabric of life that I've come to believe that it is integral to life's purpose.

We can, if we choose, replace cultures and institutions that celebrate and reward the pathologies of our lower human nature with cultures and institutions that celebrate and reward the capacities of our higher nature. We can turn as a species from perfecting our capacity for exclusionary competition to perfecting our capacity for inclusionary cooperation. We can share the good news that the healthy potential of our human nature yearns for liberation from cultural stories and institutional reward systems that have long suppressed it.

The liberation of this potential is the larger vision and goal of the New Economy agenda. It begins with clarifying our values and investing in growing the relationships of the caring communities that are the essential foundation of real wealth and security. As individuals and as a species, we can find our place of service to the larger community of life from which we separated during our species' adolescence and to which we must now return as responsible adults.

In closing, I want to take you on a brief visit to the future to see how our children may be living in 2084 if we succeed in navigating the turning from a phantom-wealth to a real-wealth economy.

EPILOGUE

▶•◆•◆•◀

THE VIEW FROM 2084

Simplification is not a commitment to abject poverty but a
choice to live more fully.

JIM WALLIS

The idea of deep and potentially wrenching change can be frightening. I have written the following fictional account of life in the real-wealth New Economy in the hope it may make such a life easier to visualize. I trust you will recognize the application of the principles outlined in previous chapters.

Some may be inclined to dismiss this hopeful vision as nothing more than a naive flight of fancy far beyond any possibility of becoming a reality. Anyone who has followed my writing knows I understand the seriousness of our situation and the immensity of the barriers against change.

Indeed, I sometimes wonder whether there is any reason not to give up, turn off the news, and wallow in self-indulgent pleasures until the inevitable system collapse. I suspect anyone who doesn't experience similar feelings from time to time is seriously out of touch with reality.

I am also aware, however, that to give in to cynicism and despair is to create a self-fulfilling prophecy. Furthermore, I know of no more fun and satisfying way to use the remainder of my days than engaging the creative challenge of helping to liberate the human spirit from cultural and institutional chains of our own making. The best part is that this work brings me into relationship with the world's most wonderfully thoughtful, creative, and inspiring people.

So join me now in a brief journey. A time machine has projected us into a future in which a real-wealth New Economy prevails. We find ourselves in a world of culturally vital, high-density communities with little evidence of either extreme poverty or extreme wealth, nestled in the midst of lush farmlands and natural habitats. These are clustered around urban centers featuring well-defined neighborhoods, efficient mass transit, walkable streets, rooftop gardens, and inviting parks. Here is my version of our report to the folks back home.

Dear friends and fellow bloggers back in 2010:

My trip to the future has been an experience far beyond my expectations. I landed in 2084 in the United States in a place very near where I grew up. I had been rather nervous about the whole thing, given the financial, social, and environmental disasters I left behind. It is pretty amazing to see how it worked out.

The history books tell of difficult times as the disasters you are experiencing played out, but people in communities all over the world rallied to the cause and created a new economy from the bottom up. The politicians eventually realized what was happening and jumped on the bandwagon just as it was about to pass them by. I love the result and would be tempted to stay and settle here permanently if that were an option, but the terms of my travel don't permit it — and I do miss you all.

Let me share a bit of what I'm seeing and experiencing. I think it will give you a sense of hope and strengthen your commitment to the New Economy agenda we were discussing before I left. Much of what I'm seeing validates the ideas we talked about. Feel free to share this report with others in the hope it may inspire them as well. So here goes:

This seems to be a truly middle-class society. I've found little evidence of more than modest distinctions between the richest and the poorest in terms of income, asset ownership, size of residence, and consumption. Most families own their own home and have an ownership stake in one or more businesses in their local economy. Paid employment seems to be organized to allow everyone ample time for family, friends, participation in community and political life, healthful physical activity, learning, and spiritual growth. People seem to be using that time fully.

Economists in this time measure wealth and well-being by indicators of the health and sustainable productivity of human, social, and living natural capital. Businesses are human-scale, locally owned, and dedicated to serving the people of the community. They take great pride in their contribution to securing the well-being of their community's children for generations to come.

I've seen no evidence of the grotesque, monotonous suburban sprawl so familiar to our own time. An old-timer told me that in the old days, as the price of oil became prohibitive, people began to abandon the suburbs. Rising energy costs and climate chaos disrupted long-distance food supply chains, and building materials became scarce. Governments responded by spending billions to deconstruct abandoned suburban buildings, salvage the materials for reuse in constructing new dwellings in compact communities, and then removed the asphalt and rebuilt the soil to support organic farming, grazing, and timber production.

Agrochemicals were banned. People seem to compost or recycle almost everything. I asked about waste dumps, but no one seemed to understand what I meant. They just don't throw things away.

I've learned that publicly traded for-profit global corporations went the way of the suburbs. Those that produced useful products were broken up into their component businesses and sold to their employees or to the communities in which they were located. Others eventually went bankrupt. Their intellectual assets were released to the public domain, and useful physical assets were sold at public auction.

The overall quantity of consumption appears modest by our standards, but the health and vitality of the children and of family and community life seem far richer. In my travels around the region, I'm impressed by the diversity of wildlife, the healthy appearance of forests and waterways, and the evident fertility of the soil.

Living off the returns from passive investments, financial speculation, collecting rents, gambling, and other unproductive activities is so unfamiliar that people are incredulous when I try to explain it to them. Their question is always the same: "Why would a civilized society tolerate anything like that?"

I get a similar puzzled response when I ask about crime and war. They say crime is rare. Some recall reading about war, terrorism, the arms industry, and outsized military budgets in history books, but they apparently have no experience of such things.

People here live in compact communities in modest but comfortable energy-efficient multifamily dwellings that run primarily on wind and solar power. Most live within walking or bicycling distance of their jobs and the local stores that supply their daily needs. Motor vehicles are relatively rare, with the exception of a few buses, taxis, and essential commercial vehicles. Travel of any distance is by public transit, primarily rail. International travel is rare and generally by rail or by wind- or solar-powered ship.

Far from a sense of isolation, however, there is a deep sense of membership in a global village. Everyone these days is connected to everyone else by a global electronic communications network that supports virtually free personal exchanges, videoconferencing, and the sharing of live cultural performances.

You all know how excited I was about using my laptop to talk for free with my wife when I was visiting Australia in 2008. Well, let me tell you, that seems so primitive given what is possible here. Holographic imaging capabilities have become so advanced I find myself forgetting I'm not actually sitting across the table from the people I'm talking with. I do miss the hugs.

The database capabilities are equally amazing. Everyone has free instant access to pretty much the total body of human experience, information, knowledge, and technology. The speed of innovation is remarkable now that everyone has a basic education and is able to so easily share the lessons of their local experiences in strengthening community and enhancing the health and productivity of their local biosystems. I must admit I experience a serious sense of information overload, but the young people seem to handle it with remarkable ease.

In my conversations with people about their way of life, I've been impressed by the pride and joy that people take in contributing to the care of their local streams and forests and participating in community life. Everywhere I go there seems to be some sort of neighborhood party, potluck, or cultural event. It reminds me of when I visited the island of Bali in Indonesia back in 1961. Everyone I meet seems to have a meaningful and dignified vocation that contributes to the well-being of the larger community and fulfills his or her basic needs for healthful food, clean water, clothing, shelter, transport, education, entertainment, and health care.

No one talks of retirement. The elders remain actively engaged in caring for children and particularly in mentoring and teaching the young for so long as they are physically and mentally able. Medical coverage, including assisted living and hospice care, is universal and locally administered.

As I dig deeper, I find that intellectual life and scientific inquiry are vibrant, open, and dedicated to the development and sharing of knowledge and life-serving technologies that address the society's priority needs. The elimination of stifling intellectual property rights monopolies has liberated creativity and positive innovation. It is amazing how motivated people are to express their creativity in ways that benefit the larger community when given the opportunity.

I'm also struck by the evident strength and stability of the families I've met. Children are all well nourished, receive a high-quality education, and live in secure and loving homes. It seems that nearly everyone is involved in civic and political life. Suicide, divorce, abortion, and teenage pregnancy are so rare that when they do occur, they are news events and spark lively discussions among people curious to learn what went wrong and how to avoid it in the future.

I guess this also explains why crime is nearly nonexistent. Those who have difficulty following the rules become the focus of a community rehabilitation program. There are a few prisons for those who seem to be beyond redemption, but prisons are considered a sign of social failure, and the goal is to eliminate them.

Perhaps my biggest shock was finding that people here respect their politicians for their wisdom, integrity, and commitment to the public good. I'm told that in this time people go into politics out of a sincere desire to serve and find that the political system encourages and rewards integrity. Maybe that's because after pouring trillions into a Wall Street bailout following the credit collapse of 2008, the government eventually shut down Wall Street in response to citizen demands and brought an end to its perverse influence over our culture and politics.

This brings me to my long-standing interest in the dysfunctions of the money system that caused the economic devastation in our time. I've met a local ecologist — yes, economics in this time is a subdiscipline of ecology — who explained that they have restructured the money system to keep money in circulation while adjusting the overall money supply and allocating it to where it is most needed in response to changing circumstances, right down to the local level. The system they have worked out seems to do this amazingly well.

All jobs pay a family wage, with no more than a small differential between the highest and lowest paid. Because current income covers daily expenses, there is no need for consumer credit except for the largest purchases, such as a car or home, for which credit can be arranged at a fair interest rate.

Some people choose to consume less than their incomes allow. Generally they put these savings into a term savings account, the equivalent of a certificate of deposit, in a local mutual savings and loan association, community bank, or credit union. In return for agreeing to leave their money in the account for a minimum specified time, they receive a modest interest rate of between 2 and 3 percent.

Many local financial institutions are organized as nonprofit cooperatives that lend the money deposited by members to members who are buying a home or investing in a local business. The association charges 5 or 6 percent on the loan. The interest spread covers administrative costs and funds a reserve for bad debts. Any surplus at the end of the year not needed to augment the reserves is distributed to the members as a dividend. This means that the money received as interest continues to circulate in the community and is available to future borrowers to pay the interest as well as loan payments as they come due.

Everyone participates in the local financial institutions over time in relatively equal measure as saver and borrower. This mitigates the tendency for money and real wealth to concentrate in the hands of lenders. Temporary imbalances are resolved by progressive tax policies.

A relatively stable money supply and the continuous recycling of interest pretty much eliminate business cycles and inflationary pressures. Debts are modest and associated with real purchases to meet real needs. In contrast with our current reality, this may sound like some imaginary fairyland, but in fact it is simply a sound design for a real-wealth financial services system.

As I came to understand how it works, I realized it is a sophisticated version of the traditional rotating credit associations I encountered in Africa and Asia, whose members each make a monthly contribution to a pool, then draw lots for their turn to receive the pot for various projects and expenses. The money continues to circulate in the community and there is no distinction between lenders and borrowers.

Local financial institutions here can create additional credit within modest limits, based on a combination of their deposits and their equity capital, as required to respond to special needs and opportunities.

The federal government can further expand or contract the national money supply as needed with a few simple accounting entries to stimulate or contract consumption, without the risk of collapsing the money system and thereby the economy. If there is need to shrink the economy and overall consumption to restore ecological balance, the government simply reduces its spending relative to its tax receipts and extinguishes a portion of tax receipts by reversing the accounting entries by which it created that money in the first place.

Each state government now has its own state bank, which allows it to similarly create its own credit, at least within strict federal guidelines. The whole system operates as a well-regulated public utility responsive to the needs and opportunities of the real-wealth economy rather than to the whims of financial speculators.

People here really seem to understand the nature and role of money. Young people learn about the money system as a part of their education for active citizenship. Even elementary school children understand the role of money and the difference between phantom wealth and real wealth.

So that pretty much covers this report. Hope you are all well.

   With much love and hugs,

   David

▶•◆•◆•◀

My greatest source of sadness comes from an awareness of the profound gap between our human reality and our human possibility.

My greatest source of joy and hope is my awareness of the vitality of the human spirit as demonstrated by the millions and millions of people who are working to realize their shared vision of a just and sustainable world that works for all.

My greatest source of motivation is the knowledge that it is within our collective means to unleash the positive creative potential of the human consciousness and make that vision a reality.

We are privileged to live at the most exciting moment of creative opportunity in the whole of the human experience. Now is the hour. We have the power to turn this world around for the sake of ourselves and our children for generations to come. We are the ones we have been waiting for.

NOTES

Chapter 1: Looking Upstream

1. Mark Pittman and Bob Ivry, "Financial Rescue Nears GDP as Pledges Top $12.8 Trillion (Update1)," Bloomberg.com, March 31, 2009, http://www.bloomberg.com/apps/news?pid=20601087&sid=armOzfkwtCA4&refer=worldwide (accessed February 25, 2010).
2. Jared Diamond, *Collapse: How Societies Choose to Fail or Succeed* (New York: Viking, 2005), 248–76.

Chapter 2: Modern Alchemists and the Sport of Moneymaking

Epigraph. John Maynard Keynes, *The General Theory of Employment, Interest, and Money* (Cambridge: Macmillan Cambridge University Press, for Royal Economic Society, 1936), chap, 12, sec. 6.
1. John C. Edmunds, "Securities: The New World Wealth Machine," *Foreign Policy*, no. 104, Fall 1996, 118–19, http://faculty.babson.edu/Edmnds/English/worldwealthmachine.pdf.
2. Kevin Phillips, *Bad Money: Reckless Finance, Failed Politics, and the Global Crisis of American Capitalism* (New York: Viking, 2008), 96–97.
3. For more detail, see Les Leopold, *The Looting of America: How Wall Street's Game of Fantasy Finance Destroyed Our Jobs, Pensions, and Prosperity and What We Can Do About It* (White River Junction, VT: Chelsea Green Publishers. 2009); and George Soros, *The New Paradigm for Financial Markets: The Credit Crisis of 2008 and What It Means* (New York: Public Affairs, 2008), xiii–xxiv.
4. Ibid., xvi. I also recommend "The Giant Pool of Money," an episode of the NPR program *This American Life*, featuring interviews with people who had a variety of roles in the events that led up to the subprime mortgage meltdown, describing how it looked from the inside. Broadcast May 9, 2008; accessible at http://www.thisamericanlife.org/Radio_Episode.aspx?episode=355.
5. Michael Mandel, "How to Get Growth Back on Track," *BusinessWeek*, October 27, 2008, 34–38.

Chapter 3: A Real-Market Alternative

Epigraph. Martin Luther King Jr., "Where Do We Go from Here?" Southern Christian Leadership Conference, Atlanta, Georgia, August 16, 1967. http://www.famous-speeches-and-speech-topics.info/martin-luther-king-speeches/martin-luther-king-speech-where-do-we-go-from-here.htm.
1. The historian Fernand Braudel gives a detailed account of the origins

and definitions of the terms *capital, capitalist,* and *capitalism* in *Civilization and Capitalism* (Berkeley: University of California Press, 1982), 2:232–39.

Chapter 4: More Than Tinkering at the Margins

Epigraph. James Gustave Speth, "Proposal for a New Economy Network," draft, August 6, 2007, 9.

1. This comparative review of Sachs and Speth is adapted from David Korten, "After the Meltdown: Economic Redesign for the 21st Century," *Tikkun,* November–December 2008, 33–40 et seq.
2. Peter Passell, "Dr. Jeffrey Sachs, Shock Therapist," *New York Times,* June 27, 1993, http://query.nytimes.com/gst/fullpage.html?res= 9F0CE7D7143EF934A15755C0A965958260&sec=&spon= &pagewanted=7.
3. Jeffrey Sachs, *Common Wealth: Economics for a Crowded Planet* (New York: Penguin, 2008), 3–4.
4. Jeffrey Sachs, "Bursting at the Seams," lecture presented at the Royal Society, London, April 11, 2007, and broadcast on BBC Radio 4, http://www.bbc.co.uk/radio4/reith2007/lecture1.shtml.
5. James Gustave Speth, *The Bridge at the Edge of the World: Capitalism, the Environment, and Crossing from Crisis to Sustainability* (New Haven, CT: Yale University Press, 2008), 57.
6. David G. Myers, "What Is the Good Life?" *YES! Magazine,* Summer 2004, 15, quoted in Speth, ibid., 138.
7. Speth, *The Bridge,* 199–200.

Chapter 5: What Wall Street Really Wants

Epigraph. Attributed to Sir Josiah Stamp, from a talk at the University of Texas in the 1920s, but unverified; noted in *Wikipedia,* s.v. "Josiah Stamp, 1st Baron Stamp"; http://en.wikipedia.org/wiki/Josiah _Stamp,_1st_Baron_Stamp.

1. Paul Krugman, *The Conscience of a Liberal* (New York: W. W. Norton, 2007), 5–6.
2. Robert Weissman, "Wall Street Still Out of Control," presentation to Public Citizen Members January 15, 2010, slide 13, http://www.citizen .org/documents/Wall%20Street%20Webinar.pdf.
3. *Journal of Accountancy,* "Rubin Calls for Modernization through Reform of Glass-Steagall Act," May 1, 1995, http://www.allbusiness .com/government/business-regulations/500983-1.html.
4. WGBH, "The Long Demise of Glass-Steagall," Public Broadcasting Service, http://www.pbs.org/wgbh/pages/frontline/shows/wallstreet/ weill/demise.html.

5. *Wikipedia.* s.v. "Robert Rubin," http://en.wikipedia.org/wiki/Robert _Rubin.

6. Phillips, *Bad Money*, 31–32 (see chap. 2, n. 2).

7. Ibid., 6.

8. Ibid., 45.

9. Jane D'Arista, "Financial Section Borrowing Drives the Credit Expansion," *Flow of Funds Review and Analysis*, Fourth Quarter 1999, quoted in Phillips, *Bad Money*,, 45–46.

10. Sarah Anderson et al., "Executive Excess 2008: How Average Taxpayers Subsidize Runaway Pay," 14th annual CEO Compensation Survey (Washington, DC: Institute for Policy Studies, 2008), 3.

11. Nelson D. Schwartz and Louise Story, "Hedge Fund Pay Roars Back," *New York Times*, April 1, 2010, B1, B10.

12. Charles R. Morris, *The Trillion Dollar Meltdown: Easy Money, High Rollers, and the Great Credit Crash* (New York: Public Affairs, 2008), 139–40.

13. Sam Pizzigati, "Our Plutocracy: A Sobering New Portrait," *Too Much*, February 20, 2010. http://toomuchonline.org/our-plutocracy-a-compelling-new-portrait/.

14. U.S. Department of Commerce, Bureau of Economic Analysis, "National Economic Accounts, National Income and Product Accounts Table," table 2.1: Personal Income and Its Disposition, http://www.bea.gov/national/nipaweb/TableView.asp?SelectedTable =58&ViewSeries=NO&Java=no&Request3Place=N&3Place=N& FromView=YES&Freq=Year&FirstYear=1959&LastYear=2008& 3Place=N&Update=Update&JavaBox=no#.

15. For fascinating insider accounts of the way this played out and the underlying patterns of corruption, see John Perkins, *Confessions of an Economic Hit Man* (San Francisco: Berrett-Koehler, 2004); and Steven Hiatt, *A Game as Old as Empire: The Secret World of Economic Hit Men and the Web of Global Corruption* (San Francisco: Berrett-Koehler, 2007).

16. James B. Davies et al., "The World Distribution of Household Wealth," December 5, 2006, University of Western Ontario, UNU-WIDER, and New York University, http://www.wider.unu.edu/publications/ working-papers/discussion-papers/2008/en_GB/dp2008-03/. See also James B. Davies, ed., *Personal Wealth from a Global Perspective* (Oxford: Oxford University Press, 2008).

17. International Labour Organization, *World of Work Report 2008: Income Inequalities in the Age of Financial Globalization* (Geneva: ILO, 2008), 1.

Chapter 6: Buccaneers and Privateers

Epigraph. Bertrand Russell, *Freedom in Society*, chap. 13, quoted in *Wikipedia*, s.v. "Bertrand Russell, http://en.wikiquote.org/wiki/Bertrand_Russell.

1. This historical review is adapted from a more detailed account in David Korten, *The Great Turning: From Empire to Earth Community* (San Francisco: Berrett-Koehler, 2006), 127–33.
2. *Encyclopaedia Britannica 2003*, deluxe ed. CD, s.v. "Hernando de Soto."
3. *Encyclopaedia Britannica 2003*, deluxe ed. CD, s.v. "Morgan, Sir Henry."
4. Kevin Phillips, Wealth and Democracy (New York: Broadway Books, 2002), 11, 14.
5. *Encyclopaedia Britannica 2003*, s.v. "Privateer."
6. Ron Harris, *Industrializing English Law: Entrepreneurship and Business Organization, 1720–1844* (Cambridge: Cambridge University Press, 2000), 41–42, 46–47.
7. Edward McNall Burns, *Western Civilizations: Their History and Their Culture*, 5th ed. (New York: W. W. Norton, 1958), 467; and *Encyclopaedia Britannica 1998*, CD, s.v. "British East India Company."

Chapter 7: The High Cost of Phantom Wealth

Epigraph. Nicolas Sarkozy, quoted in Bill Baue, "Is Capitalism Broken?" CSRlive Commentary, http://www.csrwire.com/csrlive/commentary_detail/1743-Is-Capitalism-Broken- (accessed February 24, 2010).

Epigraph. Paul Krugman, "All the President's Zombies," *New York Times*, August 23, 2009, http://www.nytimes.com/2009/08/24/opinion/24krugman.html.

1. Thornton Parker, *What If Boomers Can't Retire? How to Build Real Security, Not Phantom Wealth* (San Francisco: Berrett-Koehler, 2000).
2. John Cavanagh and Chuck Collins, "The New Inequality: The Rich and the Rest of Us," *The Nation*, June 30, 2008, 11.
3. U.S. Central Intelligence Agency, *The World Factbook*, s.v. "United States," https://www.cia.gov/library/publications/the-world-factbook/geos/us.html (accessed December 6, 2008).
4. Nicholas Varchaver and Katie Benner, "The $55 Trillion Question," *Fortune*, September 30, 2008, http://money.cnn.com/2008/09/30/magazines/fortune/varchaver_derivatives_short.fortune/index.htm.
5. Bank for International Settlements, table 19: Amounts Outstanding of Over-the-Counter (OTC) Derivatives, *BIS Quarterly Review*, December 2009; available at http://www.bis.org/statistics/otcder/dt1920a.pdf (accessed February 28, 2010).

6. Mark Pittman and Bob Ivry, "U.S. Pledges Top $7.7 Trillion to Ease Frozen Credit (Update3)," Bloomberg.com, http://www.bloomberg .com/apps/news?pid=newsarchive&sid=a5PxZ0NcDI4o# (accessed December 8, 2008).

7. Pittman and Ivry, "Financial Rescue Nears GDP" (see chap. 1, n. 1).

8. Shadow Government Statistics, "Inflation, Money Supply, GDP, Unemployment and the Dollar – Alternate Data Series," *John Williams' Shadow Government Statistics: Analysis Behind and Beyond Government Economic Reporting*, http://www.shadowstats.com/ alternate_data.

9. See, for example, Richard Wilkinson, *Unhealthy Societies: The Afflictions of Inequality* (London: Routledge, 1996); Stephen Bezruchka, "The (Bigger) Picture of Health," in John de Graaf, ed., *Take Back Your Time: Fighting Overwork and Time Poverty in America* (San Francisco: Berrett-Koehler, 2003); WHO Commission on Social Determinants of Health, *Closing the Gap in a Generation: Health Equity through Action on the Social Determinants of Health* (Geneva: WHO, 2008); Richard Layard, *Happiness: Lessons from a New Science* (New York: Penguin, 2005); and Michael Marmot, *The Status Syndrome: How Social Standing Affects Our Health and Longevity* (New York: Holt, 2005).

10. Ed Diener and Martin E. P. Seligman, "Beyond Money: Toward an Economy of Well-Being," *Psychological Science in the Public Interest* 5, no. 1 (July 2004): 10, http://www.psychologicalscience.org/pdf/pspi/ pspi5_1.pdf.

11. Carol Estes, "Living Large in a Tiny House," *YES! Magazine*, Summer 2009, 28–29.

12. Robert Frank, *Richistan: A Journey through the American Wealth Boom and the Lives of the New Rich* (New York: Crown, 2007).

Chapter 8: The End of Empire

Epigraph. Carl Anthony, "America: The Remix," a panel moderated and reported by Sarah van Gelder, *YES! Magazine*, Spring 2010, 18–23.

1. This chapter is based on the historical accounts developed and documented in much richer detail in Korten, *The Great Turning* (see chap. 6, n. 1).

2. Riane Eisler, *The Chalice and The Blade: Our History, Our Future* (New York: HarperCollins, 1987), 66.

3. Ibid., 66–69. For a fascinating exploration of the forces underlying this early turn to Empire and the specifics of how it played out, I highly recommend Brian Griffith, *The Gardens of Their Dreams: Desertification and Culture in World History* (Halifax: Fernwood, 2001).

4. This estimate is from Internet World Stats, "Internet Usage Statistics: The Internet Big Picture," table, World Internet Users and Population Statistics, http://www.internetworldstats.com/stats.htm (accessed February 5, 2010).

Chapter 9: Greed Is Not a Virtue; Sharing Is Not a Sin

Epigraph. Jim Wallis, *Rediscovering Values on Wall Street, Main Street, and Your Street: A Moral Compass for the New Economy* (New York: Simon & Schuster, 2010), 1. Kindle location 118-22.

1. Weissman, "Wall Street Still out of Control," slide 21 (see chap. 5, n. 2).
2. Pittman and Ivry, "Financial Rescue Nears GDP" (see chap. 1, n. 1).
3. Bradley Keoun, "As Banks Exit TARP, Obama Seeks New Ways to Boost Credit," *BusinessWeek*, December 16, 2009, http://www .businessweek.com/magazine/content/09_52/b4161024244392.htm.
4. Joseph E. Stiglitz, "Harsh Lessons We May Need to Learn Again," op-ed, *China Daily*, December 31, 2009, http://www.chinadaily.com.cn/ opinion/2009-12/31/content_9249981.htm.
5. Keoun, "As Banks Exit TARP."
6. Bank for International Settlements, table 19 (see chap. 7, n. 5).
7. Mara Der Hovanesian, "Magic Tricks on the Corporate Books," *BusinessWeek*, November 2, 2009, 26-7; available at http://www .businessweek.com/magazine/content/09_44/b4153000349169.htm.
8. Nelson D. Schwartz and Sewell Chan, "In Greece's Crisis, Fed Studies Wall St.'s Trading," *New York Times*, February 25, 2010, http://www .nytimes.com/2010/02/26/business/global/26greece.html?dbk; Beat Balzli, "How Goldman Sachs Helped Greece to Mask Its True Debt," S*piegel Online International,* February 8, 2010, http://www.spiegel .de/international/europe/0,1518,676634,00.html.
9. Jane Sasseen, "Hiding behind Their Hedges: How Some Executives Are Selling Their Companies Short," *BusinessWeek*, March 8, 2010, 44-50; available at http://www.businessweek.com/magazine/ content/10_10/b4169044647894.htm.

Chapter 10: What People Really Want

Epigraph. Noam Chomsky, in *Manufacturing Consent: Noam Chomsky and the Media,* a documentary by Mark Achbar and Peter Wintonick, Humanist Broadcasting Foundation, 1992.

1. Portions of the following are adapted from David Korten, "We Are Hard-Wired to Care," *YES! Magazine*, Fall 2008, 48-51, http://www .yesmagazine.org/article.asp?ID=2848.
2. For information about the Earth Charter Initiative, visit http://www .earthcharter.org/.

3. Michael Lerner, "Closed Hearts, Closed Minds," *Tikkun*, vol. 18, no. 5, September/October 2003, 10.

4. Vision of Humanity, "Global Peace Index," http://www .visionofhumanity.org/gpi/about-gpi/overview.php (accessed February 16, 2010).

5. Puanani Burgess is on the boards of *YES! Magazine* and the People-Centered Development Forum. She shared this story at Navigating the Great Turning, a leadership gathering in Columbus, Ohio, in March 2007 and in a subsequent personal communication with the author.

Chapter 11: At Home on a Living Earth

Epigraph. Adam Smith, *The Theory of Moral Sentiments,* D. D. Raphael & A. L. Macfie, eds., Liberty Fund Edition (Indianapolis: Liberty Fund, 1984), 235.

Epigraph. Elinor Ostrom as interviewed by Fran Korten, *YES! Magazine*, Spring 2010, 13.

1. *Wikipedia*, s.v. "Biosphere," http://en.wikipedia.org/wiki/Biosphere.

2. Kenneth Boulding, "The Economics of the Coming Spaceship Earth," originally published in Henry Jarrett, ed., *Environmental Quality in a Growing Economy* (Baltimore: Johns Hopkins University Press, 1968), 3–14.

3. Bradford Snell, "The StreetCar Conspiracy: How General Motors Deliberately Destroyed Public Transit," Lovearth Network, http://www.lovearth.net/gmdeliberatelydestroyed.htm (accessed March 12, 2010).

4. For a more extended treatment of lessons from the biosphere relevant to organizing human economies, along with examples and documentation, see David C. Korten, *The Post-Corporate World: Life after Capitalism* (West Harford, CT: Kumarian Press, and San Francisco: Berrett-Koehler Publishers, 1999). Note especially part II: "Life's Story," 85–133.

Chapter 12: New Vision, New Priorities

Epigraph. R. Martin Lees, "To Master the Threats of Climate Change We Have to Redefine and Reorient Economic Growth," *Club of Rome News*, January 15, 2010, http://www.clubofrome.org/eng/cor_news_bank/20/ (accessed February 6, 2010).

1. John Kenneth Galbraith, *A Short History of Financial Euphoria* (New York: Penguin, 1990).

2. For an extensive, authoritative review of this research, see Richard Wilkinson, *The Spirit Level: Why More Equal Societies Almost Always Do Better* (London: Penguin Books, 2009).

3. Glenn Greenwald, "The Bipartisan Consensus on U.S. Military Spending," *Salon*, January 2, 2008, http://www.salon.com/opinion/greenwald/2008/01/02/military_spending/.

4. Seth G. Jones and Martin C. Libicki, "How Terrorist Groups End: Lessons for Countering al Qa'ida," Rand Research report (Santa Monica, CA: Rand Corporation, 2008).

Chapter 13: Seven Points of Intervention

1. This frame draws on the work of the New Economy Working Group (NEWGroup), http://neweconomyworkinggroup.org/.

2. For the report and an opportunity to calculate your own Happy Planet Index, go to http://www.happyplanetindex.org/.

3. *Wikipedia*, s.v. "Cooperative Banking," http://en.wikipedia.org/wiki/Cooperative_banking (accessed February 20, 2010).

4. The country's remaining small and medium-size banks control only 22 percent of all bank assets, but they account for 54 percent of all small business lending. Stacy Mitchell, "Banks and Small Business Lending," New Rules Project, February 10, 2010, http://www.newrules.org/retail/news/banks-and-small-business-lending (accessed February 13, 2010).

5. Working Group in Extreme Inequality, "How Unequal Are We?"; http://extremeinequality.org/?page_id=8 (accessed February 14, 2010).

6. Richard Wilkinson, "What Difference Does Inequality Make?" A paper presented at Well-being: The Impact of Inequalities, Dundee, Scotland, 26 November 2008, p. 2. http://www.thpc.scot.nhs.uk/presentations/Wellbeing/Wilkinson.pdf.

7. United Steelworkers, "Steelworkers Form Collaboration with MONDRAGON, the World's Largest Worker-Owned Cooperative," *USW News*, October 27, 2009, http://www.usw.org/media_center/releases_advisories?id=0234.

8. This powerful idea comes from Marjorie Kelly, personal e-mail to the author, February 16, 2010.

9. For further discussion of the living economies building blocks and examples of leading edge initiatives, see BALLE, Business Alliance for Local Living Economies, "Building Blocks of a Local Living Economy," http://www.livingeconomies.org/Entrepreneurs (accessed February 21, 2010).

Chapter 14: What About My . . .?

1. Ellen Hodgson Brown, "The Battle of the Titans: JPMorgan vs. Goldman Sachs, or Why the Market Was Down for Seven Days in a Row,"

Truthout, January 30, 2010, http://www.truthout.org/the-battle-titans-jpmorgan-vs-goldman-sachs-or-why-market-was-down-7-days-a-row56526 (accessed February 21, 2010).

2. Sarah Anderson et al., *Responding to Main Street: A Sensible Plan for Recovery* (Washington, DC: Institute for Policy Studies, October 1, 2008), 2; available at http://www.peaceworkmagazine.org/responding-main-street-sensible-plan-recovery.

3. Shannon Hayes, *Radical Homemakers: Reclaiming Domesticity from a Consumer Culture* (Richmondville, NY: Left to Write Press, 2010); available from http://radicalhomemakers.com/.

4. Sarah Varney, "Did Blue Cross' Mission Stray When Plans Became For-Profit?" *Morning Edition*, National Public Radio, March 18, 2010, http://www.npr.org/templates/story/story.php?storyId=124807720.

5. Gar Alperovitz, "Retirement Crisis, Real or Imagined? Moral and Economic Questions on Social Security," *YES! Magazine*, Fall 2005, http://www.yesmagazine.org/article.asp?ID=1285.

6. Marjorie Kelly, *The Divine Right of Capital: Dethroning the Corporate Aristocracy* (San Francisco: Berrett-Koehler Publishers, 2001), 33–4.

7. Thornton Parker, "From Wall Street Bird Nests to Main Street Growth Cycles," May 7, 2009, EthicalMarkets.com, http://www.ethicalmarkets.com/2009/05/07/from-wall-street-bird-nests-to-main-street-growth-cycles/.

Chapter 15: A Presidential Declaration of Independence from Wall Street I Hope I May One Day Hear

1. "Obama's Corporate Messaging," interview with Barack Obama, *BusinessWeek*, February 22, 2010, 34; available at http://www.businessweek.com/magazine/content/10_08/b4167032896448.htm.

2. Adapted from Korten, "After the Meltdown" (see chap. 4, n. 1).

Chapter 16: When the People Lead, the Leaders Will Follow

Epigraph, Howard Zinn, excerpt from *A Power Governments Cannot Suppress*. (San Francisco, City Lights Publishers, 2006), http://www.alternet.org/media/145499/howard_zinn:_"we_should_not_give_up_the_game_before_all_the_cards_have_been_played"_/.

1. For more of this history, see Korten, *When Corporations Rule the World*, 2nd ed. (San Francisco: Berrett-Koehler, 2001), 307–314.

2. Patrick E. Tyler, "A New Power in the Streets," *New York Times*, February 17, 2003, http://query.nytimes.com/gst/fullpage.html?res=9902E0DC1E3AF934A25751C0A9659C8B63.

3. Roger Wilkins, *Jefferson's Pillow: The Founding Fathers and the Dilemma of Black Patriotism* (Boston: Beacon, 2001), 18–19.

Chapter 17: A Visionary President Meets Realpolitik

1. Daniel Wagner and Matt Apuzzo (AP), "Wall Street Has Geithner's Ear," *Washington Post*, October 9, 2009, http://www.washingtonpost.com/wp-dyn/content/article/2009/10/08/AR2009100804132_pf.html (accessed February 28, 2010).
2. Gary Langer, "In Supreme Court Ruling on Campaign Finance, the Public Dissents," *The Numbers*, ABC News, February 17, 2010, http://blogs.abcnews.com/thenumbers/2010/02/in-supreme-court-ruling-on-campaign-finance-the-public-dissents.html.
3. Tea Party, "About Us," http://www.teaparty.org/aboutus.html (accessed March 15, 2010). A subsequent site redesign removed these jokes.
4. Coffee Party, "About Us," http://coffeepartyusa.com/content/about-us (accessed March 15, 2010).

Chapter 18: Change the Story, Change the Future

1. See Paul Ray and Sherry Anderson, "A Culture Gets Creative," interview by Sarah Ruth van Gelder, *YES! Magazine*, Winter 2001. Ray and Anderson make the link between the civil rights movement and a widespread cultural awakening. Their insight triggered for me the realization that something far more profound is at work than simply a shift in values. In subsequent personal discussions Ray has affirmed his support for the thesis that what his research has uncovered is in fact evidence of a step to a new level of human consciousness that has profound implications.

Chapter 19: Learning to Live, Living to Learn

Epigraph. Margaret J. Wheatley, "Restoring Hope to the Future through Critical Education of Leaders," published in *Vimukt Shiksha*, a bulletin of Shikshantar — the People's Institute for Rethinking Education and Development, Udaipur, Rajasthan, India, March 2001, http://www.margaretwheatley.com/articles/restoringhope.html.

1. The Interfaith Amigos regularly blog for *YES! Magazine* (see http://www.yesmagazine.org/blogs/interfaith-amigos/) to share the insights of their interfaith exploration as a path beyond the fear and distrust that so characterize our present time.
2. Raffi, "No Wall Too Tall," http://www.raffinews.com/feature/no-wall-too-tall.
3. I am a member of the advisory council for Raffi's Child Honouring Initiative (http://www.raffinews.com/child-honouring/what-is-child-honouring), which is devoted to advancing the idea that if we focus our attention as a society on creating a world that works for our children, it will work for everyone and the whole of life.

4. Milenko Matanovic, "Turning the Sword," *YES! Magazine,* Summer 2002, 12–15.

5. Bill Cleveland, *Art in Other Places: Artists at Work in America's Community and Social Institutions* (New York: Praeger, 1992) and *Art and Upheaval: Artists on the World's Frontlines* (Oakland, CA: New Village Press, 2008). For evidence that low-income communities well populated with small arts centers are more cohesive, peaceful, and economically vital than those without such centers, see Mark J. Stern and Susan C. Seifert, "From Creative Economy to Creative Society," *Creativity and Change,* January 2008; available at http://www.trfund.com/resource/creativity.html.

6. Because this work falls below the radar of corporate media, keeping its scale and power in focus can be difficult. *YES! Magazine* readers tell us that the publication is a useful tonic in moments of personal despair, because each issue tells the story of the larger movement's growing power, scope, and influence.

Epilogue

Epigraph. Jim Wallis, *Rediscovering Values* (see chap. 9, epigraph), Kindle location 1591–96.

INDEX

enterprises
  debt and, 38, 39, 171, 203, 215
  living, 169, 176–178, 181–183
  local economy and, 143–150,
     212
  Main Street and, 44–45, 145,
     214
  ownership of, 180, 212
  privateers, 83
  speculation and, 26
  Wall Street and, 54, 178, 204
  worker owned, 180, 212, 213
  See also banks, cooperative
     environment
  agriculture and, 211
  crisis, 17
  Earth Charter, 132
  ecological balance, 23, 154, 163,
     257
  ecological footprint, 170
  free market and, 5, 46–47,
     56–61
  Gore, Al and, 235
  institutions and, 9–10, 15–18,
     42, 57, 79, 111–112
  living buildings and, 162
  microenvironment, 147–148, 156
  movement, 109, 224–228, 253,
     255
  resource allocation and, 24, 40,
     152, 160, 168
  wealth and, 154, 174–175
  See also biosphere; climate
     change; living system
Egypt, 103
equitable distribution, 111, 154–155.
  See also shared prosperity
executive compensation, 75–76,
  204

Falcon, Ted, 267
Federal Reserve
  Federalize the Fed, 173, 217, 239
  M3 reporting, 94

money supply management
  172–173, 217
mortgage bubble and, 33
phantom wealth and, 31
regulation of, 217–218, 239
role in bank bailout, 74–75, 92,
  94, 116, 193
role in deregulation, 73, 117–118
speculation and, 74–75
The Feminine Mystique (Friedan),
  254
financial bubble, 22, 29–39, 41,
  153, 188
Financial Markets Center, 74
Fletcher, Andrew, 245
food. See agriculture
Forbes list of richest people, 26, 66,
  78, 99
Ford Foundation, 9
Foreign Policy journal, 29, 30, 32
fractals, 146
Frank, Robert, 100
fraud
  climate change and, 122
  free market and, 47
  insurance, 188
  mortgage, 32
  regulation of, 190, 193
  securities, 188
  speculation and, 173
  Wall Street as, 54
  See also credit; confidence
     games; speculation
free market. See markets
free trade. See trade agreements
Friedan, Betty, 254
Friedman, Milton, 237
Gaia hypothesis, 139
Galbraith, John Kenneth, vii
Geithner, Timothy, 235
General Motors, 142
Glass–Steagall Act, 71
Global Peace index, 134

ABOUT THE AUTHOR

Dr. David C. Korten worked for more than thirty-five years in preeminent business, academic, and international development institutions before he turned away from the establishment to work exclusively with public interest citizen-action groups. He is the cofounder and board chair of *YES! Magazine,* the founder and president of The People-Centered Development Forum, a founding board member of the Business Alliance for Local Living Economies, an associate of the International Forum on Globalization, and a member of the Club of Rome and the Social Ventures Network. He is co-chair of the New Economy Working Group formed in 2008 to formulate and advance a new economy agenda.

Korten earned his MBA and PhD degrees at the Stanford University Graduate School of Business. Trained in organization theory, business strategy, and economics, he devoted his early career to setting up business schools in low-income countries — starting with Ethiopia — in the hope that creating a new class of professional business entrepreneurs would be the key to ending global poverty. He completed his military service during the Vietnam War as a captain in the U.S. Air Force, with duty at the Special Air Warfare School, Air Force headquarters command, the Office of the Secretary of Defense, and the Advanced Research Projects Agency.

Korten then served for five and a half years as a faculty member of the Harvard University Graduate School of Business, where he taught in Harvard's middle management, MBA, and doctoral programs and served as Harvard's adviser to the Central American Management Institute in Nicaragua. He subsequently joined the staff of the Harvard Institute for International Development, where he headed a Ford Foundation–funded project to strengthen the organization and management of national family planning programs.

In the late 1970s, Korten left U.S. academia and moved to Southeast Asia, where he lived for nearly fifteen years, serving first as a Ford Foundation project specialist and later as Asia regional adviser on development management to the U.S. Agency for International Development. His work there won him international recognition for his contributions to the development of strategies for transforming public bureaucracies into responsive support systems dedicated to strengthening the community control and management of land, water, and forestry resources.

Increasingly concerned that the economic models embraced by official aid agencies were increasing poverty and environmental destruction and that these agencies were impervious to change from within, Korten broke with the official aid system. His last five years in Asia were devoted to working with leaders of Asian nongovernmental organizations on identifying the root causes of development failure in the region and building the capacity of civil society organizations to function as strategic catalysts of positive national- and global-level change.

Korten came to realize that the crisis of deepening poverty, inequality, environmental devastation, and social disintegration he observed in Asia was playing out in nearly every country in the world — including the United States and other "developed" countries. Furthermore, he concluded that the United States was actively promoting — both at home and abroad — the very policies that were deepening the crisis. If there were to be a positive human future, the United States must change. He returned to the United States in 1992 to share with his fellow Americans the lessons he had learned abroad.

Korten's publications are required reading in university courses around the world. He has written numerous books, including the international best seller *When Corporations Rule the World, The Great Turning: From Empire to Earth Community,* and *The Post-Corporate World: Life after Capitalism.* He contributes regularly to edited books and professional journals, and to a wide variety of periodical publications. He is also a popular international speaker and a regular guest on talk radio and television.

Berrett–Koehler Publishers

A community dedicated to creating
a world that works for all

Visit Our Website: www.bkconnection.com

Read book excerpts, see author videos and Internet movies, read our authors' blogs, join discussion groups, download book apps, find out about the BK Affiliate Network, browse subject-area libraries of books, get special discounts, and more!

Subscribe to Our Free E-Newsletter, the *BK Communiqué*

Be the first to hear about new publications, special discount offers, exclusive articles, news about bestsellers, and more! Get on the list for our free e-newsletter by going to **www.bkconnection.com**.

Get Quantity Discounts

Berrett-Koehler books are available at quantity discounts for orders of ten or more copies. Please call us toll-free at (800) 929-2929 or email us at bkp.orders@aidcvt.com.

Join the BK Community

BKcommunity.com is a virtual meeting place where people from around the world can engage with kindred spirits to create a world that works for all. BKcommunity.com members may create their own profiles, blog, start and participate in forums and discussion groups, post photos and videos, answer surveys, announce and register for upcoming events, and chat with others online in real time. Please join the conversation!

Also by David Korten

When Corporations Rule the World

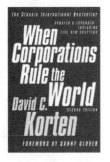

In this modern classic, called "a searing indictment of an unjust international economic order" by Archbishop Desmond Tutu, David Korten details the threat economic globalization poses to long-term human interests and outlines a strategy for empowering local communities to resist corporate power.

"This book will agitate your mind, elevate your soul, and engage your civic spirit."
—Ralph Nader

ISBN 978-1-887208-04-8

The Great Turning
From Empire to Earth Community

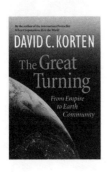

David Korten exposes the destructive and oppressive nature of "Empire," the organization of society through hierarchy and violence. Drawing on evolutionary theory, developmental psychology, religious teachings, and other sources, Korten shows that "Earth Community"—an egalitarian, sustainable way of ordering human society—is indeed possible, and he lays out a grassroots strategy for achieving it.

ISBN 978-1-887208-08-6
PDF ebook, ISBN 978-1-57675-539-6

Berrett–Koehler Publishers, Inc.
www.bkconnection.com   **(800) 929-2929**